UNDERSTANDING EARLY YEARS POLICY

SAGE was founded in 1965 by Sara Miller McCune to support the dissemination of usable knowledge by publishing innovative and high-quality research and teaching content. Today, we publish over 900 journals, including those of more than 400 learned societies, more than 800 new books per year, and a growing range of library products including archives, data, case studies, reports, and video. SAGE remains majority-owned by our founder, and after Sara's lifetime will become owned by a charitable trust that secures our continued independence.

Los Angeles | London | New Delhi | Singapore | Washington DC | Melbourne

4TH EDITION

UNDERSTANDING EARLY YEARS POLICY

DAMIEN FITZGERALD
& JANET KAY

Los Angeles | London | New Delhi
Singapore | Washington DC | Melbourne

Los Angeles | London | New Delhi
Singapore | Washington DC | Melbourne

SAGE Publications Ltd
1 Oliver's Yard
55 City Road
London EC1Y 1SP

SAGE Publications Inc.
2455 Teller Road
Thousand Oaks, California 91320

SAGE Publications India Pvt Ltd
B 1/I 1 Mohan Cooperative Industrial Area
Mathura Road
New Delhi 110 044

SAGE Publications Asia-Pacific Pte Ltd
3 Church Street
#10-04 Samsung Hub
Singapore 049483

Editor: Jude Bowen
Assistant editor: George Knowles
Production editor: Nicola Marshall
Project manager: Jeanette Graham
Copyeditor: Sharon Cawood
Proofreader: Rosemary Campbell
Indexer: Anne Solamito
Marketing manager: Lorna Patkai
Cover designer: Wendy Scott
Typeset by: C&M Digitals (P) Ltd, Chennai, India
Printed and bound by CPI Group (UK) Ltd,
Croydon, CR0 4YY

© Damien Fitzgerald and Janet Kay 2016

Previous editions © Peter Baldock, Damien Fitzgerald and
Janet Kay.
First edition published 2005; reprinted 2006.
Second edition published 2009; reprinted 2009, 2010, 2011.
Third edition published 2013; reprinted 2014.

Library of Congress Control Number: 2015950875

British Library Cataloguing in Publication data

A catalogue record for this book is available from
the British Library

ISBN 978-1-4129-6189-9
ISBN 978-1-4129-6190-5 (pbk)

At SAGE we take sustainability seriously. Most of our products are printed in the UK using FSC papers and boards.
When we print overseas we ensure sustainable papers are used as measured by the PREPS grading system.
We undertake an annual audit to monitor our sustainability.

CONTENTS

ABOUT THE AUTHORS

Damien Fitzgerald has worked as a registered nurse, teacher and special needs coordinator in early years and primary education, and as an LEA support teacher. He is currently Head of Area (Early Childhood Studies) at Sheffield Hallam University, and is engaged in varied research.

Janet Kay worked as a qualified social worker with children and families for some years before moving into teaching in further and then higher education. She has retired from full-time work, but still regularly lectures at Sheffield Hallam University, and is also working to promote better support for adoptive families in the UK.

ACKNOWLEDGEMENTS

We would like to acknowledge the many and valuable contributions of our co-author, friend and colleague Pete Baldock, who co-wrote the first three editions of this book with us. His work on the structure, style and range of topics covered in this book has shaped it from the start. He has been greatly missed since his death in 2011.

Janet Kay would also like to thank Sharon Moore and Nicola Green for their comments on and conversations about their practice experience as childminders of the Early Years Pupil Premium and other early years developments. It's lovely to talk policy at playgroup!

We would also like to thank Jamie Barr at SAGE, who helped us enormously by researching the further readings, useful websites and the timeline.

PREFACE

Policy has an important impact on the daily life of early years practitioners, whatever their role or setting. The policies of central and local government establish expectations of settings, practitioners and practice and do much to determine the level of resources available. Although we may not talk about policy much, or even at all, it is reflected in everything that early years practitioners, parents and settings do. This has not always been the case to the extent it is now. Before New Labour came to power in 1997, there had been a long period of time when there was very little attention paid to early years policy. However, since then, early years has become a major election issue and focus for government policy, as 'getting it right in the early years' has become a key feature of wider social policy.

When we wrote the first edition of this book, there were few similar books available designed primarily to help students or practitioners negotiate their way around early years policy. In fact, our motivation to write the book was to provide our own students with a reliable early years policy text. We saw the need for a book that would help students and practitioners learn how to understand the process by which policy developed, identify the context in which new policies arise and work out how to influence policy themselves.

It was not a detailed account of the policies of the government in power at the time we wrote it. Such a reference book would have duplicated information already available and it would have needed updating on a regular, at least annual, basis to remain accurate. What we tried to do was to explain what policy is and how it comes about in a way that would be relevant for some time to come through any likely changes in detailed policy. We seem to have been successful in this, but policy changes since we wrote the third edition have suggested the need for this new, updated, fourth edition. The intensified focus on early years mentioned above has meant more developments in policy in this area and more government policy goals to achieve. Getting early years policy right, so that children get a better start in life, achieve well at school and are healthy, despite poverty and deprivation, is now seen as the means to prevent or reduce later social problems such as crime, anti-social behaviour, chronic health problems, unemployment, poverty and a reliance on welfare. In recent years, there has been a lot resting on early years policies which are not always to do with the immediate needs of young children, and we have tried to reflect the significance of this in this new edition. As such, we have divided up Chapter 2 to reflect the increased focus on early years policy in recent years and the aims and goals of different governments and how these have affected policy development.

We have also updated and extended the chapter on early years policy in the devolved countries in the UK and the international chapter, as these have proved to be very popular and many of our reviewers have suggested this. The international chapter now includes two new countries, the USA and Finland, as well as updates on the original six countries in the last edition. As we have widened the scope of this chapter, we have also introduced more discussion on the value of international comparisons and some of the potential pitfalls of simplistic contrasts between countries.

The book now has ten chapters. Chapter 1 explains what policy is and why it is important. Chapter 2 outlines the development of policy in this field up to New Labour and Chapter 3 discusses policy post-New Labour. Chapter 4 describes the factors that influence the development of the aspirations and objectives that constitute basic policy. Chapter 5 describes the process by which aspirations and objectives are translated into specific legislative and administrative measures. Chapter 6 deals with the impact of devolution on policy-making. Chapter 7 looks at the international dimension of early years policy. Chapter 8 looks at the impact of policy on practitioners, children and parents. Chapter 9 deals with the analysis of policy and considers the relevance of different perspectives (of politicians, professionals, parents and children) and the extent to which a coherent early years policy is in the making. Finally, there is a concluding summary in Chapter 10. Chapters 1–9 include activities, discussion points or suggestions for reflection designed to help you think further about the issues raised, and each chapter has further reading at the end. Chapter 3 also includes a timeline (Table 3.1) as a summary of developments in the period from 1945 to 2015. A glossary of terms used as further aids and a list of useful websites follow this Preface.

The authors owe a debt of gratitude to the students, colleagues and practitioners with whom we have worked over the last few years, and to our reviewers, whose questions, observations and comments during discussion have done much to inform the development of this book over four editions. We remain responsible for the final outcome.

GLOSSARY

This glossary contains explanations of terms that may not be familiar to the reader. Terms which are used in the text but fully explained or discussed so their meaning is clear are not included.

Area Child Protection Committee (ACPC): a multi-agency committee established in every local authority to determine local policy and oversee child protection processes. ACPCs have been replaced by **Local Safeguarding Children Boards**, which are statutory bodies introduced by the Children Act 2004.

Birth to Three Matters: a framework of effective practice for those working with children aged birth to 3 issued by the Department for Education and Skills (DfES). This was replaced by the **Early Years Foundation Stage** (birth to 6 years) in 2008.

Children's Centre: there is a centre based in each of the 20% most disadvantaged wards in England. There were approximately 3,600 in 2010, although the numbers have fallen since then. Children's Centres originally provided early education integrated with full day care, identification of and provision for children with special educational needs and disabilities, parental outreach, family support and health services, among others. Many now provide more limited services.

Children's Trust: a multi-agency body established to ensure that joint planning and implementation of plans for children and young people within local authorities are effective. The philosophy of Children's Trusts is underpinned by the Children Act 2004 duty to cooperate and to focus on improving outcomes for all children and young people.

Children's Workforce Development Council (CWDC): a body set up to promote the development and integration of the children's workforce. The body was disbanded in 2012 and its work was split between the Teaching Agency and the Department for Education.

Civil Service: in Great Britain, the Civil Service helps the government of the UK, the Scottish Executive and the National Assembly for Wales to formulate their policies, carry out decisions and administer public services for which they are responsible. Civil servants are servants of the Crown, meaning the government of the UK, the Scottish Executive and the National Assembly for Wales.

Curriculum Guidance for the Foundation Stage: statutory guidance for early years practitioners in the Foundation Stage (3–5 years) on developing a curriculum to support teaching and learning towards the Early Learning Goals.

This was replaced by the **Early Years Foundation Stage** (birth to 6 years) in 2008 and it was updated again in 2014.

Daycare Trust: a national childcare charity established in 1980, campaigning for high-quality affordable childcare for all. It has now been rebranded as the Family and Childcare Trust.

Desirable Learning Outcomes: learning goals that set out what children should have achieved by the time they enter compulsory education. These were replaced by the **Early Learning Goals**.

Early Excellence Centre: an early years setting that has been highlighted as offering a level of excellence. These became rebranded as Children's Centres.

Early Intervention: early recognition and assessment of additional needs.

Early Learning Goals: the basis of the Foundation Stage curriculum in any early years setting in England.

Early Years Educator: a level 3 qualification, the criteria for which are set by the National College for Teaching and Leadership.

Early Years Foundation Stage: the statutory curriculum for children from birth to 6 years.

Early Years Professional (EYP): the aim of the Early Years Professional was to lead effective high-quality practice in the early years sector. The government's aim was to have at least one EYP in every early years setting by 2015. The EYP was replaced by the **Early Years Teacher (EYT)**.

Early Years Professional Status (EYPS): a graduate status that was achieved by following one of the recognized training or validation pathways to demonstrate a range of skills and attributes. EYPS was seen as having equivalence with Qualified Teacher Status. The EYPS was replaced by the **Early Years Teacher Status (EYTS)**.

Early Years Pupil Premium (EYPP): additional funding for early years settings to support the learning and development of eligible 3–4-year-olds.

Early Years Teacher (EYT): a graduate and specialist in early years care and education, expected to lead practice, support colleagues, influence change and improve outcomes for babies and young children in early years provision.

Early Years Teacher Status (EYTS): a graduate role, given to an individual who can demonstrate they meet the Teachers' Standards (Early Years). It is awarded to graduates who are leading education and care and who have been judged to have met all of the standards in practice from birth to the end of the Early Years Foundation Stage (EYFS).

Education and Healthcare Plan (EHCP): the outcome of a multi-professional assessment for children with SEN and/or disabilities.

Family and Childcare Trust: carries out a range of research to promote quality and affordable childcare for families.

Foundation Stage: the curriculum in England for children from birth to 6 years (see **Early Years Foundation Stage**).

Local Government Association (LGA): formed in 1997 to represent the 500 local authorities of England and Wales and to promote better local government.

Local Safeguarding Children Board: a multi-disciplinary statutory body responsible for child protection issues in each local authority (see **Area Child Protection Committee**).

National Childminding Association (NCMA): promotes and supports quality childminding expertise, provides information for parents looking for childminders, and provides information and news updates for childminders.

National College for Teaching and Leadership: a newly formed body in 2013. Its remit includes teacher training, continuous professional development and supporting school improvement to address underperformance in the education system. Also see **Teaching Agency**.

Neoliberalist policy: sees market forces as the best way to run the economy, with little role for government. Government intervention (and funding) is seen as driving inefficiency. This approach would support private intervention in the ECEC sector. It shares some similarities with neo-conservatism.

Office for Standards in Education (Ofsted): a non-ministerial government department established under the Education (Schools) Act 1992, Ofsted has expanded over time and now takes responsibility for the inspection of all schools, LAs, teacher training institutions, youth work, colleges and early years childcare and education provision in England.

Organisation for Economic Co-operation and Development (OECD): Aims to promote policies to improve the economic and social well-being of people around the world by working with governments and other national bodies.

Political ideology: this is about the values, beliefs and views of what contributes to a positive society and outcomes for individuals. Traditionally, political ideologies were classified as either to the right or left of centre, although this dichotomy has become increasingly blurred in recent years. Historically, Labour was classified as a centre-left political party (focused on social justice, equality, state provision and the redistribution of wealth), and the Conservatives as centre-right (focused on promoting private property ownership, free trade and a reduction in state bureaucracy). Also see **Third way**.

Pre-school Learning Alliance (PLA): an educational charity that represents and supports 15,000 community pre-schools in England.

Primary Care Trusts: disbanded in 2012, these were 302 free-standing statutory bodies that controlled local health care and received their budgets directly from the Department of Health.

Private sector: refers to the business or profit-making sector providing services in the early years, such as private day nurseries and childminders.

Private, Voluntary and Independent Sector (PVI): the range of non-maintained providers (e.g. school nurseries and nursery schools) that make up the ECEC sector. This includes childminders, private nurseries and voluntary providers, amongst others.

Public sector: refers to the local or central government sector providing services in the early years, such as schools.

Socialist: a political approach which views a role for the state that aims for social equality and justice through the redistribution of wealth within a welfare state. For example, raising the top rate of tax for high-income earners (as was policy under the later years of New Labour and still supported by the Scottish government) would be seen as one way of increasing equality and achieving social justice.

Standard assessment tests (SATS): these are completed at the end of Key Stages 1, 2 and 3 to assess progress in the core subjects of the National Curriculum. At Key Stage 1, there is now a less formal style of testing, with schools able to choose when pupils complete the assessment tasks. They are also referred to as National Curriculum tests.

Sure Start local programme: an area-based initiative with the aim of improving the health and well-being of families and children from pre-birth to age 4. There were 524 such programmes in neighbourhoods where a high proportion of children lived in poverty. The majority have now been transformed into **Children's Centres.**

Sure Start Unit: part of the Children, Young People and Families Directorate in the Department for Children, Schools and Families (DCSF), working with a wide range of other agencies to develop services for children and families in line with government policy, including services to socially excluded children and families.

Teachers' Standards (Early Years): published by the DfE in July 2013 and coming into force September 2013, they are a set of professional standards that must be reached for a teacher to be awarded Early Years Teacher Status (EYTS).

Teaching Agency: an executive agency of the DfE (now disbanded), it was responsible for supply and, with others, retention of the workforce; the quality of the workforce; and regulation of teacher conduct. It subsequently combined with the National College for School Leadership to form the National College for Teaching and Leadership.

Third way: any approach seen as alternative to the political ideologies of left and right. Also see **Political ideology.**

Universal services: available to all in a stated category (not means-tested), for example primary education is available to all families with children.

Voluntary sector: non-government or non-profit-making charitable or voluntary organizations such as the NSPCC and Barnardo's.

USEFUL WEBSITES

As explained throughout the book, policy is constantly developing and new initiatives are being trialled or implemented. One way to keep up to date with policy developments is to consult websites from government departments, professional organizations and other relevant bodies. In addition to the websites mentioned in the text, the following websites are likely to be helpful in this task. Some of the websites also offer the facility to receive regular email updates on new developments. This is an invaluable way of keeping abreast of ongoing policy developments. Many of these departments and organizations also have Twitter feeds, and this is an excellent source for new information.

Government departments

Each of the countries of the UK have a specific department for ECEC as this is a devolved area:

- Department for Education England: www.education.gov.uk/
- Department for Education Northern Ireland: www.deni.gov.uk/
- Department for Education and Training Scotland: www.gov.scot/Topics/Education
- Department of Education and Skills Wales: http://gov.wales/topics/education andskills/?lang=en

These detail current government policy and initiatives in education, including early learning and childcare.

Coalition policy 2010–15: www.gov.uk/government/publications/2010–to–2015–government-policy-childcare-and-early-education/2010–to–2015–government-policy-childcare-and-early-education

Other websites

British Association for Early Childhood Education: www.early-education.org.uk/ – this provides information and commentary on the latest policy and practice developments

Family and Childcare Trust: www.familyandchildcaretrust.org/ – a national child-care charity with information on and responses to policy developments in childcare

Healthy Child Programme: www.gov.uk/government/uploads/system/uploads/attachment_data/file/167998/Health_Child_Programme.pdf – a government pro-gramme focused on improving the health and well-being of young children

Joseph Rowntree Foundation: www.jrf.org.uk/ – a social policy research charity that produces reports on a range of social policy issues, including issues relevant to children and families

National Children's Bureau: www.ncb.org.uk/ – provides comment, analysis and an overview of issues relevant to children

Nursery World: www.nurseryworld.co.uk/ – a weekly publication with news and comment on all aspects of ECEC

Ofsted Childcare and Early Education: www.ofsted.gov.uk/early-years-and-child care – provides information about current issues for the registration, regulation and monitoring of early years provision

1

WHAT IS POLICY AND WHY IS IT IMPORTANT?

THIS CHAPTER EXPLORES

- the role practitioners can play in influencing policy development and implementation
- the significance of policy
- three levels of policy-making: the basic assumptions about values and facts that usually underpin policy decisions; the broad objectives; and the detailed arrangements required to meet those objectives
- the characteristics of policies
- written statements of policy
- controversy in the debate on policy.

Working with young children every day is fascinating and demanding. It is easy to see why so many early years practitioners remain entirely focused on the task in hand and do not spend time discussing policy, which is typically seen as something produced by people in suits somewhere else that just has to be implemented. A common joke has the person in charge explaining: 'There is no reason for it – it's just our policy'. Those who are actually working with children and their families may feel they can do little but put up with the consequences of changes in policy. Thinking about them and their implications is for someone else to do.

This book takes a different approach. We believe that the policies adopted by those in power make an enormous difference to the way practitioners are able to work. We also argue that policies are not just conjured up out of thin air. People who make policies have reasons *for* what they do. We may not agree with them, but they are reasons, not mere whims. We need to understand those reasons in order to implement more effectively those policies that appear to be useful and to challenge more effectively those that do not. We want to argue against the sense of helplessness. Practitioners can do more than just cope, particularly when policies are not seen as appropriate or effective.

Among the sources of policy are what practitioners themselves have to say, and they can have a considerable impact on the way that policies are implemented. An effective practitioner will give time to thinking how he/she can help policy develop in useful directions. This can take varied forms, from responding to consultations at a national level to implementing policies at a local level in a way that takes account of the local context.

What is policy?

Levin (1997) points out that the word 'policy' is used in several different ways and identifies four of these. The examples given are not from Levin himself, but have been chosen because of their relevance to our overall subject:

- A stated intention – for example, in 2013 the government consulted on its intention to simplify the childcare registration system and strengthen the approach to safeguarding. This was confirmed in 2014 and led to a number of changes, including the updating of the Childcare Regulations (2014) and the amendments to the Early Years Foundation Stage (EYFS) with a new statutory version from September 2014.
- Action taken on an issue by those with responsibility – for example, the issuing of new guidance on the transition to the Special Educational Needs and Disability (SEND) system covering children and young people aged 0–25 years old. Sometimes the word 'policy' is used to cover all the actions the government or some other body has undertaken in a particular field. Thus, we speak of 'the government's SEN policy', meaning everything it has done in relation to SEND.
- An organizational or administrative practice – for example, if the government sets up a funding regime for early years settings, there will be policies governing the type of setting that is eligible to receive the money.
- An indication of the formal status of a course of action – policies on, for example, childcare are to be found in documents that have some status, such as a government Green Paper or a manifesto published for a general election by a political party.

Although the word does carry different meanings and it is important to be aware of these, there are common elements. Levin states that any policy will entail:

- belongingness: a policy will belong to some body or another – a political party, a government department, an individual setting, and so on
- commitment: a policy entails a commitment to a particular approach or course of action on the part of that body
- status: the fact that a proposal or set of ideas is described as a policy suggests that it has been formally adopted in some way by the body that owns it
- specificity: a policy will entail specific ways of dealing with specific issues, although the extent to which it is specific on the detail will vary.

These four attributes of policy reflect the fact that policies are considered. People do not usually do things in a completely random way in their everyday lives. The same is also true of policy-makers. We define 'policy' as: an attempt by those working inside an organization to think in a coherent way about what it is trying to achieve (either in general or in relation to a specific issue) and what it needs to do to achieve it. And an organization can vary from a large government department (e.g. the Department for Education) to a professional association (e.g. British Early Childhood Education Research Association (BECERA)) or to a school or private nursery. Social policy is also set in an historical context, which has been influenced by successive governments since the inception of the welfare state and in an increasingly complex environment with devolved national and local governance (Blakemore and Griggs, 2013).

Such thinking is conducted at three levels (although any policy statement may focus on one or two of these):

- basic assumptions about the relevant facts and the values that should inform the approach to them
- broad objectives
- detailed arrangements required to meet those objectives.

In many statements of policy, the underlying values and principles about what are described as the facts of the situation are presented almost as factual, as though there can be no argument about them. This is because such statements usually come from people in charge and, however much they may have consulted people before issuing the document, they now want to get on with things. It should become clear, in the chapters that follow, that the facts of the situation and the values people bring to bear on them are constantly changing and are often matters of controversy. It is also the case that the distinction between values and facts is far from clear much of the time and people may state as matters of fact things that merely reflect their personal beliefs. In short, we should not take for granted the basic assumptions about values and facts that usually underpin policy decisions, even when there is wide consensus on these, perhaps especially when there is consensus.

In the same way, we need to look critically at the second level of policy-making – the broad objectives. Objectives have to be defined clearly, otherwise the policy-makers do not know whether they have been successful and cannot think clearly about the further measures their objectives might imply. However, clarity is not always in evidence in actual policy documents.

Policy-makers will often argue in favour of a policy on one set of grounds while also having other considerations in mind. For example, both the Coalition and Labour governments from 1997 to 2015 often adopted policies that have restricted the powers and autonomy of local councils. There is an inevitable tension between central government, which wishes to set policies for the nation, and local authorities (LAs) that have to implement policies (especially as the political party controlling a local council may be the one in opposition in Parliament). Yet, it is difficult to identify a situation where a government has stated explicitly that restricting the autonomy of local government is one of its major aims. Instead, governments are more likely to argue that proposed policies are designed to secure greater fairness, effectiveness or efficiency in the delivery of services.

Clarity can also be undermined by ambivalence on the part of policy-makers. For example, a policy designed to give more families access to affordable childcare may look to give parents greater freedom of choice or to reduce dependence on benefits by assisting parents to return to work (so that it is expected most parents will take up these opportunities). Yet it may be the case that the policy is not described consistently in terms of either of those alternative objectives in spite of the fact that they can be in conflict with each other.

In a large organization, such as the national government, there can also be actions in different areas of policy, which may or may not lead to coordinated actions in different areas of the education system. For example, at the time of the 2015 general election, the Conservative Party, who secured a small majority and formed the subsequent government, had policies (enacted through the parliamentary process) intended to promote:

- the expansion of funded childcare provisions in England for families with working parents to 30 hours (for families where a parent does not work or with high income levels, the level of funded provision will remain at 15 hours for 38 weeks of the year); as childcare is devolved, measures in other countries of the UK are dealt with by devolved government
- the provision of more and clearer information on childcare provision in each local area
- the intention to speed up the adoption process for children and the expectation for local authorities to work more effectively together to remove geographical boundaries
- further devolution of powers from central to local government through elected mayors, mainly in city areas, but with potentially extended boundaries across traditional local authority areas.

At the same time, it intended to fund the growing demand for post-16 education among young people, partly by depending more on employers as trainers and employers of this group through apprenticeship schemes, as announced in the July 2015 budget. A case could be made for each of these policies, but there is often tension between them, as discussed further in Chapters 8 and 9. For example, the majority of work is organized on a local authority basis but there is clear evidence of these barriers being eroded in some areas (e.g. adoption). There are also changes in governance at a local level with local devolution, including the election of mayors with substantial powers over many aspects of local services, focused on large cities in the north of England.

The third level of policy-making is that of the detailed arrangements that need to be made if the broad objectives are to be achieved. The law may have to be changed. Organizational structures may have to be put in place. New funding may have to be found. Particular efforts may have to be made to secure support for the broad objectives. Chapter 5 gives many examples of these and other aspects of implementation of policy.

There are always choices to be made in determining what kinds of arrangements will best meet the stated objectives. For example, if it is decided to make it easier for parents to afford childcare, this can be done by:

- measures (such as Child Tax Credit) to support family income and support parents to find the money for childcare
- subsidies paid directly to independent childcare providers or subsidized provision by local authorities or other parts of the public sector.

Whichever of these is chosen (and governments often adopt measures that have elements of both approaches), the arrangements are likely to be connected with the way in which broad objectives are conceived and with objectives in other fields (such as general economic policy).

Policy-makers might also want to offset possible disadvantages in one set of arrangements by creating others without changing the first. For example, the recent Conservative–Liberal Democrat Coalition Government sought to increase access and improve the quality of childcare in England by:

- raising the status of the workforce by introducing new qualifications and enhancing the standard of level 3 qualifications (e.g. through Early Years Teacher (EYT) and Early Years Educator (EYE) status)
- making the EYFS a statutory requirement and putting a greater emphasis on learning and development (which is increasingly expressed in terms of school 'readiness')
- focusing on the quality rather than the quantity of practitioners through amendments to required staffing ratios in early years settings
- improving the regulatory regime by simplification of the Ofsted registration function and focusing on child outcomes more explicitly in inspection judgements
- offering more parental choice in choosing childcare.

So far, this chapter has focused primarily on a discussion of government policy, but if policy is the attempt to think coherently about objectives and the means to achieve them, then policy-making is something that will occur at every organizational level.

Politicians in government will have their own policies, but the UK is not a tightly controlled hierarchical organization where the prime minister decides what he wants to happen and everyone does as he wishes. As described in Chapter 4, the policies of government are heavily influenced by the views of a wide range of organizations as well as by the media and the general public. A new phenomenon to influence policy-making at governmental level has been Coalition government, where two parties have had to work together to command an overall majority in the House of Parliament. The impact of this on policy is that it has to broadly reflect the Coalition agreement (which was drawn up following the result of the 2010 general election). This agreement sets out the position of each party on overriding policy objectives and subsequent policy had to reflect this. Once policies have been determined, the government is dependent on many different agencies, and, again, the general public, for their successful implementation, as discussed further in Chapter 5.

It is also important to bear in mind that in the field of early childhood education and care (ECEC), the national government and Parliament have direct responsibility mainly for England, and the devolved regimes in other parts of the UK now take the lead on this issue in their own countries, as described in Chapter 6.

Different departments of the Civil Service and government agencies such as Ofsted (or Ofsted's equivalents in Wales, Scotland and Northern Ireland) will need their own policies to work up the general directions from the politicians into detailed organizational and financial arrangements.

Local authorities and the National Health Service (NHS) will have their own policies for young children. The Labour governments of 1997–2010 took various steps to secure cooperation between them, but the Coalition Government that came to power in 2010 had strong reservations about some of the mechanisms it employed. An example of this was the demise of many Children's Centres and local Sure Start schemes due to funding cuts in local authorities. Different spending priorities can also impact on how policy is implemented. For example, funding for Child and Adolescent Mental Health Services (CAMHS) is often split between the NHS and local authorities, and the priorities of each organization can impact on how policy informs practice.

Early years settings will have their own policies and procedures on a whole range of practice issues. In some cases, the individual setting will be part of a wider organization, such as the education department or one of the national nursery chains, and will have policies common throughout the wider body. At this level, settings can be seen as just implementing policy. However, it is the setting that has the most impact on how policies are implemented in practice, and this in turn can impact most directly on public views and the response of other organizations, which in turn inform the response of government, making clear the cyclical nature of policy development.

ACTIVITY

Take one of the early years policies of the government or of your local authority as an example (e.g. Free Early Education Entitlement (FEEE)).

Describe the effects of that policy on any setting with which you are familiar.

The policy could be relevant to the general situation of the setting. It could have helped to make the setting more or less financially viable than it would otherwise have been or it could have affected the type of service offered (for example, the age range or the number of children with special needs received). The policy could also have affected daily practice in a variety of ways.

How has the policy come to have those effects? Have they always been what the policy-makers intended?

What are the characteristics of policies?

If a policy is the outcome of an attempt to think clearly and coherently about a particular issue, then it should have certain characteristics:

- The underlying assumptions about values and facts will be apparent.
- The broad objectives will be clear. It will be obvious who is intended to benefit from the policy and in what way, and objectives will be compatible with each other.
- The costs will be known and accepted by those responsible for implementation.
- Structural, financial and other arrangements will be made that are best designed to meet those objectives. Resources of all kinds will match the objectives adopted.
- The implications for day-to-day practice will be clear or, at least, the basis will be laid for those implications to be determined.
- Plans will be in place for communicating the policy and its implications to all those who need to know about it.
- The body making the policy will ensure that this particular policy is compatible with other policies on related topics that it has in place.
- The implementation of policy will be reviewed periodically in an effective way, so that policy can be modified if necessary.

Of course, many policies fail to meet all of these requirements all of the time. No one is perfect.

To take one example, those outlining a policy may be clear as to the identity of those it is hoped will benefit, but less clear on the identity of those who may be put at a disadvantage (a key part of the costs). Thus, it may be understood but not clearly stated that:

- tax advantages are being given to families with young children, *but* these will not be shared by other taxpayers
- financial assistance with childcare costs must be as simple as possible for parents, *but* this may mean additional paperwork or delays in payment for providers
- minimum standards will be required of early years services, *therefore* those unable to reach those standards will be forced to cease operation
- services may be required to cooperate more closely to the benefit of users *and* this may mean a loss or renegotiation of professional identity and status for some particular groups of staff.

Of course, the claim will often be made that *in the longer run* the whole of society will benefit from the improvements the policy will bring, so that the short-term disadvantages to some people are acceptable.

Written statements of policy

Policies are normally formed as a written document, although often in different formats at different levels – for example, written policy at national level which is sometimes enshrined in law through an Act of Parliament; written policy at local/national level that is presented as regulations or guidelines; written policy at institution level (e.g. a setting's special educational needs policy) that is informed by Acts, guidelines and/or codes of practice produced at a national and local level. This is not, however, always the case. Custom and practice can govern what is done in the absence of any written policy. Sometimes custom and practice can be more powerful than written policy and can guide practice in different directions to that of the written policy. This is true of central and local government, but is often more obvious in the case of an individual setting. A nursery may have a written policy that it should promote close cooperation with parents, but this policy could be undermined by administrative or security practices or the use of professional jargon that have the effect of 'freezing out' parents.

Sometimes policy can be created by inaction rather than action. A kind of negative policy creation can take place. For example, the absence of measures designed to make a setting inclusive and welcoming to children with special needs or from minority cultures can become, in effect, a policy to be exclusive and discriminatory, even though no one would state that it was intended (or, probably, even think it).

Policies should be clear about all the aspects defined in the previous section. Written statements of policy help to achieve this in two ways:

- The process of composing a written statement can itself help to clarify ideas that may be shared but not sufficiently articulated, or uncover disagreements that had not previously surfaced so that these can be resolved.
- A written statement is an essential step in communicating the policy to others, even though it is not usually adequate in itself. For practice to reflect the policy, it needs to be adopted and implemented by practitioners.

Written policy statements can take three basic forms:

- general statements that focus on the underlying assumptions and broad objectives and may be seen more as guidance
- those statements that spell out the assumptions and objectives in more detailed terms – this might include the identification of issues and possible ways forward on which the policy-makers' views are still tentative and on which they wish to consult
- detailed statements about the manner in which policy will be implemented – this form of policy is often statutory (it has been enacted through parliamentary statute and is a legal requirement).

Written policies are only useful to the extent that reference is made to them on a regular basis and their effectiveness is monitored and reviewed. Again, it may be easier to consider this at the level of the individual setting. Childcare inspectors have sometimes found that settings have excellent sets of written policies and procedures of which the staff seem completely unaware. This is pointless. The important thing is the quality of the experience of the children, not the quality of the document in the manager's office. The procedures are only important to the extent that they are helpful to staff and both govern and reflect their responses to the situations they encounter.

This is why it is dangerous to leave the composition of policy documents to a few experts. If a group of parents new to this kind of thing are trying to set up a pre-school in the local church hall and struggling to raise funds and do the other things they need to do, it may seem helpful if someone from outside offers to produce all their policy documentation for them. In the long run, it can be a recipe for disaster.

ACTIVITY

Select a policy statement from a setting in which you are working or have worked (including work as a volunteer or student on placement) and consider the following questions:

- Have you read the policy statement?
- Have you received any kind of briefing or training in its implementation?
- Were you involved in any way in the drafting of the document?
- Do you understand the reasoning behind the requirements it makes of staff?
- Are there any changes you would like to see made to the statement? If so, which changes and why?
- Do you understand what the policy statement requires you to do as a member of staff?
- Does your ability to understand the policy statement depend on your involvement in developing it?

Controversy in the debate on policy

Chapters 2 and 3 provide accounts of the development of government policy up to 2010, concluding with the end of the Labour Government and developments from May 2010 onwards. Chapter 4 deals with the influences that lead to broad changes in policy, while Chapter 5 explores the ways in which policies are put into practice through changes in the law or administrative arrangements. Our main focus is on what are conventionally called early childhood services (day care for young children, pre-school education, playwork and some support services for parents). We also say a little about services that cater for all children, but do not usually have special agencies for younger children, such as child protection services. We say very little about some areas of general policy that also have an important impact on the lives of young children – economic policy, the welfare benefits system or management of the built environment, for example. All four chapters underline some of the problematic aspects of policy. It can be easy to present the development of early years services as something inevitably moving in a single direction, with the main question being how quickly we will get to what is seen as the desired state of affairs. It is a key message of this book that change is a more complex process than that.

In the year or so before the general election of 2010, clearer differences began to emerge between the two major parties, with, for example, Labour showing itself willing to make Sure Start Children's Centres an increasingly universal service, while the Conservatives wanted them to focus on those families most in need. In March 2015, the government announced in the Budget a commitment to spend an extra £1.25 billion over five years on CAMHS. The Liberal Democrats argued that they had championed this and it followed the publication in the same month of a taskforce report into CAMHS. Again, this shows how differences between political parties can influence policy. It remains to be seen in the years following the 2015 general election whether this commitment becomes a reality as announced at the end of parliament, under the Conservative–Liberal Democrat Coalition, and the current Conservative majority government.

There are also controversies among the general public and practitioners around issues such as the possible disadvantages of day care, the role of different professions in early years services, the best ways of working with young children to help them benefit from later schooling and whether the state should or should not interfere more in family life (Simpson and Envy, 2015).

All of these disputes are important and, at the time of writing, it is still unclear whether the Conservative Government will take policy in a significantly new direction in relation to any of these issues.

SUMMARY

- There is nothing simple about the subject with which this book deals. However, that is not a reason to run away from policy issues and attempt to concentrate exclusively on the day-to-day job with all its problems and rewards.

- Policy is important because we have to think about what we are trying to do and why and how we are doing it.

- There are opportunities for influencing policy.

- If we ignore policy issues, they will not go away. With or without our participation, people will make decisions on the organizational context in which early years practitioners operate, the qualifications they need, their pay and other conditions, the resources that will be made available and, above all, what they should be doing with the children day by day.

- Children need more than our enthusiasm. They need us to think about what we are doing. In the end, that is what 'policy' means.

FURTHER READING

The field is changing rapidly, but earlier publications are still useful in spelling out some of the general issues and showing how far things have (and have not) moved in the recent past. Among books that can be recommended are:

Pugh, G. and Duffy, B. (eds) (2014) *Contemporary Issues in the Early Years: Working collaboratively for children* (6th edn), London: Paul Chapman Publishing.

Robertson, L. and Hill, D. (2014) 'Policy and ideologies in schooling and early years education in England: implications for and impacts on leadership, management and equality', *Management in Education*, 28, 4, 167–74.

Policy advice documents can also be a useful source to identify potential strengths and limitations of current policy. Professional associations, such as the British Educational Research Association (BERA), the British Early Childhood Education Research Association (BECERA) and the Association for the Professional Development of Early Years Educators (TACTYC), often produce policy advice papers that can assist this critique and make suggestions for further development. For example:

BERA (2014) *Policy Advice and Future Research Agendas: Early Years*, BERA/TACTYC. Available at: http://tactyc.org.uk/pdfs/BERA-TACTYC-Advice-document.pdf (accessed 19 October 2015).

It is also worth looking at early years policy in the context of wider social policy. Levin, P. (1997) *Making Social Policy*, Buckingham: Open University Press, was quoted earlier in this chapter. It will help you to understand the complexity of policy-making as a human endeavour, although it was written too early to reflect the changes in ECEC policy prior to the Labour government of 1997. More recent advances in educational social policy and the impact of devolved governance are relevant. There are chapters covering this in Blakemore, K. and Griggs, E. (2013) *Social Policy*, Maidenhead: Open University Press.

For those who want to keep up to date on developments in ECEC policy, there are different sources:

The weekly publication *Nursery World* has useful news items and a lively letters page, and often covers significant policy issues in its longer articles.

Government websites are an important source of official information, as are the websites of such bodies as your local authority children and families pages and national voluntary organizations, such as the Day Care Trust. (See 'Useful Websites' earlier in this book.)

An increasingly helpful source of the latest policy information is the social media site Twitter. Following relevant organizations (e.g. Children's Commissioners (for each of the countries of the UK); DfE; DfES Wales; Joseph Rowntree Foundation; Nursery World; Ofsted; Pre-school Alliance) can provide access to the latest policy documents and debates.

2

THE DEVELOPMENT OF EARLY
YEARS POLICY PRE-1997

THIS CHAPTER OUTLINES

- the relevance of the historical background to a fuller understanding of current policy on ECEC services

- some key features of the development of those services up until the election of the Labour Party to power in 1997.

This chapter and the next outline the history of ECEC services and policy-making up to the present. The chapters are divided by the election of a New Labour Government in 1997 because of the very significant focus on, and changes to, early years policy that took place during this period of government. This is discussed in Chapter 3.

However, the importance that the Labour Government of 1997–2010 attached to ECEC services was relatively new, as was the role of government in directing the development of ECEC services. There were few such services at all until the early years of the 19th century and those that were established in that period (or before-hand) relied mainly on philanthropists and voluntary organizations rather than on central or local government. Things began to change in the 19th century, but never at the pace that was achieved in France, for example, and it was only towards the end of the 20th century that the idea that ECEC services could be an important aspect of government policy began to take hold.

The historical background is significant because it underlines the fact that there is nothing guaranteed or permanent about policy on ECEC services. The disman-tling of the New Labour Every Child Matters (ECM) policy framework (DfES, 2003, 2004b, c) under the Coalition Government 2010–2015 exemplifies this. ECM introduced the greatest changes to early years policy both in the volume of policies and the scope of state intervention possibly ever to take place, but it was rapidly sidelined under the Coalition and then lapsed.

However, in spite of this, the historical background is rarely taken into account when such services are discussed. There are books that acknowledge its significance in relation to specific issues (Bilton, 1998) or services in general (Penn, 2005). There are also studies of specific aspects of our history, such as the valuable work by Brehony on the influence of Froebel and his followers in this country (in, for example, a book chapter published in 2000). Such publications tend to be exceptions. It is only relatively recently that a comprehensive survey of the history of ECEC services in England has been published, and that book reflects, as much as it corrects, the relatively low coverage of the topic elsewhere (Baldock, 2011).

Developments from the 16th century to the mid-20th century

The development of ECEC services followed on from changes in attitudes to childhood itself. There were many reasons for change, but the most fundamental explanation lies in the way the economic organization of our society was transformed from the time of the Tudors and with increasing rapidity from the end of the 18th century. The escalating pace of agricultural modernization, industrialization and urbanization gradually broke up the family as a unit of production and turned it into a unit of consumption. The worlds of work and home became increasingly separated. The roles of men and women within the family became differentiated in new ways. A world of childhood more strongly separated from adult society began to emerge (at least in the homes of families in more comfortable circumstances).

While the main driving force was economic change, other factors also came into play. Religion was one. The Reformation and the Civil War of the 17th century undermined the already limited role the church had formerly played in providing care and education for children whose parents were unable to do so. Debate on the responsibilities of parents followed. One particularly influential figure across Europe was the Czech Protestant theologian Comenius who, in a book first published in 1633, argued that children under 7 should be educated in the 'school of the mother', i.e. kept at home with mothers who would devote much of their time to the upbringing of those children (Comenius, 1956). Catholic thinkers were more prepared to see a role for the institutional church in work with young children. Long after most people had forgotten the theological origins of the differences, it remained the case that countries that had been largely Protestant (such as Britain) were more reluctant to see very young children cared for or educated outside the family home than countries, such as France and Spain, that had remained largely Catholic.

As religious belief began to fade from the picture, science became more significant in shaping attitudes to early childhood. From the 1890s, people began to study the cognitive development as well as the physical growth of small children, and in the early 20th century the picture was further modified with new perspectives on emotional development, especially those put forward by Freudians such as Melanie Klein.

In the 18th century, England failed to follow Scotland in the development of a system of basic education. In fact, fewer English children were in school in 1800 than there had been when Elizabeth I came to the throne in 1558. As the pace of industrialization and urbanization grew, many people saw the need for schools for children under 7. Infant schools were established by philanthropists on a voluntary basis, first in London then across much of the UK. The ideas of Froebel on education were spread by the many German immigrants in London, Manchester and other major cities from the middle of the century onwards. Central government became tentatively involved. A key date was 1839 when the Privy Council established its own Education Committee. However, the state's involvement was opposed by many (because it would limit the influence of the churches) and progress was slow. A universal system of elementary schooling was established by an Act of Parliament in 1870 and measures to strengthen that reform followed later. There was still a reluctance to accept fully that government now had the leading responsibility in this field. The age at which schooling should start was set at 5 years. This was lower than in much of Europe because English policy-makers believed that the schooling of the majority of children by the state was something of an unfortunate necessity and should be got out of the way as soon as possible.

If there was a reluctance to see the state take on responsibility for schooling, there was an even greater reluctance to see it provide day care for working mothers. A few employers recognized the potential benefits to themselves of providing their female employees with childcare where it was needed. There were also a large number of women called 'baby-farmers' who were paid by working-class parents to provide childminding and fostering services and who even acted as unofficial adoption agents. However, many opposed paid employment by the mothers of young children. A day nursery system for lower-paid families had barely begun to emerge by the 20th century and the number of day nurseries in the UK actually dropped quite drastically between the two world wars. There was some pressure on the school system from parents to take very young children, and this was seen as a source of difficulty in itself, since schools lacked the skills, equipment or space to cope with toddlers. It is also worth noting that while lower-income mothers were blamed for seeking the paid help of others to care for their children, mothers in more affluent families found themselves increasingly unable to cope without the help of nannies, and in 1892 Emily Ward opened the first training college for them – the Norland Institute.

The First World War reinforced a lesson that had been learned from the Boer War a few years previously – that many working-class men were in too poor a state of health to be adequate soldiers. There was a new emphasis during that war on the need for advice and other forms of support for young mothers and on the provision of play opportunities for older children in order to secure the health of future generations of soldiers. The impact was so significant that it led Dwork to give her book about maternal and child welfare services in this period the deliberately disconcerting title *War is Good for Babies* (1987). The period after the war might have seen further improvements. However, concerns about the health of pre-school children meant that the medical profession often had a dominant say in education and day care for children under 5. This was resented by leaders of the teaching profession (who opposed, for example, the development of separate nursery schools). More significantly, the economic problems of the inter-war years discouraged any real investment in ECEC services, which – as in later recessions – were seen as being among the most obvious forms of expenditure to cut.

There were, nevertheless, many arguing for better services. This is an aspect of the history of the period that is frequently forgotten. When the Women's Liberation Movement was formed in the 1970s, its adherents often described it as the 'second wave of feminism', as though nothing had happened between the victory of the Suffragettes in securing votes for women in 1918 and their own movement. In fact, feminist struggles continued throughout the inter-war period. When Bradford City Council closed down many of its nursery schools and play centres in the early 1930s, the politicians making the decisions were mainly men and those opposing them mainly women. More significantly, the gender dimension of the dispute was highlighted in the arguments in the local press and elsewhere.

The pressure for better childcare that was there already played an important part in securing such services during the Second World War. It is sometimes said that the government opened up day nurseries soon after the start of the war because it needed women for wartime production and took the cynical decision to close them down afterwards when it was no longer dependent on their contribution. There is some truth in this, but it is an over-simplification. Other aspects of what happened should be taken into account:

- Initially, the pressure for wartime day nurseries came from women's organizations. Many in government and among their professional advisers were reluctant to agree. They believed that, as children's day care is very labour intensive, the provision of nurseries would make no substantial difference to the war effort. There were also fears that children in nurseries would be especially vulnerable to both infectious diseases and enemy bombing.
- In so far as the government did want to see mothers freed up for wartime production, they would have preferred to see this being made possible by some kind of childminding. However, the two officially sponsored forms of childminding – the Volunteer Housewives Scheme and the Guardians Scheme – both had limited success due to costs and complex administrative procedures which led to low levels of take-up.
- A good deal of the day care that was provided during the war came not just from day nurseries, but also from play centres and extended hours nursery classes – services whose importance has often been ignored.
- The pace of closure of wartime nurseries after the war varied from place to place. In Sheffield, for example, it was not until 1953 that large-scale closures took place.

Before the war, many women had looked forward to improved ECEC services as the economic difficulties eased. After the war, the same women assumed that such services would form part of the new welfare state. It did not happen. The UK was in serious financial difficulties after the war and ECEC services were again among the first casualties of restrictions on public expenditure.

Developments from 1951 to 1997

In 1951 a long period of Conservative rule began (interrupted by periods of Labour Party rule in the 1960s and 1970s). This did not mean an immediate retreat from the newly established 'welfare state'. There was a considerable consensus on matters of policy, with the Conservatives accepting the welfare state and the Labour Party supporting many of the policies of the Conservatives on foreign affairs and defence. However, consolidation of the welfare state meant working within the framework already established (building more council houses, for example) rather than developing new institutions. The trauma of the war led many to seek a return to what was seen as normality, only with more financial security and better health services. There was little challenge to the established model of family life – many people wanted to get back to it again. The age at which couples married and had their first child dropped to a lower level in the 1950s and 1960s than at any other point in the 20th century.

However, as material comfort became better established, other problems began to emerge. The separation of work and home was being reinforced by the development of new residential areas – council estates, new towns and owner-occupied suburbs. Life in these areas was more comfortable, but in many ways more lonely than in older working-class neighbourhoods. Doctors began to talk about the spread of 'sub-clinical neurosis', the press of 'new town blues' (Alexander, 2009). The reduction in the amount of hard physical work involved in running a home (because of the then greater availability of domestic equipment, such as vacuum cleaners and washing machines) left women with time on their hands. The cost of those new homes also made the idea of paid employment more attractive. More and more women looked to go out to work even when their children were young.

The government was unhappy about this. One of the major policy changes introduced towards the end of the 1940s was an Act of Parliament regulating childminders and private nurseries, which were seen as a potential problem rather than as a resource for families. Local authority day nurseries were intended for families that were failing in some way. There were moves to improve the training of nursery nurses, but the qualifications offered by the National Nursery Examination Board were at a low level and many of those that secured them became nannies rather than day care workers. Innovation came from community organizations – not the government or the professions. The best-known example was the pre-school playgroup movement launched by a group of London housewives in 1960, which soon became a national organization (now called the Pre-school Learning Alliance). There were also moves to establish holiday playcare schemes that were similarly based on very local initiatives. Both playgroups and playschemes were designed primarily for the benefit of children rather than to make it easier for mothers to seek paid employment. However, they did undermine the idea that care in organized settings was only needed for families that were in some sense failing. They provided positive lessons of what could be achieved with young children and facilitated greater cooperation between providers and parents in planning for them than many of the services provided by the state.

The Labour Party, which was in power for much of the period from the middle of the 1960s to the end of the 1970s, made only tentative efforts to improve ECEC services. In 1968 the law on regulation was revised to bring more childminding arrangements within its scope and to encourage attention to avoiding accidental harm as well as infectious diseases. The Family Advice Centres, launched in a few places towards the end of the 1960s, anticipated in some ways the later Sure Start Children's Centres, but had too little support and died out. The Plowden Committee, set up to consider nursery classes and schools in England, and the similar body under Professor Gittins in Wales, had a significant impact on approaches to teaching but favoured only modest increases in the scale of nursery education, and even the degree of expansion they supported was lost in the economic problems of the 1970s.

The pressure from parents for more ECEC services grew only gradually. Little was done by the state. There were ventures from the voluntary and commercial sectors, but the major expansion in childcare was in the number of registered childminders. However, research conducted in the 1970s highlighted the poor quality of many registered childminders, who lacked any consistent form of training or support, not to mention the many unregistered ones.

In 1979, Margaret Thatcher became the UK's first woman prime minister. It might have been expected that this would bring about a new and improved situation for other career women. However, the Conservative Party was anxious to bring back adherence to older 'family values' and also wanted to restrict rather than enhance the role of the state in social life. The one really important contribution to ECEC services the party made was to set up a much more effective regulatory regime for children's day care and childminding as part of the 1989 Children Act. Even that was something taken on reluctantly under pressure from voluntary-sector organizations, and, once the Act was implemented, Conservatives expressed dissatisfaction with the way local authorities were implementing it. When Thatcher's successor John Major was prime minister, there were new moves on pre-school education. A serious start was made on devising a curriculum for children aged 3–5 and a system of vouchers was devised for nursery education. Even the latter was a half-hearted measure since it appears that the primary motivation was to try out the idea of vouchers before applying the scheme to the main school system.

Initiatives to develop ECEC services in the 1980s took place largely outside government. The number of private and voluntary day nurseries increased. Several voluntary bodies that had been set up some time earlier to provide health services for families with young children lost much of that role with a major reform of the National Health Service in 1974 and began to focus on day nursery provision and parent support. Teams set up in the social services departments to regulate childminding and nurseries began to offer advice and support as well as to regulate. Leaders of the teaching profession began to argue that there was a lack of direction in ECEC services and that giving a clear lead role to education was the best way to tackle this.

Pressure from outside government and the established professions grew significantly. A critical aspect of this was the establishment of a number of new third-sector organizations:

- The National Childminding Association (NCMA), which had been established in 1977, continued to develop its role in the improvement of childminding as a profession.
- In 1980 a National Child Care Campaign was launched in London.
- In 1982 the National Out of School Alliance (later called 4Children) was set up as an independent body to press for better out-of-school care.
- In 1986 the Daycare Trust was launched with plans to strengthen the case for better day care by publishing research.
- In 1987 an independent Children's Information Service was opened in Sheffield, specifically as a pilot for a possible nationwide network of such agencies.
- 1989 the National Children's Bureau set up the Early Childhood Forum, an important medium of exchange between people pressing for change.
- In 1990 the Childcare Association, representing private nurseries, was established, although this body did not survive for long and was effectively replaced in 2000 by the National Day Nurseries Association (NDNA).

ACTIVITY

Think about the developments in ECEC services discussed in this chapter and consider the following questions:

- What were the various reasons for developing ECEC services and how did they change over time?

- To what extent do you think ECEC services met the needs of children and families in the second half of the 20th century?

- What were the issues in ECEC facing the new government in 1997?

SUMMARY

This chapter has described:

- some of the factors that have influenced the opinions of the public, professionals and politicians on the place of ECEC services in the general scheme of things

- the slow progress made before the end of the 20th century in establishing services for young children

- the continuing difficulty that such services are not seen as being as integral to the welfare state as certain other services, and that, as a consequence, they are especially vulnerable in times of economic recession.

FURTHER READING 📖

The following readings explore policy development over time and offer an insight into the development of services in the past:

Baldock, P. (2011) *Developing Early Childhood Services: Past, present and future*, Maidenhead: Open University Press.

Cunningham, H. (2006) *The Invention of Childhood*, London: BBC Books.

The above two texts offer a good introduction to the historical study of childhood in this country.

Parker-Rees, R. and Willan, J. (eds) (2006) *Early Years Education: Major themes in education*, Oxford: Taylor & Francis Group. This piece outlines the history and tradition of early years education and is a useful source to explore the influences on policy development.

Wright, H. (2015) *The Child in Society*, London: Sage.

3

THE DEVELOPMENT OF EARLY YEARS POLICY FROM NEW LABOUR

THIS CHAPTER OUTLINES

- the relevance of the historical background to a fuller understanding of current policy on ECEC services

- the ways in which policy on ECEC developed from 1997 to 2010 under New Labour

- changes to early years policy under the Coalition Government 2010–2015

- directions for policy on ECEC services from 2015 under the new Conservative Government.

As discussed in Chapter 2, state involvement in the early years had been very limited and piecemeal prior to 1997. Despite a growing understanding of the significance of early years development in determining life chances, and the examples of more comprehensive systems of early years care and education from other countries, the early years remained on the back shelf in terms of policy and spending.

> Until 1997 maternity leave provision had been among the least generous in Europe (OECD, 2001) and state spending on childcare was almost non-existent. Some inner city areas provided free nursery education in nursery classes or schools, but for the most part playgroups and toddler groups were organized by the voluntary sector. With the exception of health checkups and payment of universal child benefit, the state largely stepped out of a baby's life after birth and only stepped back in when she arrived at primary school more than four years later. (Stewart and Obolenskaya, 2015: 6)

This was all to change. When New Labour won the election in 1997, the government went on to introduce the most wide ranging and comprehensive changes to early years policy ever to take place. This was in line with other nations which have focused on early years policy development in recent years, due to increases in the numbers of women working and a recognition of the importance of the early years to development and life chances (OECD, 2011). With a key focus on reducing child poverty and supporting early years development, it seemed in the period that Tony Blair was prime minister that a new consensus was developing on the place of ECEC services in the welfare state.

The Labour governments of 1997–2010 and the new emphasis on early years services

In 1985, while in opposition, the Labour Party produced a booklet explaining how it would – on securing power – initiate a new deal for ECEC services. Twelve years passed before the party was able to win a general election and put these ideas into practice. It was, however, able to initiate changes in many of the large cities where it controlled the local authorities. In particular, several of these set up 'integrated' services for young children and encouraged employers to consider workplace nurseries or other ways of subsidizing their employees' childcare costs. It was widely expected that Labour would do a great deal when the party came to power nationally in 1997.

However, there were important differences of perspective within the Labour Party's leadership. Tony Blair, who became leader of the party in 1994 and was prime minister from 1997 to 2007, supported moves to facilitate both day care and preschool education, but his own interest in and knowledge of the subject appear to have been slight. This is clear from the fact that ECEC services go unmentioned in the many books that describe his time in power, whether from vantage points on the inside or from a more distant perspective. It is also clear from the scant mention Blair gave the topic in a book outlining his political creed. He speaks in one brief passage of childcare being important so that single mothers can get off welfare and back to work, but has nothing else to say on the subject (Blair, 1996: 68). His own direct interventions in the field as prime minister were ill-judged and poorly informed. One occurred quite early in his premiership when he contemplated taking responsibility for early years services from his Education Minister and handing it back to Health. This seems to have resulted from his impatience with the slow pace of progress in establishing enough services to make a significant dent in welfare dependency, rather than from any principled position as to where such services should fit within the welfare state (Blunkett, 2006: 156–7). Another intervention occurred just before he resigned as prime minister when he said that Sure Start was one of the public services that he believed was doing badly, but failed to identify what he thought the problems – or the solutions – were (Wintour, 2006). Some of his ministers agreed with him. Estelle Morris, the Minister for Education, said in 2002 that she considered that everything that needed to be done to improve ECEC services had been accomplished and it was time the government turned to other issues. The reaction was so hostile that she back-tracked a little, but her statement was one indication of the low importance some senior members of Blair's government ascribed to the issue (Tweed, 2002).

Blair may not have seen ECEC services as a priority, but statements from the Labour Party had stimulated activity amongst those in the field and pressure began to build for more to be done. Moreover, Blair's Chancellor Gordon Brown seems to have seen the issue as more crucial than Blair himself did (Blunkett, 2006: 28). Thus, during Blair's second period of office, partly as a result of the scandal caused by the death of Victoria Climbié and the report of events compiled by Lord Laming in 2003, there was a renewed emphasis on the reform of ECEC services. Once Brown was prime minister himself and his close ally Ed Balls was put in charge of the new Department for Children, Schools and Families, the issue climbed even higher up the political agenda.

There were three main strands to the policy on ECEC services during Blair's first period in office:

- A National Childcare Strategy was published in a Green Paper (DfEE, 1998). The objective of the strategy was to encourage the development of new services, and at the same time to maximize the choice for parents. Because of the centrality given to the principle of parental choice, provision was not to be secured by any central plan that might have entailed establishing an early years centre in every neighbourhood, but by helping parents to pay for both childcare and pre-school education through tax credits and in other ways. In other words, the emphasis was entirely on assisting those with demands to secure the services they wanted, rather than on the state supplying services either directly or by sub-contracting providers from the voluntary or commercial spheres. The option of setting up a national system of local services was just not considered. It was too 'old Labour' (with a focus on welfare provided by the state) and too expensive.
- To offset some of the potential defects of a market-led policy, effort was put into securing greater coherence. In part, this was one aspect of the wider system of regular spending reviews instituted by Labour, although it was significant that work with children required a special set of arrangements within that system because so many departmental boundaries were crossed. Local authorities were required to establish Early Years Development and Childcare Partnerships (EYDCPs) to pull together the work of different local authority departments, the NHS at local level and various agencies outside the state. These were later judged not to have worked well (with most going out of existence by the end of 2004). However, the principle of partnership, which lay behind them, also underpinned later legislation to establish Local Area Agreements within local authority areas and Children's Trusts.
- A new system of regulation of childminding and day care was established in England under Ofsted, with a similar system in Wales under the new Welsh Assembly (later developments were to follow in Scotland and Northern Ireland). The Care Standards Act 2000 was not implemented until after the general election of 2001, but it entailed a number of significant changes. It highlighted the fact that the argument over which profession was to take the lead in ECEC services had been won by Education. It made it possible to combine the inspection processes for day care and nursery education. It paved the way for a system of regulation based on actual outcomes (i.e. what the experience of being cared for was like for the children involved) rather than inputs (i.e. detailed regulations on how providers were expected to operate). This required a new professionalism of both providers and childcare inspectors. The new system also laid the basis for

consistency across England in the judgements that were made on services that were inspected, and arranged for their publication on the Internet. It separated quite radically the arrangements for regulation from those for support of services (which stayed with LAs), with the intention at least of ensuring proper attention to both tasks. These were all important changes. They also marked a shift from preventing the bad to supporting improvements in quality. They must be seen alongside a number of initiatives that were taken to encourage the development of innovative services at local level. There are likely to be changes in the system of regulation in the future, but 2001 was probably the last time that a change in the law on regulation was a major part of any government's policy on ECEC services.

Blair's second period of office saw the consolidation of much of this. As well as the implementation of changes in the law, it also saw:

- the publication of *Birth to Three Matters*, an important official document on the quality of work with children under 3 that complemented the *Curriculum Guidance for the Foundation Stage* (Abbott, 2002)
- the Green Paper *Every Child Matters* (which laid down principles for work with all children and young people, including changes in the system to safeguard them from neglect or abuse) (DfES, 2003)
- the development of a network of Sure Start Children's Centres, starting in the poorest parts of the country, the purpose of which was to secure cooperation between agencies and innovative work at local level.

What undermined much of this was that the National Childcare Strategy was failing in its primary objective. Despite improvements in the quality of childcare, largely as a result of developing a better trained and qualified workforce, it was not sufficiently easy for parents to access good quality and affordable childcare and, therefore, to reduce child poverty and welfare dependency to the extent that was hoped for. There were detailed arguments between academics and others as to the scale on which these failures were happening, and there was no doubt that many local Sure Start projects were making a positive difference to the families that used their services. The fact remained that (as has happened in other countries) the impact of tax credits, nursery grants or other systems to help parents secure access to pre-school education and to childcare (including out-of-school-hours care for younger school-age children) did not lead to improvements in availability on the scale that had been anticipated.

When Brown became prime minister in 2007, Ed Balls attempted to deal with these difficulties, largely by the expenditure of enormous energy:

- Great effort was put into promoting the idea of Sure Start Children's Centres.
- Children's Trusts were given a new legislative basis as part of an Act of Parliament passed in 2009.
- A Children's Workforce Development Council (CWDC) was established to promote new ideas on ways in which professions concerned with children could be helped to work together more effectively, including a significant expansion in the amount of shared elements in professional training.

- Local authorities and NHS Primary Care Trusts in particular were leaned on to work more closely together on the elaboration and implementation of joint plans for children and young people.
- The Foundation Stage curriculum guidance introduced in 2000 was heavily revised and the 'stage' itself extended from covering children aged 3–5 years to children from birth until close on their sixth birthday.

Much of this was to the good, although there were complaints that too many resources were going into high-level discussions on joint planning and too few into implementation, and that the new Foundation Stage curriculum was too detailed and lent itself to burdensome paperwork.

Serious problems were also still arising in child protection. While the Laming Report (2003) had triggered new ways of working to prevent and identify abuse by involving all workers with children, whatever their role, issues of training and low skill levels in detecting and responding to abuse in some disciplines seemed at times to have left children more vulnerable than before. The introduction of the Common Assessment Framework (CAF), intended to promote multi-disciplinary work to reduce the incidence of abuse, was welcome, but it also put many childcare professionals such as teachers and early years workers, who did not have specialist safeguarding training or roles, into the frontline of child protection. Brandon et al. (2006) found that workloads increased with CAF, and that it was not always understood, often being used as a referral rather than an assessment tool. Different professional groups had different understandings of CAF, depending on professional roles and experience, and this led to confusion about the CAF process. The training provided was found to be inadequate to resolve these issues for some groups of staff.

Joined-up working was also harder to achieve than anticipated, with poor communication, lack of common systems and protocols, and professional distrust cited as reasons for difficulties in achieving integration both in services and working practices. The new Children's Service Authorities (CSAs), comprising children's social care services and education, were designed to bring services together to improve coordination and integrated working, but many concerns were expressed that as most of the directors came from education authorities, this meant a lack of effective leadership in safeguarding services, of which they had little experience. In addition, attempts to share information about children across different services and professionals through ContactPoint, an electronic database, were fraught with technical and ethical difficulties, and the system was dropped in 2010 when the Coalition came to power.

Despite these problems, there were significant improvements for families with young children with the introduction of 39 weeks' maternity leave, Sure Start Children's Centres in the most deprived areas of the country, and increased cash benefits to families (whether working or not) through tax credits and other means-tested benefits. However, reductions in child poverty, which seemed significant in the early years of New Labour, soon reached a plateau and evidence from the exhaustive research by the National Evaluation of Sure Start (NESS) was mixed in terms of the impact of Sure Start Local Programmes SSLPs on children's outcomes. Although NESS showed some improvements in parenting, such as increased numbers of mothers who were breastfeeding and fewer who were smoking, overall it was not clear that children's development had been impacted on significantly in Sure Start areas as opposed to other similar areas (DfE, 2010).

One of the main problems which remained was that of the *supply* of ECEC services. The Daycare Trust warned in 2009 that childcare costs were continuing to rise in a way that caused parents enormous problems without any obvious gains being made by providers or their staff. The number of providers was falling. Some of this may have been due to inadequate providers leaving the business and some providers offering a wider range of services, but it was clear that major difficulties lay ahead.

ACTIVITY

Talk to an experienced early years practitioner who has been in the field for some years:

- Ask them about the ways in which things have changed since they started work in early years. Which are the most important of the changes that have taken place in that person's opinion?

- What is their understanding of the thinking behind the changes of which they are most aware?

- Do they see the changes as making things better, on the whole, or worse for practitioners, children and parents?

- What do you make of their experience?

The Coalition Government 2010–2015

In the spring of 2010, the general election resulted in defeat for Labour, but no overall majority for the Conservatives who went into coalition with the Liberal Democrats to form a government. Although Sarah Teather, the first Minister for Children in the new government, was a Liberal Democrat, it was evident that the Conservatives had a stronger and more detailed approach to the issue, and that ECEC services were one of the areas where their views were likely to prevail. In the period from the electoral defeat of the Conservatives in 1997 to the rise of David Cameron to the leadership of the party at the end of 2005, Conservative leaders had made little reference to the Labour Government's new emphasis on young children. It seemed safe to assume that, while considerably less enthusiastic about policy developments than some in the Labour Party, they had no intention of reversing them. It gradually became clear that, with Cameron as Conservative leader, this was no longer a safe assumption.

Before the election of 2010, David Willetts, a leading Conservative, had twice made public statements about the need to slow down the development of Sure Start (Morton, 2009; Faux, 2010). In response, Balls highlighted the progress of Sure Start as one of the successes of the Labour Government. Even so, there was little reference to early years policy in the Conservative manifesto (Stewart and Obolenskaya, 2015). Once the Coalition Government was established, work began on chipping away at the changes the Labour Party had introduced. Some of these moves were symbolic. The crucial government department was once more called simply the Department of Education, although the functions relating to children that the previous government had transferred to that sphere were retained. This signalled a new and more limited focus on educational achievement and a move away from the five outcomes for children established under ECM. This was also evident in the discouragement everyone was given from making use of the phrase 'Every Child Matters' or referring to the five outcomes for children that policy should be serving. Since no one is ever likely to object to children being healthy, safe, materially secure or able to enjoy life and make a positive contribution to society, this step can only have been a re-branding exercise, underlining the split from the past. Other measures included a reduction in the funding and role, and eventual closure in 2011, of the Children's Workforce Development Council.

The key change – one signalled by the Conservatives long before the election – was to abandon the idea of Sure Start being a universal service and to concentrate effort on those families in greatest need, with a view to supporting low-income families in order to reduce child poverty and improve children's life chances (Stewart and Obolenskaya, 2015). Teather, in an article published in 2011, spoke of Sure Start as a 'universal service' whilst saying she wanted to 'better target those most in need'. If this was not confused thinking, the statement was certainly confusing. The new prime minister was rather clearer on the principle. In a speech given in August 2010, Cameron said that the 'sharp-elbowed middle classes' should keep out of Sure Start, which was 'for those who are suffering the greatest disadvantage' (Hope, 2010). This was in sharp contrast to the stated aim of the Labour Government to develop Sure Start as a universal service. Many were worried that it threatened a return to the situation that had prevailed for much of the period from the 1950s to the 1990s where local authority day nursery provision was seen as a service for failing families and consequently stigmatized. The collapse of a large number of community-based ECEC services, as their funding was withdrawn or drastically reduced, added to the potential for this to happen, since the manner in which those services were established and operated had produced some reduction of the distance between providers and their clientele.

Another key change was removing the focus from childcare and education services by aiming to recruit 4,200 more health visitors and doubling the number of places on the Family Nurse Partnership programme (supporting teenage parents), in order to achieve a greater focus on support for families in their own homes rather than in group settings (Stewart and Obolenskaya, 2015). However, support for ECEC services was reduced in real terms with 'spending per child on early education, childcare and Sure Start services falling by a quarter between 2009–10 and 2012–13, from £2,508 to £1,867' (2015: 5).

Despite their initial lack of focus on early years policy, the Coalition commissioned an independent review of poverty and life chances with a focus on the early years within a very short time of taking office. Following on from this, independent reviews of early intervention, the Early Years Foundation Stage and the early years workforce were also commissioned (Stewart and Obolenskaya, 2015). Collectively, these reviews recommended developing ECEC services to reduce poverty and improve life chances. Frank Field's (2010) review on poverty and life chances suggested shifting funding to 0–5-year-old provision, and Graham Allen's influential report on early intervention drew on a range of examples of well-established programmes and research to argue that focusing services on young children was both effective and a good use of resources (Allen, 2011). Allen made a persuasive argument that spending on late intervention in children's lives, where there are additional needs, was an ineffective use of resources, which, therefore, should be shifted to early intervention where change was more likely to happen. His proposal to introduce an Early Intervention Foundation primarily to support the development and dissemination of effective early intervention programmes and strategies was achieved in 2013.

The Tickell review of the Early Years Foundation Stage (EYFS) (2011) and Nutbrown's review of the early years workforce (2012) both recommended strategies for improving levels of qualifications in the early years workforce, and Tickell made recommendations on improving the EYFS curriculum. The reviews also recommended programmes of intervention which were seen as proven to work and more research into early intervention strategies (Allen, 2011). Together, these reviews strongly suggested considerable investment in the early years to improve health, educational attainment and the quality of family life for young children.

Early years policy started to emerge as a central part of the Coalition's child poverty and social mobility strategy under the Child Poverty Act 2010. However, the clear message was that their stated aims were to invest in support services for young children of lower-income families, to promote health and development, good quality early education, good parenting and early intervention for children with additional needs, but that enhanced cash benefits to low-income families were no longer a part of the package, as they had been under New Labour.

Despite what seemed a more promising start than was expected, in fact what was most notable at the time was the lack of early years policies in comparison with the previous regime. As Every Child Matters withered away, it was remarkable that very little was introduced to replace this vast raft of inter-linked strategies and interventions. As the new austerity chipped away at local authority budgets and new funding structures left Sure Start Children's Centres more vulnerable to cuts, services to young children came under attack from budget cuts and closure. Despite efforts to spend mainly on more vulnerable families and focus resources on more disadvantaged areas, the outcome was loss of services in many areas exacerbated by the removal of ringfencing to Sure Start budgets.

The changes to early years education are generally not seen as positive as they include removing the requirement for a qualified teacher in Sure Start Children's Centres, closing the Graduate Leader Fund which had provided for graduates in every centre, and closing the CWDC, as mentioned above. In addition, the Early Years Professional role has been replaced by the Early Years Teacher, a move that has been described as re-branding rather than genuine change, as the role does not require qualified teacher status. The EYFS was simplified in line with the recommendations of the Tickell Review, and new development checks were introduced at 2 and 4 years of age. The 4-year-old check focuses more on school readiness in line with the aims of the new EYFS. Concerns about these changes focus on the move away from supporting the child's overall development through early education services to a more narrow focus on preparation for school and improving school attainment.

Not all the changes are negative. Stewart and Obolenskay's 2015 review of the Coalition's early years policies suggests that there were links between New Labour and Coalition policies which provided some level of continuity in policy. Chiefly, the Child Poverty Act 2010, passed as the government was about to change, has been instrumental in keeping the reduction in child poverty on the political agenda, albeit with a different focus of social mobility under Conservative control. According to Stewart and Obolenskaya (2015), what the Coalition did achieve in early years policy development was:

- arrangements by which maternity/parental leave can be shared flexibly between parents
- free nursery provision of 15 hours for the 40% most disadvantaged 2-year-olds
- extension of free provision for 3–4-year-olds from 12 to 15 hours a week and more flexibility in how this can be used
- introduction of the Early Years Pupil Premium for families eligible for free school meals, albeit at a lower rate than for primary school children
- recruitment of 4,200 more health visitors by this year (2015) and an expansion of the Family Nurse Partnership programme to support more children and parents aged under 20 for the first two years of the child's life through intensive home visiting.

The impact of Coalition policies has been felt mainly through the reduction and abolition of benefits to families, including stricter eligibility criteria for some benefits and freezing of others such as Child Benefit. However, the impact on Sure Start Centres has also been difficult, with centres closing and merging, and loss of funding resulting in fewer services being offered despite growing demand. These changes have also been uneven, with some of the most disadvantaged authorities being hit hardest. Despite this, some centres have continued to provide a wide range of services and to meet demand, in authorities where early years provision has been protected from cuts and prioritized (4Children, 2014). This means, however, that the sustainability of Children's Centre services now rests on local authority spending decisions and a willingness to promote ECEC services at the expense of other commitments, leaving families with a postcode lottery as to what is available.

In conclusion, although the outcomes of the Coalition Government's policies on early years are not fully documented as yet, as it takes time for the full picture to emerge, there are clear indicators that young children and their families have lost out under the Coalition in comparison to New Labour. Overall, there has been a reduction in policy for early years in comparison with the previous New Labour's raft of legislation. The comprehensive approach of Every Child Matters has been dropped, with increased targeting of services such as Sure Start Centres, and the emphasis on childcare and education has been replaced by extending health services to young children. The focus on improving social mobility and reducing child poverty through services rather than cash benefits has been compromised by cuts to childcare support and Sure Start Centres, although New Labour plans to provide free nursery places for 2-year-olds and extended free hours for 3–4-year-olds have been honoured.

In addition, Stewart and Obolenskaya (2015) argue that the cuts to benefits for families with young children are the most significant for any group in England, with 'the abolition of the Health in Pregnancy Grant and Baby Tax Credit and the restriction of Sure Start Maternity Grant to first-borns only ... These three cuts together take £1,230 out of a family's budget between the sixth month of pregnancy and the baby's first birthday' (p. 51). Concerns have also been expressed about the failure to upgrade Early Years Teachers (who have replaced EYPs) to qualified teacher status and the removal of financial and other support for a graduate workforce in early years.

The Conservative Government 2015

In May 2015, the Conservatives were elected to government with an overall majority, with work and childcare as their first legislative targets. Their key proposals for early years legislation are:

- to double free childcare for 3–4-year-olds to 30 hours a week for families where all parents are working a minimum of 8 hours a week
- to increase rates to nursery providers to fund this increase, including capital funding to expand school nursery provision.

However, concerns have already been registered that this increase must be properly funded in order to ensure that providers can supply quality childcare and education at this level. Questions remain as to whether there will be sufficient capacity and whether the quality of provision can be maintained in light of the increased demand. Childcare and education organizations have emphasized that this development needs to be in the best interest of children and not just to improve maternal employability. A report published by the Nuffield Foundation in 2015 (Hillman and Williams, 2015) suggests that the rapid expansion in childcare and education that has taken place over the last two decades, within a mixed economy of providers, has already resulted in differential quality between private/independent provision and state provision. Despite the fact that most of the growth has taken place in the private, voluntary and independent (PVI) sectors, state provision continues to be of higher quality (Hillman and Williams, 2015).

This has implications for another period of fast expansion to accommodate the increase to 30 hours per child, as the Nuffield study showed that while children in high-quality provision experienced positive effects from childcare and education until they were in their teens, overall this effect was much less when looking at all provision, and the impact disappeared earlier on in the primary years. While variable quality may be the reason for the limited efficacy of childcare and education overall, it is also important to note that the report found high quality to be associated with graduate leadership in settings, whether state or PVI (Hillman and Williams, 2015). Without proper uplift of funding to providers or new initiatives to support a graduate workforce in early years (something which the Coalition failed to continue to fully support), then the issue of quality may become crucial.

SUMMARY

This chapter has described:

- the unprecedented extent and range of early years policy under New Labour which aimed to tackle child poverty, improve employment rates and reduce disadvantage for all children through benefits and services designed to support health, welfare and educational attainment

- the change in focus to social mobility and targeted services for disadvantaged families under the Coalition Government, against the backdrop of benefit and budget cuts as part of the new austerity

- proposals for continuing to focus on early years policy to drive social mobility and higher rates of maternal employment under the new Conservative Government.

FURTHER READING

The following readings explore aspects of Labour policy on ECEC:

Baldock, P. (2011) *Developing Early Childhood Services: Past, present and future*, Maidenhead: Open University Press.

Faulkner, D. and Coats, E.A. (2013) 'Early childhood policy and practice in England: twenty years of change', *International Journal of Early Years Education*, 21, 2/3, 244–63.

Lewis, J. (2011) 'From Sure Start to Children's Centres: an analysis of policy change in English early years programmes', *Journal of Social Policy*, 40, 1, 71–88.

Penn, H. and Randall, V. (2005) 'Childcare policy and local partnerships under Labour', *Journal of Social Policy*, 34, 1, 79–97.

Table 3.1   Key dates in the development of early years policy 1962–2015

This timeline sets out some of the principal dates in the development of early years in the UK over the last half-century (starting in 1962), in order to give you an overview and help you put particular events in their historical context.

NB: Only those general elections that led to a change of government are included.

1962	• The Nursery Schools Campaign becomes the National Association of Pre-School Playgroups (now the Pre-Schools Learning Alliance)
1963	• The Children and Young Persons Act provides the legislative base for Family Advice Centres
1964	• The Labour Party wins the general election
1965	• The Ministry of Health conducts an inquiry on childminding
1966	• The Handicapped Adventure Playground Association is launched – a significant event in the development of inclusion in play settings
1967	• The Plowden Report is published
1968	• The Health Services and Public Health Act tightens up the regulation of day care and childminding
1969	• The Children and Young Persons Act (among other things) increases the powers of local authorities to intervene in families
1970	• The Conservatives win the general election
1971	• Social Services Departments begin operating
1972	• The White Paper *Education: A Framework for Expansion* urges education departments to cooperate more closely with the voluntary and community sector in early childhood provision
1973	• A major research project on childminding undertaken by Brian and Sonia Jackson begins
1974	• The Labour Party wins the general election
1975	• The Children Act is passed in response to child abuse scandals
1976	• The DES/DHSS report *Low Cost Day Care for the Under-Fives* is produced • The National Conference at Sunningdale speaks of the dangers of emotional deprivation for children in day care – this is highly influential for many years to come
1977	• The National Childminding Association (NCMA) is launched
1978	• A government circular on the coordination of early childhood services is released
1979	• The Conservative Party wins the general election
1980	• The National Child Care Campaign is launched

(Continued)

Table 3.1   (Continued)

1981	• The Brierley Report leads to reforms at the National Nursery Examination Board
1982	• The National Out of School Alliance (Later 4Children) is launched
1983	• Changes in tax law create difficulties for assistance with childcare which employers offer their staff
1984	• The Workplace Nurseries Campaign is launched
1985	• The Labour Party presents its 'Charter' for under-5s
1986	• The Daycare Trust is launched • An 'integrated' service for early childhood is formed in Strathclyde (this is copied over the next decade in several local authorities run by the Labour Party)
1987	• The Clark Report speaks of the need for greater coordination of early childhood services
1988	• The National Curriculum is introduced in schools
1989	• The Children Act (among other things) extends the system of regulation of early years day care and childminding • The UN Convention on the Rights of the Child is published
1990	• The Rumbold Report on the education of 3–5-year-olds is published • The Scottish Childminding Association is launched
1991	• Guidance on the regulation of early childhood services is published by the government • The number of playgroups and childminders reaches an all-time high • The UK formally adopts the UN Convention on the Rights of the Child
1992	• The Schools Act establishes Ofsted • Part X of the 1989 Children Act (on regulation of early childhood services) is implemented
1993	• A government circular accuses local authorities of being too rigid in the regulation of early childhood services • The *First Class* report by Ofsted on reception classes is produced
1994	• The Council for Awards in Children's Care and Education (CACHE) is formed
1995	• A hearing in the High Court confirms that official Guidance and Regulations on the registration and inspection of early childhood services does not have the force of law
1996	• *Desirable Outcomes for Children's Learning on Entering Compulsory Education* is published by the Schools Curriculum and Assessment Authority – the start of what later became the Early Years Foundation Stage (EYFS) • The Nursery Education and Grant-Maintained Schools Act sets out the voucher system for nursery education

1997	• The Labour Party wins the general election

1998	• The National Childcare Strategy is launched

1999	• Working Families Tax Credit is introduced
	• The National Early Years Training Organisation is launched
	• The Protection of Children Act comes into force

2000	• The National Day Nurseries Association is launched
	• *Curriculum Guidance for the Foundation Stage* is published
	• The Care Standards Act (among other things) lays down the legislative basis for the transfer of early childhood services regulation from local authorities to Ofsted in England and the Assembly in Wales

2001	• Local authorities are obliged for the first time to provide information, advice and training services in the early years field
	• New regulatory regimes take over in England and Wales
	• The First Children's Commissioner is appointed in Wales
	• *For Scotland's Children* is published by the Scottish Executive

2002	• The Criminal Records Bureau begins work
	• *Birth to Three Matters* is published by the Sure Start Unit
	• The *Inter-departmental Review of Childcare* is published
	• A single Sure Start unit is established in the DfES

2003	• The Laming Report on the Victoria Climbié case is produced
	• *Every Child Matters* is published
	• A 'Children's Centres' programme is announced
	• The Children's Commissioner for Northern Ireland takes up their position

2004	• The *Common Core Prospectus* for early years is drafted
	• A system of 'light touch' regulation of nannies is announced
	• The EPPE (*Effective Provision of Pre-School Education)* report is published
	• The ten-year strategy for childcare in England is published
	• The Children Act comes into force
	• The Children's Commissioner for Scotland is appointed
	• The Childcare Working Group is set up by the Welsh Assembly Government

2005	• The Children's Commissioner for England is appointed
	• The Children's Workforce Development Council for England is launched
	• The evaluation of Sure Start is published

2006	• The Childcare Act comes into force
	• The first set of candidates secures the new EYPS
	• The Welsh Assembly publishes its strategic plan for education for 2006–2010

(Continued)

Table 3.1 (Continued)

2007	• A critical report on Children's Centres is published by the National Audit Office
	• Ofsted's range of responsibilities is significantly extended
	• The new SNP government in Scotland appoints the country's first Minister for Children and the Early Years
	• A new Department for Children, Schools and Families is established
	• The final version of the Welsh Foundation Stage guidance is published
	• The new qualifications framework for Scotland is published
	• The Department for Education in Northern Ireland assumes responsibility for Sure Start in the province
	• Critical reports on the ways in which government policy on funding early childhood services is working are issued by the Child Care Trust and HEDRA Consulting
2008	• The new EYFS in England is implemented
2009	• The Apprentices, Skills, Children and Learning Act (among other things) alters the law in relation to Children's Centres, Safeguarding Boards and Children's Trusts
2010	• The general election leads to a coalition government being formed by the Conservative Party and the Liberal Democrats
	• A review of the Early Years Foundation Stage is set up
	• Cuts in public spending begin
	• Ofsted figures show an 'alarming' drop in the number of childcare places in England
	• Private providers threaten to pull out of the nursery education grant system
	• Dunford reviews the role of the Children's Commissioner for England
	• The Frank Field report, *The Foundation Years: Preventing poor children becoming poor adults – the report of the Independent Review on Poverty and Life Chances*, is published
2011	• There is a continued decline in the number of childcare places
	• A survey by 4Children and the Daycare Trust suggests that some 250 Children's Centres in England could close
	• 4Children is asked to set up a group to lead work with the government on early childhood services, as part of the Department for Education's grant programme for the voluntary sector
	• An advisory group on early years policy is set up by the government
	• Funding is announced for childcare strategy in Northern Ireland
	• The government Green Paper, *Support and Aspiration: A new approach to SEN and disability*, sets out a new approach to supporting children and families with special educational needs and disabilities
	• The Tickell report on EYFS is published
	• The Munro review of child protection (final report) is produced

	• The Graham Allen report, *Early Intervention: The next steps*, is published • The Education Act 2011 is the first major education legislation from the Coalition Government. It focuses on many areas, including extending early years provision for 3–4-year olds and eligible 2-year-olds
2012	• Nutbrown reviews education and childcare qualifications (interim report March 2012, final report June 2012) • A Revised Statutory Framework for the Early Years Foundation Stage is produced
2013	• *More Great Childcare* is published, including details on planned reforms to raise the standard and quality of the early years workforce • The government publishes *More Affordable Childcare*, setting out plans to help working parents access childcare • The Early Years Teacher Status (EYTS) (replacing the Early Years Professional Status programme) and early years teacher training are introduced • The Teachers' Standards (Early Years) are published by the DfE • Funding for eligible 2-year-olds is introduced nationally in England (570 hours annually)
2014	• The Children and Families Act 2014 is given Royal Assent and passed into law (applicable to England) • A revised framework for the Early Years Foundation Stage (EYFS) is published, introducing Early Years Educator qualifications in September 2014 • Guidance is issued on the duties of local authorities, health bodies, schools and colleges on the SEND system for children and young people • The new SEND code of practice: 0 to 25 years is published • Legislation is passed removing the requirement for schools to register separately with Ofsted if they take 2-year-olds and allowing childminders to provide care on school premises under their childminding registration • Children and Young People (Scotland) Act 2014 is published with a focus on improving well-being and increasing the entitlement to funded early learning provision to 16 hours from 2015 (600 hours annually) • Scotland votes to reject independence and remain part of the UK in the referendum • Wales publishes a draft 10-year plan for the early years, childcare and play workforce
2015	• The general election returns a majority Conservative government • Early Years Pupil Premium (EYPP) is introduced for eligible 3–4-year olds • Childcare Bill is published – outlining a commitment to provide families, where all parents are working, with an entitlement to 30 hours of free childcare for their 3–4-year-olds • Funding for 2-year-olds is introduced for eligible children in Scotland (600 hours annually)

4

INFLUENCES ON
EARLY YEARS POLICY
DEVELOPMENT

THIS CHAPTER EXPLORES

- the range of influences on the formation and development of early years policy
- the ways in which policy is developed
- the first two levels of policy-making as described in Chapter 1 (underlying factors and broad objectives). The third level (detailed arrangements required to meet those objectives) is discussed in Chapter 5.

In this chapter, we explore case studies of policy development to demonstrate who is involved in policy-making and how particular policies come into being. The social and cultural contexts of early years policy development are discussed, along with the influence of social change and public opinion on the policy process. The roles of central and local government and key government agencies are also discussed with reference to the influence of early years agencies, organizations, practitioners and academics on how policy is developed.

Early years policy has been at the forefront of government policy-making for the last 20 years after a long period of previous neglect. But who and what influences the development of early years policy and how do particular policies come into being? There is nothing inevitable about the existence of specific early years policies – they are developed through human processes that are subject to many variables. The development of early years policy is usually part of much wider policy agendas, and the goals of early years policy may be broader than simply developing and structuring services for young children and their families. For example, within the New Labour political agenda (1997–2010), much of the development of ECEC services was part of a much bigger strategy to tackle poverty and raise standards of educational outcomes for children. The Coalition Government (2010–2015) also placed early years policy at the heart of its aims to improve social mobility and reduce child poverty. As such, the aims of early years policy have become multi-layered and complex, interweaving the development of ECEC services with other social goals.

For example, over the last 20 years early years policy has at some point been linked with the following policy goals:

- improving educational standards, particularly basic skills, especially among socially disadvantaged children
- increasing employability among school-leavers
- providing childcare so parents (particularly mothers) can go into work, education or training
- reducing the number of people dependent on state benefits in both the short and the long term
- ensuring better standards of health and welfare for all children
- reducing anti-social behaviour and crime rates.

This complexity of goals for early years policy can lead to tensions as to whether the policy will truly improve the quality of life for young children or whether goals such as reducing the benefits bill and getting more women into the labour market are more significant. For example, providing 30 hours' childcare a week for working families, as the current Conservative Government has promised, may seem a positive goal but is being in childcare for 30 hours a week best for children? This will, of course, depend on many factors such as the quality of care available and the child's age and circumstances, but there have to be concerns that the policy focus may be on improving maternal employment rates rather than improving life for children.

As illustrated in Chapters 2 and 3, which look at early years policy over recent years and through changes of government during those years, developments in early years policy cannot be viewed in isolation from the wider political agendas which shape them. A change in government not only produces new policies but also new policy goals and underpinning principles, depending on those agendas. But, why is it important to have an understanding of where early years policy comes from, and what determines the content of such policy? Practitioners need to understand the varied and interrelated factors influencing policy development in the early years, in order to be able to understand their own and others' roles in this process. It is also important to recognize that policy is neither exempt from trends nor made in isolation, but that it is a product of the prevailing social context within which it develops. Practitioners need to understand that policy will change and develop; that it can be questioned; can be considered wrong; and can be influenced by their own views and actions.

Early years policy as a social construct

Social policies, including early years ones, are not created in a vacuum but develop within a historical, cultural and ideological framework. Policy is subject to trends and the influence of dominant viewpoints. It is based on previous policy, which may continue to shape it. It may be influenced by single events or long-term trends. It can be influenced by feedback from those who implement it or research by academics or practitioners. Policy is not developed outside 'real life' but is dependent on what happens in practice whilst at the same time influencing this.

Early years policy can be described as a social construct because its nature and content are dependent at any point in time on the social and cultural context within which it is made and implemented. As such, early years policy will change over time and develop within the society in which it is made. Early years policy is subject not only to wider social and cultural trends and developments, but also to specific events within the field of early years. Often, policy developments are a result of the interactions between a complex range of factors.

Historical perspectives on early years policy, like any other policy, are dependent on viewing past events from the ideology and value-systems of the present, resulting in changed perceptions of the relevance of those policies. For example, Moss (2003) discusses how childcare policy has changed over time and how 'best practice' in the past seems 'grotesquely inappropriate' today. Moss concludes:

> care – policy and practice is situated within particular temporal, spatial and cultural contexts. What we see as best practice today may not seem so in another generation, nor will it necessarily be viewed as such from the perspectives of those countries and groups who prefer different approaches or who have different traditions. An historical perspective is a reminder of the provisional and contingent status of all policies, and the practices and provisions to which they give rise. (2003: 16)

For example, one of the authors of this book remembers visiting a residential nursery in the 1970s where children under 2 were cared for either because they were waiting to be placed for adoption or because they were in the short- or long-term care of the local authority. At the time, this type of care was diminishing rapidly as changing views of the needs of infants, particularly around attachment needs, led to the development of policies which determined that all young children should be placed in family care. Within current thinking, this type of group care of young infants goes against everything we know about the needs of children of this age, exemplified by the human rights outcry against such nurseries in countries like Romania and China. However, in the past, young children were routinely raised in orphanages and children's homes, sometimes from birth, and this was considered a positive aspect of child welfare.

In the next section, the various influences on early years policy development are illustrated in an extended case study of how the original Sure Start Local Programmes were developed. This case study is intended to demonstrate the ways in which a range of influences shape policy development at a particular time and how these influences interact with each other.

CASE STUDY 4.1

Early years policy development: Sure Start

One early years policy development that clearly exemplifies the varied range of interrelated factors which come together to influence policy at a particular point in time and place is that of Sure Start. This highly significant development in early years policy has evolved over the last three governments in response to different political influences and goals. The original Sure Start Local Programmes (SSLPs) developed in the way they did because of the conjunction of a range of events at a time when the political agenda created an opportunity for this type of project. However, since that time Sure Start centres have been adapted and developed to meet different political goals and policy aims.

In 1997, New Labour came to power with a remit to tackle poverty and social exclusion. A comprehensive spending review was undertaken to look at how public money was being spent and to make reforms to take into account the spending priorities of the new government. Although most of this review was done on a department-by-department basis, some areas of policy, such as early years, were not the responsibility of one department and so were subject to 'cross-cutting' reviews across a number of departments. At this time, early years was not a major area of policy development and had certainly not gained the significance that it has now. The fact that there was no single department responsible for early years exemplifies this. The early years 'cross-cutting' review was also influenced by the perception that ECEC services were failing the most needy children and families. The departments involved were many:

> As well as the obvious departments like health (including personal social services), education and employment (including childcare), there were also social security (benefits for children and families), environment, transport and the regions (urban regeneration and housing), home office (policy on the family), the Lord Chancellor's Department (family law), culture, media and sport (children's play) and the Treasury (the money) – not forgetting the Scots, Welsh and Northern Irish, each with their own subtly different mix of policies. (Glass, 1999: 2)

The sheer number of departments involved led to the appointment of Tessa Jowell, the Minister for Public Health, as the chair of the group, not as departmental representative but in her own right. This was significant in that she strongly influenced changes in the remit to look at under 7s and refocused the review on birth to 3s and pre-conception as the period most likely to influence long-term changes in outcomes for children. Although usually this type of review would mainly have been done through the relevant departments, as outlined above, early in the review many other agencies became involved, either through being contacted by government officials or through their own interventions.

This meant that the development of SSLPs was influenced right from the start by organizations such as the Pre-school Learning Alliance (PLA), the National Children's

(Continued)

(Continued)

Bureau (NCB), various ECEC services and academics involved in the field. This involvement by those in practice led to a series of seminars where government officials and ministers met with those directly involved in ECEC services from 'a wide range of disciplines including child development, social work, health and demography as well as practitioners and local politicians' (Glass, 1999: 3). It also led to the commissioning of a review of research into 'what worked' to support children and families by Marjorie Smith of the Thomas Coram Research Unit (Smith et al., 1998).

The result of all this range of activity was the conclusion, in the review, that services needed to be developed to support children and families in their earliest years of life to combat multiple disadvantages that had a significant negative influence on children's life chances. Such services needed to be consistently targeted on under-4s, where service provision had been persistently neglected and which was, as a result, fragmented and unevenly distributed geographically. Other factors found to be significant in the delivery of such services were the need to provide community-based services, to involve parents and to provide family support at a high level. Developments also needed to be long term, sustainable, multi-disciplinary and culturally sensitive.

The influence of the US Head Start programme, which had been running since 1965, was also highly significant in the development of Sure Start. The Head Start programmes had been developed to support pre-school children from low-income families in order to improve educational attainment and general health and welfare. Early Head Start was established in 1995 to extend the programme to children aged from birth to 3 and pregnant women. The development of SSLPs drew much from the structure and philosophy of Head Start, particularly the child-focused and multi-agency approach.

And so the SSLPs were born and with them the start of the New Labour government's later wide-ranging Sure Start initiative. Some of the key factors influencing policy development, which resulted in the establishment of SSLPs, were:

- a newly elected government with a mandate to tackle social exclusion

- the decision to look at young children's needs across departments (the cross-cutting review)

- the review of research on 'what works' for young children

- the extensive involvement of agencies and practitioners in that review.

The commitment to SSLPs was significant, reflected in the growth of the number of programmes. Between the initial 250 established in 1999 and the sixth 'wave' in 2003, a total of 524 SSLPs were set up in the 20% most disadvantaged wards in the country. Evaluation of the SSLPs was achieved through a six-year-long project – the National Evaluation of Sure Start (NESS). Earlier reports showed that there were mixed results, with inconsistencies between SSLPs and some evidence that SSLPs may have failed to reach the most disadvantaged families they sought to support. Evidence showed positive developments in terms of involving parents but a more mixed and less successful set of outcomes for partnership between agencies. However, the NESS team reported that SSLPs had been successful in that:

- Parents of 3-year-old children showed less negative parenting while providing their children with a better home learning environment.

- Three-year-old children in SSLP areas had better social development with higher levels of positive social behaviour and independence/self-regulation than children in similar areas not having an SSLP.

- The SSLP effects for positive social behaviour appeared to be a consequence of the SSLP benefits on parenting.

- Three-year-old children in SSLP areas had higher immunisation rates and fewer accidental injuries than children in similar areas not having an SSLP.

- Families living in SSLP areas used more child- and family-related services than those living elsewhere. (Adapted from NESS Research Team, 2008: 1.)

After 2003, SSLPs and other existing provision such as neighbourhood nurseries and Early Excellence Centres were transformed into Sure Start Children's Centres (SSCCs), in response to further policy development which sought to mainstream the types of provision developed through SSLPs. This was in line with New Labour policy to provide universal services to young children as part of their Every Child Matters (ECM) strategy. In 2002, the Sure Start Unit and the Early Years and Childcare Unit had merged to integrate Sure Start and government childcare strategies.

SSCCs rolled out across the country, with one in every community (over 3,600) by 2011, fulfilling the policy goal to develop universal coverage from the previously targeted SSLPs, which were located mainly in deprived areas. The development of SSCCs was placed firmly within local authorities, in that since 2004 they were responsible for 'co-ordinating local planning and carrying accountability for delivery' (Arnold, 2005: 7). In addition, developing leadership in SSCCs was a key focus for ensuring effective change management, with the establishment of the National Professional Qualification in Integrated Centre Leadership (NPQICL) through the National College for School Leadership, piloted in 2004 and rolled out to Children's Centre managers from 2005 onwards.

The development of SSCCs was based on establishing holistic services for families and children under 5, aiming to provide:

- affordable, quality childcare and education

- health and family support services

- services for children and families with special needs

- co-located, integrated service provision to better meet the needs of all children and families and to provide early assessment and intervention for children with additional needs.

This was a particular example of the application of the principles associated with ECM, which aimed for all children to be healthy, safe, enjoying achievement, making a positive contribution and achieving economic well-being. The goal in this

(Continued)

(Continued)

case was to develop integrated mainstream services for all children, which would also better support the children and families most in need. In order to promote this, development work was done on mainstreaming Sure Start principles and practice through seven pilots running between 2002 and 2004. While the actual services provided varied, the pilots all focused on:

- developing parenting and family support

- training paraprofessionals (frontline workers such as early years practitioners) to provide services such as speech therapy

- co-locating and integrating service provision (including health)

- developing databases

- providing multi-disciplinary training. (Sure Start, 2008)

The evaluation of the mainstreaming pilots provided feedback relevant for the development of SSCCs:

- the use of existing local strategic networks, which was more effective than trying to build new ones

- the need for cross-agency steering groups, pilot coordinators and project managers to keep new developments on track

- feedback systems to monitor progress

- early planning and development of mainstreaming strategies

- time and resources for frontline staff

- regard for both national and local policy and priorities

- champions for mainstreaming Sure Start approaches and making the case for change. (White et al., 2005)

One of the key arguments for moving from SSLPs focused on disadvantaged areas to universal SSCCs was that some children and families with needs who lived outside Sure Start areas did not get a service. However, the development of SSCCs led to a number of concerns about the loss of SSLPs as they stood (Glass, 2005). These concerns focused on several areas:

- Spending was much lower per child as budgets were more thinly spread.

- Parental involvement and the role of the voluntary and community sectors were seen as under threat under LA control.

- Services would be less focused on the most needy and more focused on childcare and parental employability.

- Prescriptive guidelines would lead to fewer local choices.

- Professionals from some other agencies, particularly health, were not employed by the SSCCs and therefore it was more difficult to secure effective services.

An evaluation of SSCCs by the National Audit Office (NAO), published in 2006, found that:

- most families were happy with the quality of services, and centres were meeting the needs of some families

- fathers, ethnic minority groups (in areas where they were a smaller part of the population), families of children with disabilities and families with the highest level of difficulty were not yet having their needs met across the centres

- not all centres had developed effective working arrangements with health and employment services

- leadership challenges in developing effective inter-professional cooperation needed to be met

- there were difficulties in measuring the cost-effectiveness of services.

Similarly, Ofsted (2006a) found that SSCCs were meeting children's needs and were generally well managed, but that measuring the outcomes of extended services posed a challenge, as did short-term funding. Ofsted found that 'The most successful providers shaped the provision gradually to reflect their community's needs and wants in collaboration with other agencies' (2006a: 3).

In early 2008, Ofsted reported again on the progress of SSCCs, finding that:

- centres were generally successful in promoting the ECM outcomes

- parents were positive about the childcare on offer, and children using the centres were generally well prepared for school.

However, although local authorities supported the setting up of centres, Ofsted (2008) found that they gave less support for monitoring and evaluation, and despite performance management guidance issued in late 2006 this continued to be an area for development for centres (DfES, 2006). The guidance aimed to support clearer monitoring and evaluation to ensure that services also reached the most disadvantaged groups and that outcomes for children's achievement could be tracked.

Ofsted also found that:

- services within centres were not always well coordinated and this may have affected take-up

- not all types of families were using the centres fully, with ethnic minority groups and families with disabilities less likely to.

When the Coalition Government came to power in 2010, the focus of SSCCs shifted again to targeted support for families in the greatest need, rather than the universal service SSCCs had become. The Conservative Party had echoed New Labour's commitment to SSCCs, but in fact the Coalition's austerity policies led to cuts to LA spending, which in turn led to the merger or closure of over 700 SSCCs from 2010. These closures were facilitated by the removal of ringfenced funding for SSCCs. Many other centres ran with reduced services and fewer staff,

(Continued)

(Continued)

and over 55% of day care places were lost when the Coalition removed the legal requirement for SSCCs to provide this service. This is despite the steady increase in users, for example an increase of 50,000 from 2013–2014 to reach 1.05 million (Butler, 2013; McVeigh, 2014). Estimates are that budgets for SSCCs have been cut by around 35% since 2010 (Barnardos, 2015).

This case study of policy relating to Sure Start over the last 16 years demonstrates that early years policy is influenced strongly by government ideologies and the policy strategies they put in place to achieve their goals. Although Sure Start has survived into its third government, changes to funding and the focus of the centres have reflected each government's policy goals and overall strategy. This has meant significant changes to the aims of Sure Start centres and the extent to which they have been supported by the government of the day. Changes have included:

- evolution from a targeted service aimed at disadvantaged families into a universal service for all families with young children and then back to being a targeted service

- cuts to funding under the Coalition Government, as austerity policies predominated, leading to closures, mergers, loss of staff and reduced services

- removal of the legal obligation established under New Labour to provide day care in all SSCCs and consequent cuts to the number of centres providing day care

- anticipation that under the current Conservative Government a new round of austerity economies will further undermine SSCCs, affecting staffing levels, leading to more closures and further reductions in services.

Factors influencing early years policy development

As discussed in the case study above, SSLPs (and later SSCCs) were established through the conjunction of a range of influences at a particular place and point in time. In the case study, one of the key factors was the complex interaction between political agendas, politicians, civil servants and the professional groups who became involved in the process of developing SSLPs. The election of New Labour in 1997 resulted in a shift of political objectives and placed individuals with an interest in developing services for young children in positions of power. This provided a forum for the views of professional organizations such as the NCB and the Thomas Coram Foundation to become more influential. However, the development of SSLPs into SSCCs and the more recent changes to SSCCs are mainly the result of changing political agendas.

Factors influencing policy development do not operate independently, but form systems, which create policy unique to themselves. A system can be defined as a set of elements interacting to achieve a goal. The components of a system are the elements that are involved in the processes of the system, which can affect the system and may be affected by it (Levine and Fitzgerald, 1992). For example, in the development of SSLPs the elements involved in this process included the work of the cross-cutting review and the contributions of politicians, civil servants, practitioners, agencies and researchers (Figure 4.1). However, within systems theory there is a belief that in order to understand some events, we need not just see the elements contributing to an event but also the whole, recognizing patterns and interrelationships between those elements (Senge and Lannon-Kim, 1991). In the case study, the important feature of the policy development was not just which individuals or agencies were involved in the process, but also the nature and quality of the interrelationships between them. A key feature of this development was the communication that took place between different elements, and the ways in which beliefs about how the needs of children and families could be best met were shaped by these communications. The development of SSLPs was not just based on ideas about how children's needs could best be met but also on the perceived failures of previous policy. The subsequent change from SSLPs to SSCCs and then changes in the nature of SSCCs were more straightforwardly the result of political changes and the predominance of different political ideologies.

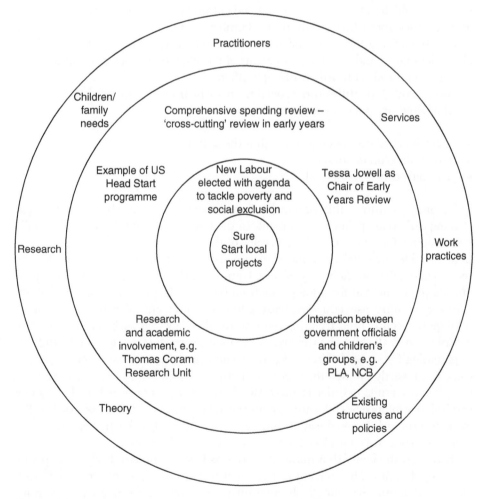

Figure 4.1   Systems diagram of the development of Sure Start

However, SSCCs continue to be supported through the All Party Parliamentary Group on SSCCs (established in 2010), which represents a range of interests in early years, both political and professional, leading us to conclude that policy in connection with SSCCs is still a product of a range of influences.

As was said at the end of Chapter 2, it is important to remember that, nationally, governments determine the direction of early years policy, and the ways in which other influences come to bear on government plans are complex. It is clear that the influence of factors such as lobbying by professional organizations and academic research may have no significant impact on policy development until it coincides with a political agenda. The ways in which political agendas are shaped and developed are discussed below.

The social and cultural context of early years policy

One of the most significant influences on early years policy is the social and cultural context in which policy is made. Social and cultural changes over time shape views and attitudes about how children and families should behave and be supported. Two of the driving forces behind more recent policy in the early years have been changes in how childcare is seen in terms of its value to children and families and changes in attitudes towards working mothers.

Moss (2003) identifies three social norms which have influenced the development of childcare policy over time:

- individualized care of children within the family
- gender division of labour
- national economic survival.

The changing nature of the relationship between these norms has been significant in shaping early years policy development. In the UK, strong cultural beliefs in family responsibility for children and the privacy of the family as an institution have been punctuated by the state's assumption of responsibility for children where families are seen to have failed in their duty of care. Until 1997, this meant that care of children outside the home had for a long time been seen as a last resort – undesirable but necessary in some cases (Daycare Trust, 2005). However, attitudes towards childcare have more recently been reconfigured towards the view that such care is a positive contribution to all children's welfare, rather than a compensation for poor standards of parenting for some children. This sea change in attitudes towards childcare has come about partly through the necessity of bringing women into a labour force hungry for new recruits in order to meet Moss' (2003) third norm: national economic survival. Acceptance of childcare as a universal benefit to children was aided by the integration of early years education and care and the growing belief that early learning is crucial to positive educational outcomes for children later on.

However, the belief that maternal care was best dominated early years policy for many decades. The concept of the superiority of one-to-one care of children within the family has largely hinged on perceptions of women's gender roles within the family and workforce. Historically, early years policy has been strongly influenced by views on the role of women and the 'best' care of young children. The belief that young children should be cared for by their mothers until school age was highly significant in the development of childcare policy throughout the period between the Second World War and the 1980s (Moss, 2003). For example, most of the day nurseries that opened during the Second World War, to allow women to work while men fought, closed rapidly after the war finished, as women were encouraged to return to their traditional roles, which included caring for children.

Even the Plowden Report (DES, 1967), which led to the expansion of nursery education through an increase in provision, clearly stated that part-time places should be offered because they discouraged women from working, and children needed to be with their mothers at least part of the day. Only in an exceptional and limited number of cases where financial need overruled the objections to mother–child separation were full-time places considered. Although the report recognized the strong links between social class and educational success, it also emphasized the role of nurseries in compensating for disadvantage rather than as a universal service for all young children. The Plowden Report continued to influence nursery education until the 1990s by perpetuating the split between education and care; ignoring the under-3s – and ignoring the needs of working parents.

The principle that children were best off at home with their mothers was challenged by the steady rise in the numbers of women working from the 1970s onwards as, increasingly, the woman's wage became an essential part of the family income. In addition to individual families needing to increase their income, the changing roles of women, driven by the women's movement throughout the 1970s and 1980s, and changing labour market needs, have resulted in social changes around perceptions of women's gender roles. More recently, the need to fill gaps in the labour market with increased numbers of women workers has been a strong factor in policy development. Demographic changes have led to concerns relating to national survival in terms of meeting labour market needs and supporting the increasing proportion of older people in the UK. As Brannen and Moss (2003) point out, an increased focus on early years policy has been partly influenced by falling birth rates and an ageing population.

Although women continue to have the main responsibility for young children, large numbers of women are in the workforce. In the UK, the number of working women with dependent children has grown. In 2013, 72% of married or cohabiting women with dependent children were in the workforce compared with 67% in 1996. Over the same period, the number of lone women with dependent children in employment rose from 43% to 60% (Office for National Statistics, 2013). Women are more likely than men to work part-time, particularly if they have dependent children. Nearly 40% of women with dependent children work part-time compared to 23% of those without.

Women's changing role in the labour market has influenced the development of ECEC services as demand for childcare rose steadily through the 1980s onwards. In the absence of a coherent policy to support the growing need for childcare, the growth of private day nurseries filled some of this gap, but this only met the needs of better-off families with well-paid jobs, as private day care was not affordable for many parents. The introduction of tax benefits under New Labour to reduce childcare costs to parents improved this situation for some but the cost of childcare still remains outside the reach of many families (Daycare Trust, 2005). More recently, the reduction in cash benefits to families has increased the cost of childcare to some.

The availability and affordability of childcare places for less well-off families continues to be a thorny problem for many, despite the growth of places since the National Childcare Strategy and other subsequent childcare policies. Despite the increase in women working, Britain still lags behind much of the industrialized world in terms of maternal employment rates. For British mothers who's youngest child is aged 3–5 years, the average employment rate is 58% compared to 64% across the industrialized world. Traditionally, families have relied on relatives to help out with childcare but there are fewer extended families and higher levels of geographical mobility now. As a result, fewer parents can rely on relatives to help out with childcare and their reliance on other forms of care has increased.

The Conservative Government's proposal of 30 hours' free childcare for 3-4-year-olds to working families appears to offer a positive solution but there are concerns about the availability of sufficient good quality places. However, the move towards state provision of free childcare at a level that offers parents a chance to work without prohibitive childcare costs is currently on the agenda of all political parties. Interestingly, the Employment Minister Priti Patel has been chosen to head the task-force set up by Cameron to oversee progress in implementing childcare policy. This signals clearly the emphasis on childcare as a means of improving maternal employ-ability rates, rather than it focusing on children's welfare and needs.

Other social trends have significance for the development of early years policy. Child poverty grew in the UK between the late 1970s and the 1990s in response to market-driven economic strategies and low investment in education, health and welfare for children. This growth in child poverty was widespread, with one in three children living in poverty in 1998 as compared to one in ten in 1979. However, between 1998/99, when Blair announced his intention to eradicate child poverty, and 2011/12, 1.1 million children were lifted out of poverty. More recently, as the recession took its toll and the Coalition Government introduced austerity measures leading to higher unemployment (7.8% in 2011), child poverty rose yet again to 3.8 million in 2009–10 – 30% of children in the UK (CPAG, 2012). Child poverty rates continue to be of deep concern, with 27% of children in Britain continuing to live in poverty (3.5 million children – End Child Poverty, 2015). Poverty was once most associated with a lack of work in families, but now two-thirds of children living in poverty are in households with at least one adult working (CPAG, 2015). To avoid poverty, families need to have more than one adult working and/or in well-paid employment. At present, one in ten men and one in five women work in low-paid jobs. Poverty is strongly linked to an inability to access well-paid work, with the gap between 'work rich' and 'work poor' families growing steadily. As part of the 'welfare to work' policy programme under New Labour, ECEC services were expanded to facilitate the return to work of more parents, particularly mothers. But many women continue to work part-time in low-paid jobs.

The Child Poverty Act was passed in 2010 with the support of all parties, with the aim of ending child poverty by 2020, as first proposed by Tony Blair. However, the Child Poverty Strategy published in 2011 as a result of the legislation was seen as disappointing and was described as 'weak' and 'empty of action' (End Child Poverty, 2011). The current Child Poverty Strategy (2014–17) has three aims:

- supporting families into work and increasing their earnings
- improving living standards
- preventing poor children becoming poor adults through raising their educational attainment. (HM Government, 2014)

The focus of the strategy is providing incentives for parents to work and some help with living costs, and an early years focus which includes the Early Years Premium, the increased free childcare hours and some support for parents. However, the emphasis is on individual family failure as the reason for poverty and the characteristics of families who may fail, and there is little recognition of any structural or institutional causes of poverty.

Poverty has an impact on many aspects of children's lives, including health and educational outcomes. It plays a key role in social exclusion and the impact of social exclusion on children's welfare, health and life chances, including possible effects on outcomes for future generations. The price of high levels of poverty is seen in high unemployment figures, high benefits bills, a poorly skilled workforce and family breakdown. High levels of poverty are linked to high crime figures and anti-social behaviour among children and young people.

The outcomes of poverty are significant for children, with one-third of all children:

- not having three meals a day
- missing out on toys, activities and school trips
- lacking adequate clothing.

Poor children also have shorter lives, lower birth weight (associated with a higher chance of infant death and disease), lower achievement in school, fewer qualifications and more chance of death or injury from accidents or fires (Ridge, 2011).

ACTIVITY

Think about the impact of poverty with reference to children you work with.
List what you think are the hopes of every parent for their child.
How do you think poverty may affect achievement of those goals?
Many families in poverty have at least one parent working. What might be the impact of recent cuts to tax credits for working families?

Political agendas

Prior to the election of New Labour in 1997, the long-term neglect of early years policy had resulted in ECEC services that were shaped as much by that neglect as by political intervention. For example, the provision of large-scale childcare by the state was seen as undesirable, and thus before 1997 there was a reduction rather than an expansion in local authority provision. Alongside this, there was a slow but escalating growth in the private and voluntary sector, with the development of adventure playgrounds and playschemes, mainly by voluntary bodies, the growth of registered childminding in some areas and a very slow growth in the number of private nurseries, which began to escalate in the early 1990s.

From 1997 to 2010, under New Labour, the central focus of social policy was the reduction of poverty, particularly child poverty, and early years policy came to the forefront as a key tool to drive poverty eradication and social inclusion. Tony Blair's Beveridge lecture (in March 1999; reprinted in Walker, 1999) included a pledge to eradicate child poverty within 20 years, which was subsequently supported by a raft of new policies and legislation. Roberts (2001: 53) stated that these measures were designed to 'lift around 1.2 million children out of poverty'. However, by 2006 indicators showed that progress in eradicating poverty had reached a plateau and targets were unlikely to be met. At present, between 3.5 and 4 million children live in poverty and poverty reduction remains a cross-party political goal, although there are political differences in terms of how this should be achieved. The Child Poverty Act 2010 reiterated the aim of eradicating child poverty by 2020.

The political agenda New Labour rolled out between 1997 and 2010 was a multi-layered and complex set of strategies to reduce poverty, relieve pressure on the welfare state, raise standards in young children to improve outcomes for them as school-leavers, improve employability, reduce crime and increase social stability. This agenda was also shaped by a distinctive philosophy influencing policy development – the emphasis on 'joined-up solutions' was a central influence in shaping policy responses to eradicate poverty. This 'joined up' philosophy was apparent in changes in the structure of children's services at national and local levels. One of the influences on this development in policy may have been studies by academics such as that by Peter Moss on the effectiveness of more universal ECEC services in other countries in meeting working parents' needs whilst raising educational standards. The benefits of universal ECEC services were the subject of campaigns and lobbying by organizations such as the Daycare Trust. In addition, studies such as the Effective Provision of Pre-School Education (EPPE) project have confirmed the value of early years care and education for young children in terms of benefits to their learning and development (Sylva et al., 2004).

A study by members and associates of the Centre for Analysis of Social Exclusion at the London School of Economics commented that the New Labour Government's agenda to reduce poverty involved both short-term cash and service benefits and long-term elements to improve life chances and standards for all children (Joseph Rowntree Foundation, 2005). This study also suggested that, in the short term, tax and benefits measures and the reduction of unemployment were successful in reducing poverty for about 1.3 million children.

The New Labour political agenda had its roots in the years spent in opposition to Conservative governments between 1979 and 1997. The Labour Party went through a period of bitter rivalry between right- and left-wing factions after its defeat in 1979, leading to a left-wing leadership win and the defection of the right-wing to a new party, the Social Democrats, in 1981. Failure to win the 1983 election led to reforms in the Labour Party's philosophy and policies, which became more marked after Tony Blair was elected party leader in 1994.

Effectively, the philosophy of the 'Third Way' (as it was initially called) was developed to ensure election success for the struggling Labour Party. The main theme was an economic strategy which sought to ameliorate the worst effects of laissez-faire economic policies on the most vulnerable groups. Within this broad approach, the expansion of childcare and other services for children and families was seen in terms of their advantages to parents and the labour market, rather than in terms of children themselves. This is in contrast to other European countries where childcare is seen primarily as a service to children, reflected in state subsidy to ensure investment in high-quality staff. Interestingly, both the Coalition and the new Conservative Government's approach to expanding childcare have been subject to similar criticisms, and as the plan to expand free childcare to working families unfolds, concerns about capacity and quality persist. It is clear, however, that childcare has become a central issue to political party manifestos, with the May 2015 election seeing 'bidding wars' between the different parties on how many free hours of childcare they would offer.

Although the reduction of child poverty drove a range of different social policy developments, the emphasis on improving conditions and outcomes for children has been a strong element of these. The trends in social development, described above, have led to a focus on the early years over the last 18 years after a long period of stagnant policy development and low levels of state involvement in strategic planning and development of the early years sector, as discussed in Chapter 2. Developments under New Labour included:

- increases in the number of childcare places to support working parents
- growth in the childcare workforce
- increased opportunities for training and gaining qualifications in the sector
- tax credits to support children and families, including those in low-paid employment
- extension of out-of-school care and of school provision
- development of integrated service delivery.

One of the key initiatives, the National Childcare Strategy, introduced in 1998, has included a range of developments to support early years and wider policy goals. The National Childcare Strategy was also significant in flagging up the new centrality of early years in the political agenda after years of indifference. Thirty years of neglect at national policy level had left ECEC services in a fragmented and inadequate state, with:

- a poorly paid workforce, with limited access to training and career development for many practitioners
- service provision dominated by a lack of coherence between sectors and low levels of availability and state investment
- an artificially created divide between care and education services, which meant many services failed to provide for the needs of children or parents.

The Coalition came to power in 2010 and immediately introduced policies designed to reduce national debt as a key priority. The impact on early years was significant in terms of the de-prioritization of policies aimed at supporting all families and the change in approach to reducing child poverty. While New Labour had tackled child poverty and social exclusion through cash benefits as well as service provision, the Coalition made it clear that while some services to support targeted families would continue or be developed, there would be reductions in cash benefits. Targeted services, deregulation and a focus on early intervention rather than universal services changed the nature of early years policy and practice under the Coalition considerably. The 'joined up' approach that had been significant to New Labour's ECM agenda was deprioritized, as was the focus on universal services for all children. For example, the closure of some SSCCs and the focus on family responsibility for children indicate a significant change in policy aims for young children. Despite the extension of free nursery places to 3- and 4-year-olds to 15 hours and the expansion of childcare places across the sectors, many working parents continued to struggle to find adequate day-long childcare that they could afford. Childminders continued to fill the gaps, but numbers fell and childcare places for children under 3 remained fewer and more expensive.

The net result is that, despite developments in childcare provision, at this point in time many children's care arrangements involve a number of different settings and individuals, are vulnerable to breakdown and deny the child coherence and consistency of care. For example, a child may be childminded between 2 and 3 years old or go to a day nursery. He/she may then continue at day nursery or go to nursery school for half a day and be cared for by relatives, friends or a childminder for the rest of the day. In some areas, nursery schools provide extended care for which parents pay. Most private day nurseries provide the free nursery education so that children can remain in the same setting all day, but this can be an expensive option and one not available to less well-off families. For many families, the options are bewildering and in choosing childcare it is no wonder that most parents do this on the basis of proximity and cost.

The proposed 30 hours of free childcare for working parents under the current Conservative Government may resolve this issue in terms of coherent childcare arrangements for young children, but already there are concerns about how the places are to be found, underfunding of providers, quality issues and whether the benefits will outweigh the potential costs. In one of the few studies into the effectiveness of free places on improving maternal employment, Brewer et al. (2014) found that there was a 3% rise in employment of mothers with a youngest child aged 3 due to the increase of free hours to 15. This is a very modest improvement.

Childcare organizations have focused on issues of quality and underfunding in the ongoing debate about whether the 30 free hours will work well. With 2 out of 5 private and non-profit providers not employing an early years graduate due to cost, there are concerns about the quality of placements offered to young children. Will they benefit? It is generally accepted that having an early years graduate raises quality in a setting and that for some children living in poorer conditions, attendance at a quality setting can offset some of the disadvantages of poverty. However, if the additional free hours are not just offered to quality settings, then for some children the experience will not be beneficial (Jeffreys, 2015). Concerns about underfunding already exist as private, independent and non-profit provider organizations argue that there is a funding gap already in terms of the 15 free hours, with concerns that further underfunding costs may be passed on to parents of other children. The government is planning a review aimed at raising the rates paid to providers.

ACTIVITY

Talk to some parents you know through work or as friends or neighbours and/ or consider your own experience of parenting and work:

- What issues (if any) do parents face in balancing work and childcare?

- What do children and parents experience on a day-to-day basis in order for parents to work?

- What improvements do you think 30 free hours of childcare may make for these families?

- Do you think there are any negative aspects of the current early years policy for children, parents and families?

Government bodies, professional organizations and other stakeholders

A key influence on early years policy is the role of government agencies and professional bodies in determining developments. For example, the location of early years in departmental structures has been significant in the governmental approaches to early years policy for some time now. New Labour transferred early years to the Department for Education and Employment from the Department of Health in 1998, signalling that early years policies were to be dominated by education in the future. In addition, the transfer of responsibility for standards and regulation from directors of social care services to Ofsted's Early Years Directorate and the creation of new responsibilities for support services in education departments in 2001 firmly placed childcare in the remit of the educationalists. The role of the Department of Health and social care services within local authorities became much less influential in shaping policy as a result. Despite this, the Department for Children, Schools and Families tried to reflect a multi-agency approach to early years under New Labour, which was promptly abandoned by the Coalition in 2010 as it hastily renamed the DCSF as the Department of Education. The emphasis on education as opposed to children's health and welfare is in line with policies under all recent governments that aim to improve child poverty rates through raising educational attainment.

One of the features of the rapid expansion of early years policy has been the increasing influence of professional organizations, academics and other stakeholders through their stronger links to civil servants and policy-makers. This process started under New Labour, carried on through the Coalition and is expected to continue under the Conservatives. An emphasis on evidence-based policy-making, public reviews and systematic evaluation strategies for new policies has become the norm in early years policy-making. As such, academics, research organizations and professional bodies have found a newly expanded role in policy development through government-funded research, reviews of aspects of early years, and evaluation projects. The Tickell Review (2011) on the EYFS, the Field Review on poverty (2010), the Allen Review on early intervention (2011) and Cathy Nutbrown's report on the childcare workforce (2012) were commissioned by the Coalition in order to shape and validate its early years policy.

Key professional organizations such as the National Children's Bureau, 4Children, the Thomas Coram Research Unit, the Pre-school Learning Alliance and the National Childminding Association, to name a few, have found influence in policy-making through their links with government agencies, and through the role professional organizations and children's charities have in developing policy through joint policy writing, consultations, responses to government proposals and the commissioning of research from professional organizations. This role has varied and while no government can afford to ignore influential organizations in the sector, the organizations themselves have the difficult job of maintaining their position and principles while adapting to work with different government strategies over time.

Academic institutions and individual academics have also found a steady voice in early years development through their role in developing aspects of policy, as well as through the influence of research, as discussed. However, this is not always an easy relationship as, while governments can commission studies, reviews and consultations, the providers of these may not have a say in the extent to which their recommendations are followed. For example, Cathy Nutbrown, who reviewed the childcare workforce for the Coalition, stated 'As I read beyond the headlines ... I realized that most of my recommendations had, in effect, been rejected' (Nutbrown, 2013) (cited in Stewart and Obolenskaya, 2015: 18). Nutbrown was concerned particularly that the new Early Years Teacher role (which replaced the Early Years Professional role) did not require Qualified Teacher Status, as she had recommended, and in fact was just a re-labelling exercise.

The Coalition Government did to some extent continue with evidence-based approaches to policy-making affecting early years, which became common under New Labour. The role of SSCCs was evaluated under this regime, as discussed above, and the introduction of evidence-based interventions is part of this change, aimed at reducing costs. However, as with all governments, the evidence chosen was that which reflected the government's wider policy agendas and overall aims. For example, the influential Allen Report (2011) on early intervention was cited to support this as a key aim in early years policy development under the Coalition. Recommendations in the 2011 report influenced early years policy, such as in the assessment of pre-school children; a renewed focus on parenting programmes; an early years education that focused on emotional and social development; more funding to Family Nurse Partnership schemes; and an emphasis on 'school readiness'.

Evidence-informed practice has been a significant development requiring individuals, organizations and policy-making bodies to support their decisions and practice with research findings. Evidence-informed findings and the outcomes of the evaluation of projects are increasingly gaining a significant influence on policy development. However, it is necessary to be cautious of this approach as the contested nature of most research and the possibility of the selective use of findings can impact on the value of 'evidence' as a basis for change, as discussed further in Chapter 7. Although the increased influence and involvement are generally welcome, there is a concern that the overwhelming influence of government may stifle the independent voice of professional organizations, academics and other stakeholders in the early years.

Significant events

Significant events are those that focus attention on existing failures or flaws in policy and legislation or the quality of services provided. Although these flaws and failures may already be in the public domain or part of the professional debate, key events may have a disproportionate impact as catalysts of change. Key events often draw a disproportionate amount of media attention, highlighting the need for change and shaping and directing public opinion. However, they must also resonate with government agendas in order to be influential. For example, the Utting Report (DoH/Welsh Office, 1997), drawing on research findings mainly from the voluntary organization associated with children in care, The Who Cares? Trust, determined that children 'looked after' by local authorities (those in public care) were likely to suffer dismal outcomes in terms of education, health, employment, mental health and risk of criminality, homelessness, drug and alcohol abuse. The report was commissioned in response to widespread concerns and public outrage at a series of revelations of abuse and mistreatment of children in the public care system. The policy response was rapid and broad, introducing the Quality Protects Strategy in 1998 (DoH, 1998), covering a range of measures to improve life chances for these children, including shorter waiting times for permanent placements, better monitoring of health and educational progress, and targets for improved educational achievements for children in care.

Another example was that the Green Paper *Every Child Matters* (DfES, 2003) was published in response to the recommendations of Lord Laming's inquiry report into the death of an 8-year-old girl called Victoria Climbié, who was killed by her aunt and her aunt's boyfriend in 2001 (Laming, 2003). Victoria Climbié's death brought about a sustained focus on deficits in the existing legislation and guidelines to protect children from abuse and neglect. This single case highlighted existing flaws in the management of child welfare, deficits in communication between key responsible agencies, poor-quality training and the lack of ability of staff to work effectively in protecting children. The sustained media interest in the case and the particularly tragic circumstances of the child's death were significant in the role that her death would play in influencing policy change. However, the influence of the Laming Report on the timing and content of ECM was not a simple linear relationship. Existing developments and plans within government also determined the changes and no single factor can be seen as the sole determinant of policy change.

Subsequently, the death of 17-month-old Peter Connelly in 2007 once again highlighted flaws in the child protection system. This led to a further report by Lord Laming (2009) which found that many of the recommendations of his previous report encompassed in ECM had not been fully or effectively implemented in all local authorities. Steps to improve child protection services were subsequently outlined in the Munro review (2011), leading to increased numbers of children coming into care and earlier action to protect children (Cafcass, 2012). The report showed that 'since 2008 the number of children taken into care in England has risen by 62% to more than 10,000 a year' (Bingham, 2012). The report also confirmed that in many cases, intervention was more timely and earlier. In this case, the links between the significant event and policy change are very clear.

International policy

In some ways, the influence of international policy development on UK policy is difficult to measure. However, there is no doubt that under New Labour early years policy development in other European countries was scrutinized and compared with that in the UK by academics such as Peter Moss and Helen Penn. It is also true that at that time there was a strongly Europhile influence in government. More recently, proposals to extend free childcare to 30 hours for working parents are in line with Scandinavian policies, which have provided state-supported childcare to working parents for some time. In this section, the influence of international policy on the early years is discussed in terms of its impact in the UK.

The adoption of the United Nations Convention on the Rights of the Child (UNCRC) in 1989 was a major step in establishing the rights of children as a key theme in policy development (OUNHCHR, 1989). However, within the EU there were only limited developments in policy relating to young children, which had only a small impact in the UK (Ruxton, 2001). This impact has partly been limited by resistance to the concept of EU intervention in the child and family policy field, based on the persistent ideology of non-interventionism which dominated UK child and family policy through the 1980s and 1990s, and by reluctance in most member states to extend the EU's influence in matters of social, as opposed to economic, policy. Areas where there has been an EU influence on family policy are in improving rights to maternity leave and restricting long hours of work. Both of these relate to economic affairs. However, Ruxton (2001: 69) argues that 'the EU has a very limited legal base for its action in relation to children'.

Despite this, there are common features of an agenda for early years policy in Europe. Moss (2001: 28) identifies these as:

- a legal right to parental leave
- public support for the childcare needs of employed parents
- public support for at least two years' education for all children before they start compulsory schooling.

However, he also points out that in the UK there has only been a clear commitment to this agenda since 1997. Under New Labour, there were indications that early years policy in the UK came increasingly under the influence of European developments, including the move towards universal ECEC services and integrated planning and services delivery. However, these trends were not sustained under the Coalition and are not on the Conservative policy agenda at present. While there is an all-party commitment to increase free childcare for working parents, other aspects of the much respected Scandinavian approaches, such as staffing with social pedagogues, have been dropped. The Early Years Professional was developed in line with the principles of social pedagogy, but this focus has been lost with the introduction of the Early Years Teacher. Certainly, the emphasis on qualified staff in some other European countries influenced New Labour to raise standards through the development of a graduate workforce, but this was not supported by the Coalition or, it seems, by the current Conservative Government.

CASE STUDY 4.2

Special educational needs: accumulative influences on early years policy

Special educational needs (SEN) policy provides a good example of how a number of the influences discussed above interact to shape policy and practice. In respect of SEN, the key influences on policy include:

- social and cultural developments in terms of how children with learning difficulties are viewed
- government agendas such as increasing the level of social inclusion
- stakeholder views such as voluntary and parent associations
- international policy promoting the globalization of children's rights agendas.

Before the 1980s, children with SEN were defined through medical models of disability and it was believed that many of these children could not be educated. Following an enquiry into the educational needs of children with disabilities, the Warnock Report was published in 1978 and the Education Act in 1981, establishing the concept of integration (inclusion) by legislating that children with SEN should be educated in mainstream schools if this was at all possible and that educational objectives should be the same for all children (HM Government, 2006). A proportion

(Continued)

(Continued)

of children identified as having learning difficulties are given a statement of SEN, which outlines the child's needs and how these would be met. About 17.9% of children in primary schools have SEN, and 1.4% of children in primary schools have statements of SEN. Overall, two million children have SEN and/or a disability (DfE, 2011b).

Warnock (Warnock Committee, 1978) did not ignore the under-5s in the report, focusing on the following principles for supporting children in their early years with SEN:

- support for parents as their children's primary educators

- early identification and assessment of SEN and support for children under 2

- training for all professionals involved with young children to recognize early signs of special needs and the social basis of some of these needs

- prompt and sensitive disclosure of disability to parents and access to information about support at an early stage

- a named contact for parents to provide a focus for advice and support.

The Education Act 1981 was not at the time supported by additional funding, and as such it became clear that statements of SEN were subject to resource limitations from their inception, and this tension between entitlement and resource restrictions has continued as a factor, as the number of children identified with SEN has risen and many special schools have closed (Croll and Moses, 2000). Muncey (1988) also critiques the Act, suggesting that it had many loopholes through which local authorities could choose not to make significant changes to their provision.

Additional pressures on the Warnock framework arose as testing within the National Curriculum, introduced in 1988, created competition between schools, pressuring them to focus on the children who might get good results. Moreover, in mainstream schools, 'integration' may sometimes mean segregation within the school through a number of mechanisms, including specialized units for children with disabilities, some of which are highly separate from the rest of the school (Dyson, 2005).

In the Warnock Report (1978), social deprivation was not identified as a cause of SEN. However, increasingly, clusters of children with SEN are found in particular schools, settings or areas as social disadvantage, poverty and class link to higher incidences of SEN, as do gender (boys) and ethnicity (Dyson, 2005). Moreover, families with children with disabilities are more likely to experience poverty as they may have restricted access to employment because of the child's needs and there may be additional expenses associated with the child's disability. This clustering creates particular problems for schools, which struggle to 'improve' in terms of conventional measured outcomes whilst supporting the needs of high numbers of children with SEN. As more children are identified with SEN linked to social issues such as autistic spectrum disorders (ASD), the principles of inclusion are tested as settings and schools struggle to provide for children with high levels of need. Ofsted (2006b) found that the increase in the number of children statemented for behavioural, emotional and social difficulties (BESD) meant that these children were more likely to be excluded from schools and that their inclusion was the biggest challenge to schools and settings. In the early years, too many children with emerging BESD did not get a quality response.

The Warnock Report established the principle of parent partnership to better support children with SEN, which was eventually enshrined in the Special Educational Needs Code of Practice (1993, 2001, 2015). This is a set of detailed procedures for schools, early years settings and other agencies involved in assessing and providing for children with SEN. Although parents have consistently preferred their children with SEN to be educated in mainstream schools (apart from a small number where the child has severe/complex disabilities), it is also recognized that the limitations on resources could impact negatively on successful inclusion. The concept of parent partnership in SEN is supported by the right to appeal against statementing decisions, which has introduced a 'quasi-judicial element into provision for SEN' (Croll and Moses, 2000).

Since the Warnock Report, policy has continued to focus on inclusion agendas for children with learning difficulties, including children with disabilities. Policies in the UK have been influenced throughout by international developments, including the 'globalisation of rights and entitlements' for children with disabilities (Artiles and Dyson, 2005: 38). The UNCRC articles 12 and 23 address the rights of children with disabilities in mainstream education. However, the UNCRC has been criticized for not establishing the principle that access to services according to need for disabled children should be a right (Quinn and Degener, 2002, cited in Mittler, 2005).

The United Nations Educational, Scientific and Cultural Organization (UNESCO) Salamanca Statement on Special Needs Education 1994, aligned the international inclusion agenda with children's rights campaigns and informed the Green Paper, *Excellence for All Children: Meeting special educational needs* (DfEE, 1997), which linked policies in this country to international trends (Mittler, 2005).

Other policy and legislation included:

- the SEN and Disability Act (SENDA) 2001, which provided some protection for disabled children against discrimination in schools and confirmed their right to education in mainstream schools wherever possible

- Removing Barriers to Achievement (DfES, 2004a), which set out the government agenda for children with SEN within the ECM policy agenda, focusing on early intervention; partnership with parents; inclusion; and raising achievement through teacher training and monitoring progress

- Together from the Start (DfES/DoH, 2003) and the Early Support programme, which focused on coordinating and raising standards for the youngest disabled children and delivering services to these children and their families through Children's Centres

- the Childcare Act 2006, which stated that LAs will only be deemed to have met the childcare needs of parents if there is sufficient provision for disabled children.

However, the Warnock framework was critiqued for no longer being able to meet the needs of children with SEN, not least by Warnock herself (2005). Key factors

(Continued)

(Continued)

under debate were the impact of inclusion on special school closures, changed concepts of SEN (now increasingly focused on social aspects of disability) and the impact of increased numbers of children with SEN in mainstream schools. In early years contexts, more children aged 3 and 4 had entered nursery education since the National Childcare Strategy started to promote increases in places in 1998. The earlier opportunity to assess young children's needs had led to many more children being identified as having SEN at an earlier stage, adding to the pressure on limited resources.

The *Statutory Assessment and Statements of SEN: In need of review?* document (Audit Commission, 2002) suggested that statutory assessment is both slow and expensive, and ultimately may not ensure the child's needs are met due to poor levels of monitoring and geographical variations in the availability of resources. The report also found that parents struggled with statementing, finding the process stressful to go through.

The Green Paper, *Support and Aspiration: A new approach to special educational needs and disability* (DfE, 2011b), which led to the Children and Families Act 2014 and which was implemented in September 2014, brought significant changes to the SEN system (DfE, 2014e). The rationale for change was that parents found the previous system difficult to comprehend and to be involved in, with adversarial aspects when negotiating support. There was lack of parental choice, poor information and low expectations of children. Many special needs were identified too late, and overall child and family needs were not always met (DfE, 2012).

The new arrangements were piloted through a Pathfinder programme across 31 councils, which found through evaluation that both parents and professionals welcomed the changes to the SEN system and particularly the closer involvement of families. The changes were generally welcomed by disability and SEN agencies and organizations as there was a consensus that there needed to be more emphasis on outcomes for children and on agencies working together more effectively, especially those concerned with health and LAs. In general, it seems that that this legislation was both needed and timely.

The Children and Families Act 2014 introduced a new statutory framework for identifying, assessing and providing services for children with SEND. A new Code of Practice followed in 2015 to support implementation of the Act (DfE, 2015a). Within the new legislation, SEN support replaces School Action, School Action Plus, Early Years Action or Early Years Action Plus, which, in effect, means the following for under 5s:

- a written progress check when the child is 2 years old

- a child health visitor carrying out a health check on the child if they're aged 2 to 3

- a written assessment in the summer term of the child's first year of primary school

- making reasonable adjustments for disabled children, such as providing aids like tactile signs.

Children with needs not met through this process could be made subject to an Education, Health and Care Plan (EHCP) which replaces the previous statementing system. The EHCP involves multi-agency assessment at the start of the process, higher levels of parental involvement and choice, and is considered to be more outcome-focused than previous statements, according to a review of the Pathfinder programme by Spivack et al. (2014). The EHCP can also be effective until the child is 25 if that is necessary for the child to finish their education. Parents may also have a personal budget with which they can buy services for their child. Local authorities still retain a key role in identifying, assessing and providing educational services for children with SEND and they are required now to make a 'local offer' covering such aspects as personal budgets, complaints and specialist help. Children and parents are to be involved in the development and review of this 'local offer'.

Overall, the new arrangements for children with special educational needs and disability (SEND) have been welcomed for giving families more choice and involvement and promoting greater cooperation between health services, local authorities and social care services. Challenges to the process come from questions about the ability of coordinators to meet the planning requirements for each child and whether the relevant agencies are able to work together successfully.

However, one of the goals of the changes was to reduce the number of children identified as having SEN. Before the Act, 17.9% of children in primary schools were identified as needing School Action or School Action Plus, and it was believed that this identification was linked to low aspirations and expectations, leading to poorer outcomes for these children (O'Brien, 2011). This reduction may have implications for the levels of support some children may then receive, as support is linked firmly to identification. Under the new system, children with SEN who are not subject to an EHCP may miss out compared to children with more severe needs, creating a two-tier system (Power, 2011). In addition, the inclusion of voluntary and community sector organizations in the plans may de-professionalize services for this group of children and reduce quality. Other concerns are about the levels of funding and training provision for relevant staff in the context of austerity policies and cuts to public spending.

The Children and Families Act 2014 was the most significant and wide-ranging piece of legislation relating to children's welfare for decades. The goals of the Act were in line with the Coalition Government policy principles on enhancing the role of families, privatization and early intervention. Five areas of change were identified: early identification and support; giving parents control; learning and achieving; preparing for adulthood; and services working together for families (DfE, 2011b). While early identification and parental control were key principles of Coalition Government policy, it is interesting to see that working together remained a goal, as this was not a major strand in policy-making under the Coalition.

The SEN policy agenda has been driven partly by international trends linked to children's rights movements and the need for government to better support all children to meet their potential and offset the high social cost of failing this group in terms of outcomes and life chances. These include higher chances of not being in education, employment or training than non-disabled young people and more likelihood of getting fewer or no qualifications. However, support for children with SEND has also been the subject of a powerful lobby from disability charities and alliances, which support a clearer inclusion agenda with political and financial backing.

SUMMARY

- The influences on early years policy are varied and have complex interrelationships, forming systems to create particular policy developments at certain points in time.

- That said, policy is essentially made by governments, and the receptivity of politicians and civil servants to different views and influences on early years policy development will depend on the prevailing political agenda.

- At the same time, political agendas are themselves influenced by social trends and developments, which will determine the context within which policy is framed.

FURTHER READING

The following readings look at the influences on ECEC policy development, both currently and in the recent past:

Eisenstadt, N. (2011) *Providing a Sure Start: How government discovered early childhood*, Bristol: The Policy Press.

Mukherji, P. and Dryden, L. (eds) (2014) *Foundations of Early Childhood*, London: Sage; in particular, see the chapter 'Social inequalities' by G. Knowles and P. Mukherji.

Parker-Rees, R. and Willan, J. (eds) (2006) *Early Years Education: Major themes in education*, Oxford: Taylor & Francis Group.

Pugh, G. and Duffy, B. (eds) (2014) *Contemporary Issues in the Early Years: Working collaboratively for children* (6th edn), London: Sage.

Robertson, L. and Hill, D. (2014) 'Policy and ideologies in schooling and early years education in England: implications for and impacts on leadership, management and equality', *Management in Education*, 28, 4, 167–74.

5

IMPLEMENTING EARLY
YEARS POLICY

THIS CHAPTER DISCUSSES SEVERAL ISSUES

- what is expected of policy-makers in terms of approaches to development and implementation of policy, planning and communication of policy developments, and the type of research, monitoring and evaluation activities that best support effective policy-making

- the implementation of policy at national, local and individual setting levels

- some of the ways in which policy is implemented at the different levels and issues arising from this implementation (illustrated by case studies).

The implementation of policy involves a process through which the ideas, intentions, principles and practicalities of specific policy plans and developments are made real. At national level, this can be through the enactment of legislation, the development of new organizational structures or changes to existing organizations, and the transfer or alteration of responsibilities within or between local and national government. At local level, this can be through the development of new local authority structures or agencies, new ways of working and new protocols for working arrangements between agencies and other bodies such as voluntary organizations. Policy implementation can also mean new jobs and careers, and new conditions of service and qualification structures within the workforce. At setting level, implementing policy may be through new organizational structures, changed or new policies, different ways of working, job descriptions and arrangements with other agencies.

Often, legislation is required to pave the way for significant policy changes, but other developments take place under existing law. In the simplest terms, new policy is the result of government activity in planning and delivering implementation strategies (including legislation) for policies developed by departments and agencies. However, the implementation of policy is complicated, reflecting interactions between a wide range of stakeholders in the early years, including those within and outside government.

Modern policy-making

There are certain features of policy-making at the beginning of the 21st century that are intended to promote effectiveness and value for money. Modern policy is expected to be efficient in terms of achieving planned outcomes in a cost-effective way and not delivering any unexpected side-effects that may render it ineffective or costly. Policy-making is increasingly influenced by evidence from research into the best way of achieving policy goals and on evaluations of existing policy to determine its effectiveness. In addition, policy is often piloted and then reviewed through Pathfinder projects that are aimed at testing the effectiveness of new systems and identifying any potential problems. For example, the new statutory framework for SEND was piloted through 20 Pathfinder sites prior to being rolled out. Evaluation of the Pathfinder found modest improvements to parental satisfaction, among other findings (Craston et al., 2013). To this extent, modern policy is evidence-informed and draws on lessons learned about the success or otherwise of previous policy (NAO, 2001). Recent governments have promoted improvements in the quality of policy to try to develop long-term strategies and reduce both fragmentation in policy-making and the risks of policy either being ineffective in achieving its aims or having unforeseen negative and costly side-effects.

According to the National Audit Office, there are nine characteristics of modern policy-making. It should:

- be forward-looking
- be outward-looking
- be innovative and creative
- use evidence
- be inclusive
- be joined up
- evaluate
- review
- learn lessons. (NAO, 2001)

In recent years, the central focus is on what policy actually achieves and this is supported by an expectation that there will be an evaluation of policy outcomes to ascertain whether policy goals have been met. This type of approach has become common in early years policy development, with evaluations being conducted by academics and/or professional organizations using government department or agency funding, as exemplified above in terms of the SEND Pathfinder programme. Such evaluations provide information about best implementation strategies for new or emerging policy developments and legitimize these in terms of the stake-holders involved. However, evaluation is not value-free and in itself is a political process, as what constitutes 'evidence' is contested. Similarly, evidence-based policy-making can make demands on evaluators to produce findings which fit with the remit of the political agenda (Taylor and Balloch, 2005).

Modern policy-making involves ensuring new policies are considered in terms of cost, impact, risks and priorities. Policy development now requires a considera-tion of a range of different options for achieving policy goals, and risk and cost analyses of these in order to determine the option most likely to succeed. There are also requirements to consult with stakeholders, pilot new policies and consider their impact before extending policy developments more widely. As such, departments are required to draw up implementation plans for policy developments. These plans can include:

- a timetable for delivering policy
- roles and responsibilities for those involved in delivery
- strategies for tackling barriers to policy development
- strategies for monitoring and reporting performance
- flexible approaches (listening, monitoring, reviewing). (NAO, 2001)

The ways in which implementation plans are developed in the field of early years policy are illustrated in the case studies discussed below.

ACTIVITY

Research an early years policy area of the Children and Families Act 2014 online:

- What are the expected outcomes of the policy changes?

- What evidence was offered to show the policy changes would be effective?

- How were the proposed developments tested before implementation?

- Who was involved?

Two other issues have become central to modern policy-making. First, there is using the Internet to communicate information about proposed policies, to publish policy documents, to provide a forum for debate and to conduct consultations on proposed policy. The websites of government departments and agencies and professional organizations are now major vehicles used to communicate the details of policy implementation plans and, in the case of the latter, to debate and interpret the meaning of new policy on behalf of particular audiences. Research and evaluation study reports are published on government and other websites, providing extensive information about the reasoning behind particular developments and the effectiveness of these when put into practice. Timetables for introducing new policy are published, along with the consequences of policy implementation for different stakeholders, including parents and children. For example, early years and other child-related policy developments are now usually explained in a children's version. Practitioners now have unprecedented opportunities to access information about early years policy developments and to view and take part in the critical debate that usually accompanies such developments. However, the opportunity to contribute to a consultation does not necessarily lead to making an impact on the shape that policy will take (see Barnardo's, 2003).

The Useful Websites section at the start of the book gives details of the key websites for accessing this type of information in respect of early years policies and the debate around these. Individuals and organizations within the early years can use this information to keep up with policy developments in the field and to consider the impact of policy development at service delivery level within the context of their own role and/or agency.

Stages of policy implementation

In Chapter 4, we looked at the influences on policy development and how they interact to determine policy goals. Once policy goals are determined, the government has the complex job of implementing these by directing and monitoring changes at national, local and individual practice levels. The success of policy depends on the ways in which implementation plans are introduced, communicated, debated and interpreted through practice.

Green Papers

Not all policy requires legislation to implement it, but where it does, new policy is often introduced through consultation documents called Green Papers, published by the relevant government department or agency. Originally, these contained ideas and thoughts about how policy could be developed rather than specific proposals, but this is not now always the case as Green Papers tend to contain more concrete and fully formed policy proposals than previously.

In early years policy-making, consultation is usually with local authorities and the broad range of voluntary sector organizations working with children and families and research institutes in the field. For example, there was a consultation on the Green Paper, *Support and Aspiration: A new approach to special educational needs and disability*, which proposed radical changes to support for children with SEN and disabilities (SEND) and changes to the statutory framework for identifying, assessing and providing services to children with SEND (DfE, 2011b). Organizations and individuals send their written responses to the relevant government department or agency and such responses are usually published on the Internet by the organizations involved. The extent to which consultation responses influence government plans can vary and tends to depend on the confidence the government has in implementing its plans successfully, the extent to which there is general acceptance of those plans, the anticipated difficulties of implementing policy at local level and whether the proposed amendments will change the basic structure of new policy.

White Papers

Once the consultation process is completed, the government may draw up a more specific report containing concrete proposals for policy developments called a White Paper. White Papers 'signify a clear intention on the part of a government to pass new law' (www.theyworkforyou.com/glossary/?gl=220). A White Paper is not generally a consultation document, although it may promote discussion about the detail of new legislation. A White Paper normally leads to the introduction of a Bill, which is a draft new law.

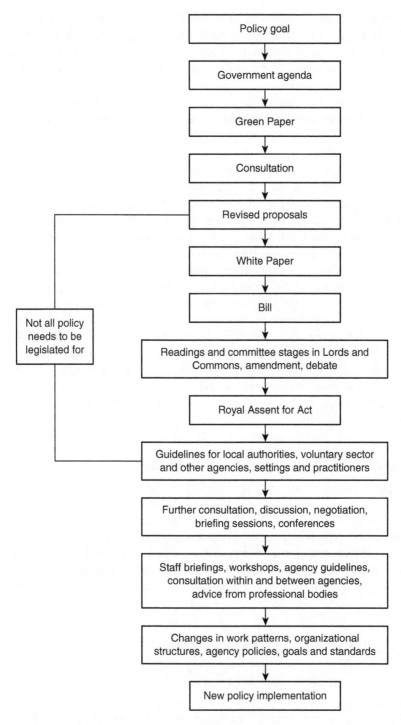

Figure 5.1   Stages of policy implementation for the early years

Effectively, a Bill travels in a predetermined process through Parliament, as outlined in Figure 5.1. The stages of parliamentary process are designed to ensure that there is time for considered debate about all aspects of the legislation, for amendments to be tabled and discussed, agreed or disagreed, and for scrutiny by relevant bodies and committees to ensure that the legislation is robust and not fatally flawed. In the case of large, complex or very influential bills, progress through Parliament will be scrutinized by the media and concerned organizations.

Acts of Parliament

After the final stage, Royal Assent, when a Bill becomes law it is known as an Act. There is often a gap in time before an Act is implemented as it may require changes in the way services are organized or delivered. This gap may vary according to the urgency of the legislative changes and the degree of complexity involved. For example, in the case of the Children Act 1989 (DoH, 1991), implementation took place over a two-year period, but sections of the Children and Families Act 2014 were implemented within months. The time between Royal Assent and implementation is used to interpret the legislation at local and national levels and to put in place policies and structures, including financial measures, to ensure that the legislation can be successfully implemented.

The process may then involve intense activity on the part of government to issue guidelines and information about how to implement the policy or legislation at local level, if this is required. This may include briefings and conferences, written advisory documents and meetings with key local government bodies. Within local authorities, information about expected changes will be disseminated through staff briefings, invitations to stakeholders to consult, and workshops to debate and plan with those stakeholders.

Examples of implementing early years policy

The implementation of two early years policies is discussed below in the form of case studies of how such policy is put into practice at different levels. The discussion includes looking at the roles of different national and local organizations in ensuring implementation, how expectations are disseminated at the local level, and the role of national and local government officers and professional bodies in developing and establishing implementation plans. Finally, the impact on different sectors of the workforce is discussed in light of the range of changes to structures and work practices.

CASE STUDY 5.1

Implementing the Early Years Pupil Premium (EYPP)

The EYPP was introduced in April 2015 to provide additional financial support for disadvantaged children aged 3–4 who have taken up at least part of their free nursery place entitlement. The main aim of the funding is to try and decrease the attainment gap for children from disadvantaged backgrounds and to improve their school readiness. The EYPP follows on from the introduction of the pupil premium for school-age children in 2011. The EYPP was intended to 'close the gap at ages 3 and 4' in additional support for disadvantaged children, between the free nursery places they can access at 2 years old and the primary pupil premium they will be entitled to on entering school (DfE, 2014b).

In order to be eligible for the EYPP, one of several eligibility requirements needs to be met, and these include the claiming of certain benefits, the child being adopted or 'looked after', or having left care under a Special Guardianship, or having a Child Arrangement Order, or the family being supported as asylum seekers. The funding is 53 pence an hour per child, which is £300 per year for children taking up the full 570 free nursery hours.

Implementation at national government level

Implementation of the EYPP was facilitated by a consultation process taking place with the publication of *Early Years Pupil Premium and Funding for Two-year-olds* (DfE, 2014b), which reported back in October 2014 (DfE, 2014d). The consultation was brief – merely two months between June and August 2014. Although there was widespread support for the proposal, there were concerns about the administrative cost of eligibility checking and the need to engage parents with this process (DfE, 2014d). There were also concerns expressed by some children's organizations about the level of funding. Grauberg (2014) suggests that as one of the objectives of the government is to try and get more children from disadvantaged backgrounds into good or outstanding early years settings, then any incentive to encourage such settings to try and attract these children would require a higher level of funding. She goes on to suggest that the EYPP should be increased over time to match the much higher primary premium.

Pilots in seven local authorities were set up in February 2015 to test the robustness of the proposed system in terms of checking eligibility and allocating funding. It was clear from the start of the implementation that concerns about introducing the EYPP centred on the difficulties in ensuring eligible children were identified and received funding, and the possible high costs of achieving this. These 'early implementer' authorities also provided case studies about how they had spent the money, which was mainly on enhancing staff skills through staff development, increasing the hours of existing staff or appointing new staff and using the additional capacity to provide direct support to eligible children and their families or to allow for staff development time (Goddard, 2015b). As the proposal that settings would be free to choose how they spent the money to enhance the attainment of disadvantaged children was strongly supported through the consultation process, it has been important to build a body of case studies and examples of how the funding can be used effectively (DfE, 2014b, 2014d).

4Children, a strategic partner of DfE, was also charged with finding and sharing best practice examples of how the funding could be used. This is in line with recent and current government practice to involve relevant agencies in policy development and implementation by commissioning them to either report on pilot projects and/or research into the best approaches to implementation. 4Children found that providers are prioritizing spending on personal, social and emotional development, and early language and communication (Robb, 2015). However, there were some suggestions that conditions should be imposed on how the funding is spent. Grauberg (2014) suggests that as there is clear evidence that

(Continued)

(Continued)

quality is improved where a setting is led by a graduate who works directly with children, the money should be spent on improving staffing quality. However, this may not be possible if the setting is small or there are few disadvantaged children in a setting as the funding may simply not be enough to cover new staff costs.

The government also had to legislate to allow the eligibility checking system already in use for free school meals to be used for EYPP – this was done by making amendments to the Small Business, Enterprise and Employment Act 2015.

Implementation at local level

There were a number of implementation issues that started to come to light as the EYPP pilot project progressed. One of the key issues in implementing the EYPP is encouraging parents to identify that they may be eligible when there is no clearly recognizable incentive to do this. In contrast, the primary pupil premium was linked to free school meals until recently, which meant eligible parents had a clear motive to register. Despite this, schools missed out on funding, as even with this incentive some parents failed to register. Moreover, as free school meals have become universal for children at KS1, this incentive has been lost for infants, and getting parents to identify themselves has become more of an issue in schools as well as in early years settings. This is an interesting example of how the introduction of new policy can impact on existing policy in negative ways. In early years settings, there is no apparent financial benefit given directly to children and their families from the EYPP. The money is intended to be pooled to provide enhancement for all disadvantaged children and therefore individual benefits are not always easily identified. As parents are asked to provide proof of eligibility and/or agree to eligibility checking, they may also be deterred from identifying themselves because of the stigma involved or because of the desire to keep personal information private (Goddard, 2015a).

One of the other concerns was that eligibility checking may be quite complex and potentially costly due to the range of eligibility criteria. LAs need to check the eligibility of the children named by settings, using the existing checking system (already used for free school meals) for this purpose under the Small Business, Enterprise and Employment Act 2015. However, childminders in one authority told the author that initially they were sent a letter asking them to check evidence relating to eligibility themselves, by asking parents they intended to name for sight of that evidence. They felt that this could have a negative effect on their relationship with parents as it felt intrusive to ask for personal information about parents' financial status or other aspects of their private lives. This is a potential problem in any setting as settings clearly need to encourage as many parents as they can to identify themselves as possibly eligible, but this then could lead to settings being perceived as pressurizing parents who do not want to be identified in this way.

In addition, the government consultation on the EYPP agreed that providers will have the freedom to spend the money as they wish, but that they would be accountable through Ofsted inspections to show evidence of how the money has benefited the eligible children. This has been identified as a cause for concern in terms of whether

Ofsted judgements on settings may be affected by the inspectors' own views on how the money should have been spent (Pre-school Learning Alliance, 2014).

In terms of supporting local implementation, the DfE has commissioned the development of case studies on how to spend the money, as discussed above. The department has also issued guidelines to LAs to explain and guide the implementation of the EYPP, mainly focused on eligibility checking and the distribution of funding (DfE, 2014c). The Education Endowment Foundation Teaching and Learning toolkit has also been extended to the early years, providing research evidence on how best to use resources to raise the attainment of disadvantaged children (DfE, 2014d). However, it will take time to develop a good level of information on effective interventions and there are also concerns about the difficulties of ensuring thorough dissemination in an industry which is highly fragmented with many very small settings (Grauberg, 2014).

Finally, evaluating the effectiveness of the EYPP in improving the quality of settings will become part of the Study of Early Education and Development (SEED), a longitudinal study of 5,000 children aged 2 to the end of KS1 to determine the impact of childcare and education on their lives. Grauberg (2014) does suggest, however, that as there are several tools in use at the moment to measure children's developmental progress, then a single child outcomes measure is needed urgently to ensure that evaluation is realistic and that Ofsted can make effective judgements on whether the EYPP is being used effectively.

While implementation of the EYPP has been generally welcomed, there are a number of questions about the potential effectiveness of the funding which are still outstanding, mainly relating to the costs involved in checking eligibility and whether the funding is sufficient to make a real difference.

To summarize, some of the issues that may prevent full take-up of the EYPP are:

1. Nurseries are required to put forward the names of children who are eligible to their LA, but there are significant variations in how aware nurseries are about the EYPP.

2. Both LAs and providers may incur high administrative costs in ensuring eligibility is checked effectively.

3. The money may not be sufficient to make a great deal of difference to disadvantaged 3–4-year-olds, particularly in small settings, or to incentivize settings to actively seek out disadvantaged children.

4. Although it is known that having graduate staff improves quality in an early years setting, there may be insufficient funding to pay for this in some settings.

5. It may prove hard to 'sell' the EYPP to parents (as discussed above) and the process of informing parents and encouraging them to identify themselves may also incur costs or create difficulties in the relationship between the setting and parents.

6. Developing a body of evidence on how best to improve quality in the early years may take some time to achieve and there may be some difficulty in disseminating this information.

7. Evaluating the outcomes of EYPP may be difficult without a single child outcome framework. (Grauberg, 2014; Goddard, 2015a)

CASE STUDY 5.2

Integrated reviews for 2-year-olds

Until recently, children aged 2 to 2 and a half have been reviewed separately by health and early years staff to determine their developmental progress across a wide range of aspects. The Healthy Child Programme (HCP) health and development review is completed by health professionals (usually health visitors) when the child is aged 2 to 2½ years old and involves assessing the child's learning, social skills, speech and language skills. The review is supported by the parent-completed Ages and Stages Questionnaire (ASQ3), an evidence-based tool used to determine developmental delay in young children, which generates data for a public health outcome measure of child development at age 2–2½. The EYFS progress check is completed by early years professionals when the child is between 2 and 3 years old and comprises a short written summary of the child's development, learning and care within the EYFS framework. The main areas where the two reviews overlap are speech and language, physical development, and social and emotional development, although both reviews also include assessment of other aspects of children's health, development, learning and welfare. Both reviews are focused on ensuring children's development is satisfactory and that where developmental delays or other issues are identified, these are responded to with service provision in a prompt and effective way.

Although health checks for 2-year-olds have been part of health policy for children for some time, the EYFS progress checks are relatively recent, introduced in 2012 as a result of the Coalition focus on early intervention (Allen, 2011; DfES, 2014). The introduction of the EYFS progress checks created a situation where the requirement for two separate developmental checks on the same group of children led to variations in review outcomes and some parents receiving contradictory advice from professionals. There is also the issue of duplication of information because of the two separate reviews (Blades et al., 2014). Concerns that potential differences between the outcomes of the reviews in respect of a child may affect the chances of early identification of any developmental issues have also driven plans to integrate the reviews. As one of the main purposes of both reviews is to identify any developmental issues and ensure early intervention where needed, this is a good example of how policy may have counter-productive outcomes if implementation is not thoroughly considered during the policy planning stage.

There were also a number of facilitating factors which supported the move towards integrated reviews. The introduction of free early education entitlement for some 2-year-olds means the reviews can cover more of the population as many more 2-year-olds are now in early years settings. Also, Coalition Government commitments to increasing the number of health visitors as part of the drive towards early intervention meant there was improved capacity to ensure more reviews could take place.

Implementation at national government level

In 2011, the DfE and DoH jointly published the policy document *Supporting Families in the Foundation Years*, which proposed the integration of health and education reviews for 2-year-olds. Following on from this, in March 2015 the Coalition Government published plans to combine the HCP review at 2 to 2½ years old and the EYFS progress check at 2 years. The integrated reviews are scheduled to be introduced in September 2015 based on the outcomes of the pilot programme which was reported on in 2014.

The aims of the new integrated review are as follows:

- to identify the child's progress, strengths and needs at this age in order to promote positive outcomes in health and well-being, learning and behaviour

- to facilitate appropriate intervention and support for children and their families, especially those for whom progress is less than expected

- to generate information which can be used to plan services and contribute to the reduction of inequalities in children's outcomes. (Blades et al., 2014)

The review covers both child factors and contextual factors influencing the child's development:

Child factors include:

- speech, language and communication

- personal, social and emotional development

- physical development

- learning/cognitive development

- physical health.

Contextual factors include:

- parenting

- home learning environment

- family circumstances

- social/community circumstances.

The pilot project ran from January 2012 in five LAs, with the formal pilot starting in January 2013. Key questions for implementation were:

- which staff would complete the reviews (early years, health or both)

- how the reviews would be coordinated and organized

- where they would take place

- how information could be shared effectively

- how parents could be fully involved

- what training and development needs had to be met.

Key issues to be resolved were how early years and health staff could work together effectively and how their separate information systems could be coordinated so that data could be shared. The pilot areas also needed to develop new systems and

(Continued)

(Continued)

protocols for organizing and completing integrated reviews and information-sharing. Three of the pilot areas developed integrated reviews for children attending Children's Centres, although only two of these introduced joint working between health and early years staff. Another pilot took place in the PVI sector but also did not introduce shared reviews. The final pilot also took place in Children's Centres but did not develop an integrated approach. Instead, an enhanced HCP review was delivered to children by health staff. None of the pilots included the development of integrated reviews for childminders or children not in early years settings.

The research report on the pilot project for integrated reviews, *Implementation Study: Integrated review at 2–2½ years – Integrating the EYFS progress check and the HCP health and development review,* was led by the National Children's Bureau in line with what is now common practice to involve stakeholders in the planning and implementation of policy (Blades et al., 2014).

The report concluded:

- In order to have successful integrated reviews, there needs to be a lead individual from health and one from early years involved.
- Working together and sharing health and early years expertise is an important element of success.
- Training in child development, communication with parents and making clinical judgements is needed.
- Take-up of the integrated review is better than that for the HCP health and development review.
- Lack of a shared information and record keeping system is a barrier to success.

One of the issues identified as a possible problem is that a higher take-up rate and possibly more thorough review may lead to higher and earlier demand for intervention services for children. There are questions as to whether there are sufficient resources to meet this additional need (ican, 2014).

Three different delivery modes emerged from the pilot:

- a single meeting with the child and parent in which the review is delivered by both early years and health staff who complete their own parts of the review but discuss outcomes jointly with parents
- two separate early years and health reviews brought together by sharing information and a joint response to any issues identified through the reviews
- a single review conducted by early years professionals only, who then share information with health staff.

While the first two options were considered viable in practice, the third was not. The report strongly suggested that having expert health staff was vital for good clinical judgements and substituting early years staff could lead to poor judgements.

In terms of positive outcomes, there were signs that the integrated reviews led to better working together and information-sharing about children between early years and health. They were also perceived to reduce duplication and confusion. However, the pilot study was not able to conclude that the integrated reviews were better quality than the single reviews or whether they led to improved early identification of developmental issues, due to insufficient data (Blades et al., 2014).

One of the limiting issues to implementation of the integrated review is that, although there have been increases, not all 2-year-olds attend early years settings and the pilot projects focused on children who did, especially those attending Children's Centres. The number of 2-year-olds attending early years settings has risen with the offer of 15 hours of free nursery provision to disadvantaged children, but this only covers 40% of the population. Although take-up of the reviews was improved in comparison to the HCP health and development check, the integrated reviews will not at present apply to all children and therefore there is still a strong need for good HCP checks for children in their own homes (Blades et al., 2014). It was also suggested that the reviews not be called 'integrated' as there is no obligation for both early years and health staff to be at the review (Corbett, 2015).

Overall, the pilot projects were quite slow to develop and deliver integrated reviews because new systems and information-sharing protocols had to be put in place in order to ensure that effective systems could be established. Integration was seen as both costly and time-consuming in some areas. Also, although effective joint working is key to the success of the reviews, some pilots found a lack of mutual trust between early years and health workers which hampered the success of the projects (Corbett, 2015).

Interestingly, the report identified an issue in terms of the extent to which policy for young children is sufficiently 'joined up' at national level to support integrated working at regional and local levels. The authors of the report urged the government to ensure that emerging national policy provided a sound base for supporting the implementation of integrated reviews (Blades et al., 2014).

Concerns from practitioners focus on the role of early years staff in making judgements about children's development and whether they have the skill and expertise to do this. It is felt that early years staff do not always have the expertise to assess all the factors contributing to a child's development and that this could affect the quality of reviews if early years staff do these alone. It is strongly felt by all involved that health staff should be involved in some way in the reviews and that early years staff may need additional training. Variations in outcome due to the extent and duration of the child's time in nursery are also a possible cause for concern as this is a factor outside the control of the setting. Parents may also be concerned about whether their children are being 'tested' unless the purpose of the review is clearly conveyed (Corbett, 2015).

At the time of publication, integrated reviews have been implemented from October 2015 onwards across England, although progress is slow and approaches vary considerably. While some authorities are introducing reviews that involve separate assessment during a single meeting, others are using information-sharing from separate meetings to integrate outcomes. Oxfordshire have introduced a model whereby health checks take place when children are 2–2½ and EYFS progress checks take place when children are 2½–3 years old. Other authorities are planning their own strategy development and/or local pilots before implementing in spring next year. How successful the integrated review will be in the long run and which models will work best in which authorities remain unclear, but many seem to see success in terms of sidestepping rather than embracing the difficulties of health and early years staff working closely together.

(Continued)

(Continued)

To summarize some of the issues affecting implementation of the integrated 2-year-old review:

- The best model for effective integrated reviews is where staff from both health and early years do a joint review, however this may be costly, time-consuming and difficult to organize.
- Other barriers to integrated reviews include differences in professional culture and lack of trust between health and early years staff, although effective working together was identified in the pilot study as a key element of success.
- Lack of common record-keeping and shared-information systems created difficulties for joint working.
- Not all early years staff have the skills to make clinical judgements about children's developmental issues and there are training implications for this.
- Not all 2-year-olds are in settings, so some will continue with just the HCP review, leading to concerns about a two-tier system.
- The pilots were slow to develop, and as a result there is still a lack of information on whether the integrated reviews will be more effective in early identification of developmental issues than the single reviews were.
- The pilots mainly covered children in Children's Centres and did not cover childminders who do the EYFS progress check with children in their care.
- There are concerns that the review is a 'snapshot' and may not take into account all factors, such as how long the child has attended the setting.

ACTIVITY

- Considering the last time you worked with practitioners/professionals from a different disciplinary background to your own:
  - o Did you focus on the same issues or have different ideas about what was important?
  - o Were your goals similar or different?
  - o How did you feel about working with someone from a different background?

- Looking at the two case studies above:
  - o What do you think were the causes of some of the issues arising from the policy?
  - o Were these to do with how the policy was implemented or the policy itself?
  - o Why do you think Blades et al. (2014) suggested that governments should do more to 'join up' early years policy?

SUMMARY

The two case studies highlight the complex process by which policy is developed and implemented and some of the key stages and tools used in this process. Both are drawn from the wider policy focus on increasing early intervention in children's lives to support families and children where there are developmental issues and to reduce the costs to the state of long-term developmental problems. This wider policy goal was introduced under the Coalition Government 2010–15 and so far has remained significant to the Conservative Government elected in 2015. The case studies show that implementation of policy is achieved through consultations on the proposals; pilot projects (and research reports on these) which test the viability of the policy, identify any problems which may arise and start to build knowledge about what best practice may be; and then dissemination of government guidance to LAs, which is then trickled down to settings and individuals.

It is usual for governments to involve stakeholders in the process of implementing policy, although the extent of their influence in making any significant changes to that implementation is debatable. However, early years staff and agencies are involved in the consultation process and the pilots, and relevant agencies are involved in the research and reporting stage, including academic institutions and children's charities.

Policy implementation is a process of negotiation between bodies with different levels of power and influence, and can involve shifts in working practices, new protocols and systems, and changes to relationships between staff, parents and children. It may also involve changes in the way professionals from different agencies or disciplines work together. As such, it is essentially a human activity with all the unpredictability and flawed nature of human activities. As the case studies show, this can lead to issues arising that affect the process of implementation, such as a professional mistrust between early years and health staff when asked to do integrated reviews.

Policy implementation can also be subject to whether those involved are in support of the policy or see it as negative. Both policies discussed above were generally seen as positive for children and families, but in the case of EYPP there were concerns about whether the money would make a difference to small settings and whether parents would see the value to their children of identifying themselves as possibly eligible. As the take-up rate depends on early years settings informing and encouraging parents to identify, and parents being willing to do this, then the take-up rate (and therefore the success of implementation) depends on the actions of individuals based on their views of whether it is worth being actively involved in the process.

Finally, policy formation and implementation are not always predictable in terms of outcomes. The introduction of the EYFS 2-year-old progress check created a problem when the results of these checks did not always agree with or generate the same professional advice as the HCP health and development checks on the same body of children. The two checks sprang from policy developed in two different government departments, who then had to work together to solve the anomalies caused. This is a direct result of having more than one central government department involved in children's welfare and development, and demonstrates that joined-up work is not always in place at any level of policy-making and implementation, as commented on by Blades et al. (2014).

FURTHER READING 📖

The main government websites for following early years policy developments and key documents are listed in the Useful Websites section at the start of the book. In addition, the texts below focus on different aspects of ECEC policy:

Meehan, C. (2015) 'Every child mattered in England: but what matters to children?', *Early Child Development and Care*. Available at: http://create.canterbury.ac.uk/13405/

Miller, L. and Cable, C. (eds) (2011) *Professionalization, Leadership and Management in the Early Years*, London: Sage. This book explores the increasing professionalization in the early years sphere and the effects this has had on implementing early years policy itself.

Palaiologou, I. (ed.) (2016) *The Early Years Foundation Stage: Theory and practice* (3rd edn), London: Sage. Part 3 of this book contains an in-depth exploration of implementing early years policy in practice.

Keeping up to date with new early years policy means reading trade journals such as *Nursery World* and *Community Care*, and newspapers such as *The Guardian* and *The Independent*, all of which can be found online.

6

EARLY YEARS POLICY IN WALES, SCOTLAND AND NORTHERN IRELAND: THE IMPACT OF DEVOLUTION

THIS CHAPTER DESCRIBES

- the structure of devolved government that has developed in the UK since 1997
- the development of early years policy under the devolved regimes in Wales, Scotland and Northern Ireland
- the impact that devolution has had on the development of early years policy across the UK
- the potential value of comparisons of policy within the UK.

Devolution and policy-making

The UK is dominated in several senses by England, the country whose population constitutes more than 80% of that kingdom as a whole and whose largest city, London, is the kingdom's capital. As Clark and Waller (2007) point out, commentators fall all too often into the error of making statements that purport to be about the UK, but are, in fact, only true of England. This chapter systematically examines early years policy in Wales, Scotland and Northern Ireland.

Some independent states have federal constitutions (national government has powers as well as regional areas, as proposed by parliament for devolved powers to large cities and counties with elected mayors) (Department of Communities and Local Government, 2015); some are much more centralized, although with local administrations that will always have some measure of autonomy. The UK is set up rather differently: 'neither unitary nor federal, but ... a union state' (Pilkington, 2002: 7). England, Wales, Scotland and Northern Ireland each have a different relationship to the kingdom as a whole, a relationship determined by different histories. The Channel Islands and the Isle of Man have constitutional positions that are different again. However, initiatives there have had less impact on the rest of the kingdom and for this reason we have left consideration of their position on one side.

The UK is not unique in having various kinds of devolution. In Spain, the 'communities' that make up the state have different degrees of autonomy, with Catalonia and Euskadi (the Basque country) coming closest to complete home rule – and these arrangements were established in one brief period during the return to democracy in the late 1970s and early 1980s. The 'asymmetric' form of devolution in Spain has proved relatively stable and the same could prove to be true of the UK. However, differences in local powers can be seen as unfair and fuel debate as to whether there should be a more systematic approach (including devolution for England or for regions within England). The dynamic nature of devolution is exemplified by the referendum in 2014, where the majority of Scots voted against becoming an independent country and breaking away from the UK. Although the vote returned a definitive 'no' to independence, this resulted in further devolved powers to Scotland, while the debate continues on this subject and the question of devolution for other countries of the UK and regions/counties of England (Mackinnon, 2015).

The support of young children has been one of the areas of policy most clearly under the control of the devolved governments in Wales, Scotland and Northern Ireland. It was also an area that had been comparatively neglected in these countries before devolution. One result of this has been that the devolved governments have often seen it as a sphere in which they could demonstrate their competence and progressive thinking. For example, in July 2001, when Northern Ireland began consultation on a strategy for children, Dermott Nesbitt, the Deputy First Minister, expressed the hope that the strategy would make his country a 'world leader' (*Nursery World*, 2001: 6). The 2010 strategy was replaced in 2013 with a revised framework, Learning to Learn (DENI, 2013). The revised strategy, similar to approaches in England, focused heavily on education and preparing children for school. It was also acknowledged that the strategy did not cover all aspects of child services, and in response to this the Northern Ireland executive developed the *Delivering Social Change Framework* (DENI, 2015a) to improve outcomes for children. The aim of the framework is to coordinate services for children and families across government departments, acknowledging that education department policy is focused on raising educational attainment rather than on increasing cooperation and coordination across services for children and families.

The interest that many politicians in the three nations take in early years policy has been encouraged by lobbyists in England. It was already established practice there to compare the UK unfavourably with other countries, particularly with Spain, New Zealand, Denmark and the region of Reggio Emilia in Italy, all of which were said to provide models we should copy. Devolution has provided a new stick with which to beat those making policy for England. Thus, in recent decades comparisons have been made between countries of the UK. In 2001 Bruce spoke warmly of her experience of early years work in Scotland (Rawstrone, 2001) and Lindon (2005) praised the Scottish guidance on the birth-to-3 curriculum, claiming that it was superior to similar moves in England. It is significant that it was in 2001 and 2002 that *Nursery World* provided unusually detailed coverage of developments in the devolved countries, since this was the period when policy there (on standards in childminding and the role of the Children's Commissioner) was more in tune with the thinking of a majority of early years practitioners than was policy in England. Variances in quality and accessibility to the mix of private, voluntary and independent (PVI) provision were something of a lottery in different parts of the UK (Bertram and Pascal, 2014).

Given the way in which developments in the three countries have been used in debate, it is worth pointing out that England is not always bottom of the league in terms of what the early years profession views as best practice. The scale of provision has often been better in England. England also took some steps to modify the artificial distinction in law and institutional arrangements between care and education before the other three nations. However, there has been much less focus on this in recent times and the main driver for early childhood education and care (ECEC) is the focus on school readiness (including the revised EYFS curriculum), leading to an overly heavy focus on education and potentially inappropriate pedagogy and less value on children and childhood (Kingdon, 2014).

Comparing Wales, Scotland and Northern Ireland

The next three sections of this chapter provide some basic information on early years policy in Wales, Scotland and Northern Ireland. Each country is considered in relation to six issues:

- the history of its devolved powers
- the integration of services for young children
- the expansion of early years services since 1997
- the policy emphasis post-2010
- quality, curriculum development and regulation
- comparison with other parts of the UK.

Wales

Devolution

The gradual conquest of Wales by England in the Middle Ages led to absorption into England under the Tudors. In the 19th century, there was a systematic attempt to eliminate the Welsh language and children were punished for using it in school, even in the playground. It was not until 1907 that the first step was taken towards separate administration for Wales with the establishment of a Welsh Section in the Department of Education. In 1951, a Ministry of Welsh Affairs was set up under the Home Office (which then had a very wide remit). In 1957, responsibility for oversight of that ministry was transferred to Housing and Local Government. A Welsh Office was set up at Westminster in 1964. That body acquired responsibility for health in 1968 and for education in 1970. However, legislation continued for some time to be written for 'England and Wales' rather than for each country separately.

At the end of the 1970s, there was a half-hearted and unsuccessful attempt by the Labour Government to establish a form of devolved government for Wales.

Two decades later, devolution was one of the commitments of the Labour Party when it won the General Election of 1997. The first Government of Wales Act was passed in 1998 and the first elections for the Welsh Assembly were held in 1999. Tony Blair seemed to assume that Wales would be content with a minimal level of autonomy and initially the posts of First Secretary of the Assembly and the Secretary of State for Wales were held by the same person. Rebellion in the Welsh Labour Party led to an end to this arrangement and later to the Government of Wales Act 2006, which gave the Assembly primary jurisdiction over all its own domestic affairs. Developments in early years are seen as key to overall education policy. In particular, they have been seen as crucial to the success of attempts to promote the Welsh language, now spoken by an increasing number of people, especially the young. These developments, including a push for greater integration of early education, care and play have continued, with the publication in 2014 of a draft plan for the development of a cohesive, integrated and high-quality workforce to support children's development and learning (DfES/DfCTP, 2014).

Integration

Across the UK, there have been moves since 1997 to break down artificial divisions between care and education in services for very young children and to establish a more 'integrated' approach. Some hoped that Children's Commissioners would have a key role to play in this process. Wales was the first country in the UK to show a strong interest in this idea, but the creation of a commissioner post was blocked by the Conservatives and, initially, by the 1997 Labour Government. An inquiry into abuse in children's homes in Wales (Waterhouse, 2000) galvanized interest in the idea of a commissioner as well as in improvements in child protection. Legislation followed, creating for the first time anywhere in the UK a post of Children's Commissioner. This was also the first piece of legislation in the UK to make specific reference to the United Nations Convention on the Rights of the Child (OUNHCHR, 1989). Peter Clarke, the first Children's Commissioner for Wales, took up post in 2001. Development in the role of Children's Commissioner has been evident. For example, in 2011 the four UK Children's Commissioners released a joint report expressing their concern over poverty, the disproportional impact of spending cuts on the most disadvantaged and the need to ensure that 'all children's rights [are] fully understood and enjoyed across the UK' (p. 16). Several years later, the four UK Children's Commissioners were still expressing concern about the disproportionate impact of austerity measures through benefit payments and welfare reform on the most disadvantaged children (Children's Commissioners, 2015). This highlights how the role of Children's Commissioner that was first instigated in Wales led to change and coordination across the UK, and shows a significant change from the early debate on whether there should even be a role for a Children's Commissioner.

Expansion

Childcare was not well developed in Wales before devolution. As late as 1986, there was only one full day care setting throughout the country. The number of such settings in England would have been much lower than it is now, but not as low as that. As recently as 2006, there was only one childcare place for every seven children under the age of 8 in Wales. Reliance on informal care by grandparents and others remained a strong factor (Clark and Waller, 2007). The Welsh Assembly has been active since its establishment in promoting childcare, education and health. The Assembly government was already committed to ensuring that early education was available to all children whose parents sought it and that out-of-school care was similarly available to all by 2010. A large-scale investment began with the 'Flying Start' programme (2005–08), under which £46 million was spent on children and families in deprived areas to fund childcare and various forms of family support. As a result of these and other initiatives, there has been a significant increase in the number of places available (nearly 19,000 in the first five years of the Assembly's operation). Emphasis was also placed on developing a pedagogically appropriate foundation phase (which covers children aged 3–7 in Wales), and although further training is required there has been an overall improvement in educational achievement and well-being, and enhanced levels of involvement of children in their education (Taylor et al., 2015). Unlike England, the focus on developing the early years, childcare and play workforce has continued, with the publication of a draft 10-year development plan in 2014 (DfES/DfCTP, 2014). This draft focuses on attracting high-quality entrants to the workforce as well as raising the skills and standards of the current workforce, suggesting a more cohesive approach to workforce development than is evident in England. This is significant not only for its difference with England but also for the focus on expansion over the past decade, which has achieved the desired increase in provision and in the attention now focused on increasing quality through workforce development.

Quality, curriculum development and regulation

Even before devolution, there was a separate approach in Wales to quality and the curriculum, partly because of the increasing readiness of Westminster to allow some concessions to the Welsh language in the education system. This was strengthened by the decision taken in 1996 on the Welsh equivalent of the framework for desirable learning outcomes in pre-school education. From the start, the Welsh framework was seen as superior to the English one, with a stronger focus on the child as learner and an open-minded approach to the value of play. This has been a source of considerable pride in Wales. The powers of the Welsh Assembly include control over curriculum issues. In 2003, a new Foundation Phase was proposed and a revised version of that guidance was produced in January 2008. In comparison with the new Foundation Stage guidance that came into force in England in September 2014 and which continues to make only a slight dent in the barrier between pre-school and school education, for the majority of children, in the child's fifth year, the Welsh Foundation Phase led to the abolition of Key Stage 1 in 2010 and research suggests that this is having a positive impact on Key Stage 2 outcomes (Taylor et al., 2015). It also continues the Welsh traditions of heavy emphasis on the role of play and of ascribing value to Welsh. Moreover, the new phase was introduced with even greater care than its English equivalent, with a formal pilot in 41 settings monitored by a team led by Iram Siraj-Blatchford and Kathy Sylva. The final version was presented in October 2007 and full implementation took place in 2011 and was followed by systematic evaluation to identify benefits and future developments (for example, the review by Taylor et al. (2015) has identified the need for development in pedagogical approaches with young children, the need for workforce training and the need to focus more attention on the role of parents/carers).

Wales also carried out a review of the registration, regulation and inspection process for ECEC. The aim of the review, unsurprisingly, was to provide the best possible start in life for children, but also to bridge the gap between the maintained and non-maintained sectors. The review argues that a single quality framework is needed – removing the historically artificial divide between school-based early years education and non-school-based ECEC. This is seen as having the potential to eradicate the distinction between care and education, where young children in school are not seen as needing care and those in day care are not being educated. To support this, the review suggests the establishment of ECEC boards, and some parallels could be drawn between the potential remit of such boards and EYDCPs, which existed in England between approximately 1998 and 2005 (Fitzgerald and Kay, 2008). This clearly highlights how the direction of travel in Wales in terms of ECEC is different to that in England.

Wales and the rest of the UK

Many of these developments have similarities with Scotland and Northern Ireland, while having differences to England. Wales has moved towards closer integration of services and seen childcare to a large extent in terms of getting parents off benefits and back to work. Under the Coalition and subsequent Conservative Government, the focus on getting parents back to work has continued but the focus for young children has been on education and school readiness (with little or no reference to ECEC) and less on the development of pedagogically appropriate and high-quality ECEC. Part of the explanation for these similarities is the political parties in power in these countries rejecting neoliberalist approaches to policy development and implementation and drawing more on socialist or third-way approaches. However, since developed government was introduced to Wales there have been areas where it has led policy and practice for ECEC, particularly in regard to:

- the energy with which the Welsh Assembly has tackled children's inclusion, typified in its determination to secure a Children's Commissioner
- the emphasis on play, which is set to continue over the next decade
- a more radical approach to the question of when formal schooling should begin
- an approach to cultural diversity that follows from a commitment to promote the Welsh language.

Scotland

Devolution

Unlike Wales, Scotland remained independent of England until the beginning of the 18th century. When the two countries were first united (in the early 17th century), it was on the basis of having the same monarch (James I and VI) rather than because

Scotland had been conquered or absorbed in some way. Scotland had its own Parliament until 1707. Divisions between different parts of the country were at that time as important politically as any division between Scotland and England. After the unification of the two Parliaments, differences remained in the legal and educational systems. A separate Scottish Office was established in Westminster as early as 1885.

When the Labour Party attempted to introduce devolution in Wales in 1979, a similar attempt was made for Scotland, one that was also unsuccessful. Margaret Thatcher was deeply opposed to devolution. However, once in power, Tony Blair moved rapidly to set up a new form of government for Scotland, and in 1998 the Scotland Act laid the basis for a Scottish Parliament with its own Executive (later re-named the Scottish Government). The areas under control of the Scottish Parliament include all those relevant to early years policy. Like Wales, Scotland continues to send MPs to the Westminster Parliament and the UK government retains control over significant areas of policy, including defence and foreign affairs. Initially, at any rate, the Scottish Parliament had wider powers than the equivalent Assembly in Wales. Devolution (rather than full independence from or full union with England) appears to have the support of a large section of the Scottish people (Bromley et al., 2006). In 2007, the Scottish National Party (SNP) emerged as the largest party in elections to the Scottish Government, although without an absolute majority. The SNP formed the new government, which included Scotland's first Minister for Children and Early Years – Adam Ingram – who spoke of his ambitions for young children. However, this was a matter of detail and emphasis rather than outright conflict between the parties. As the Chief Executive of the Scottish Out of School Care Network said, 'all the major parties seem to agree on putting money into childcare' (Marcus, 2007: 5).

In September 2014, a referendum was held to decide whether Scotland should become an independent country and separate constitutionally from the rest of the UK. There were months of debate, at times intense, about the perceived benefits and disadvantages of independence. The Scottish people voted decisively against independence (55% against; 45% for). There are, however, two notable points following the vote. First, the turnout of 85% was exceptionally high (in comparison, the turnout for the 2015 general election was 66%), confirming an extremely high level of engagement amongst the Scottish people on the issue. And second, although the vote was against independence, the debate has clearly brought centre stage the issue of devolved power for each of the countries of the UK. At the time of writing, the Scottish Bill (Scotland Office, 2015) is being debated, and this proposes the devolvement of certain aspects of tax-raising powers and control over other aspects of policy to Scotland, as laid out by the Smith Commission. It seems clear that over time the direction of travel is for further devolvement of control over many areas of policy to Scotland, Wales and Northern Ireland, as well as regions of England.

Integration

Scotland has pursued the concept of integrated services for young children with some eagerness and has won the admiration of many in England as a result. The first integrated service for young children in the UK was established in Strathclyde in the 1980s, well before local authorities in England were legally obliged to go in that direction in 2001, and ahead of those pioneering authorities in England that set up such services in the 1990s. In some respects, until recently, integration has gone less far in Scotland than in England. For example, there were still separate systems for the regulation and inspection of childcare and early education. Nevertheless, there had been significant moves towards integration, including:

- the early establishment of a post of Children's Commissioner
- the policy document *For Scotland's Children* (Scottish Executive, 2001), which laid down an overall approach to integration
- the establishment of local Childcare Partnerships, similar to the EYDCPs in England, but held by some to have been more successful
- joint inspection of child protection services
- an updated early years framework launched in 2012, promoting multi-agency, bottom-up quality improvement involving all 32 community planning partnerships
- the continued embedding of the Curriculum for Excellence for all children aged 3–18 and the development of new qualifications to support the curriculum.

In 2008, efforts to increase integration were taken forward significantly by the introduction of the umbrella policy, *Getting it Right for Every Child (GIRFEC)* (Scottish Government, 2008). Rose (2012) suggests that developing effective multi-agency services is crucial in achieving the Scottish early years policy goals of 'prevention, early identification of concerns and structured interventions' (p. 155). *GIRFEC* is based on principles of coordinated service delivery, but more importantly involves 'whole-system' changes to ensure effective service provision. The focus is on developing existing universal services such as health and education to work better together through changes to 'culture, systems and practice' (p. 156).

One of the key elements to this policy is the introduction of the role of the 'named person' to provide a point of contact for agencies and families in terms of any concerns about the child. This would be a professional from either health or education, depending on the age of the child, and is universal to all children. In respect of children with additional needs, where more than one service is involved, there will also be a lead professional to coordinate multi-agency planning. In many ways, this parallels the role of the 'lead professional' in English policy, where a child who is being assessed within the Common Assessment Framework (CAF) has a specific person to lead the multi-professional 'team around the child'. Similarly, the National Practice Model is a single or multi-agency assessment and planning tool with parallels to the English CAF. The principle underpinning this model is 'one child, one plan', and although the details differ, the approach has the same goal as the English CAF, which is to reduce assessments and complex planning for children and families to a single multi-agency assessment and child plan. The National Practice Model, however, focuses very clearly on the participation of children and young people in assessment and decision-making processes (Rose, 2012). However, the role of the lead professional receives much less prominence now in England than in Scotland, where, in contrast, further developments are planned. From 2016, all children and young people will have a statutory entitlement to a 'named person', who will offer support and advice as requested and provide early intervention when needed (Scottish Government, 2014), and can be seen in many ways as expanding aspects of the lead professional role to all children.

The Early Years Framework was introduced in 2008, covering pre-birth to age 8. The Framework focuses on developing better early intervention rather than 'crisis management', aiming to achieve 10 changes over 10 years to improve the lives of young children. These include improvements in services and in multi-professional collaboration to achieve better outcomes for children and families. However, the Framework was implemented in a restrictive economic climate, with some emphasis on the aim to reduce costs in respect of later interventions (Scottish Government/ COSLA, 2008). Further emphasis was placed on the pre-birth to 3 age range with the publication of national practice guidance to support early learning and child-care (ELCC) (Scottish Government, 2014), with the aim of promoting positive outcomes for all children and linking coherently to the 3–18 curriculum, to improve the well-being of children as laid out in the Children and Young People (Scotland) Act 2014.

Expansion

In the period since devolution, there has been significant expansion in early years services, particularly in after-school care and integrated pre-school centres. At times, this has been seen as threatening maintained provision (partly because it has happened at a time of falling birth rates that has already placed some maintained settings at risk). When it formed the new government in 2007, the SNP had a long-standing commitment to provide funding to support childcare and early education, and took a number of initiatives. These included the decision to provide £15 million to extend free pre-school education from 33 to 38 weeks as part of a set of major funding proposals for education as a whole, building on plans already formulated in 2006.

The Children and Young People (Scotland) Act 2014 increased free ELCC for 3- and 4-year-olds to 16 hours from August 2014 (previously the entitlement was 12.5 hours per week). From August 2015, 2-year-olds who are looked after or have a parent in receipt of certain benefits, will also be entitled to this same level of provision. This is slightly more than the position in England in 2015, but the proposal for the latter is to extend this to 30 hours per week for children of *working* parents in pilot areas from 2016.

Quality, curriculum development and regulation

The system of education in Scotland has always differed from that in England in several respects. Neither the National Curriculum nor standard assessment tests (SATs), nor the literacy and numeracy hours, were ever imposed in Scotland. Devolution has encouraged further change. As in Wales, ideas on the earliest phase of the curriculum are integral to plans for schooling as a whole. Thus, the work being conducted early in 2008 on curriculum guidance was concerned with the age range of 3–18 years rather than birth to 5, as in England. The Curriculum for Excellence was introduced with four key capacities: 'to enable each child or young person to be a successful learner, a confident individual, a responsible citizen and an effective contributor' (Education Scotland, 2012). The focus is on a comprehensive lifelong-learning approach to curriculum development, which until recently differed from the more fragmented approach to early years curricula in England. The focus on the pre-birth to 3 period is also prioritized by the Scottish government through the Early Years Collaborative (EYC), which is focused on improving young children's well-being by developing effective evidence-based practice, led by practitioners, and supported by each of the 32 Community Planning Partnerships (organizations that support public agencies to work together and with local communities) (Children and Families Directorate, 2014).

In 2007, the Scottish Social Services Council published new regulations on the qualifications of managers in all early years settings. In 2008, the Scottish Care Commission announced a number of changes in the inspection system, including a new grading system and a greater use of self-assessment in the inspection process. However, regulation and inspection of early learning and childcare settings continue to be undertaken by two separate bodies: the Care Inspectorate regulates services according to the National Care Standards, and Education Scotland inspects and reports on the quality of education. Both organizations work collaboratively, but this distinction is unique to pre-school education in Scotland.

Scotland and the rest of the UK

The excellent work that has been done on some aspects of curriculum development in Scotland and the pioneering initiatives taken even before devolution on the integration of early years services have won praise in England for Scottish achievements. This may sometimes give a misleading impression of the contrast. The integration of inspection in the area of child protection can divert attention from the fact that Scotland still has systems for the regulation of early years childcare and education services that are separate in a way that they no longer are in England. The fact that the country has a single set of curriculum guidance for ages 3 to 18 can divert attention from the fact that the guidance for children under 3 remains quite separate.

GIRFEC (2008) and the *Early Years Framework* (2008) have in some ways paralleled some of the developments within the *Every Child Matters* policy framework, but the emphasis on early intervention was echoed by recent policy shifts in England under the Coalition Government (Scottish Government/COSLA, 2008). However, *Every Child Matters* no longer figures in English policy for ECEC, and, even more starkly, the emphasis of English policy has moved towards a focus on school readiness, with very little reference to care.

Northern Ireland

Devolution

If there was violence in the history of England's relationships with Wales and Scotland, that fact was largely forgotten in modern times – at least in England. Both Scotland and Wales have political parties that are seeking full independence from the UK and the process of devolution has been marked by bitter argument, evident most recently in the debate and vote for Scottish independence. Nevertheless, devolution itself has been implemented with nothing much worse than the odd shouting match. The history of Northern Ireland is different. It has entailed not only wars in the distant past, but rebellion in the early 20th century and armed conflict for much of the last part of that century. Previous forms of devolution have foundered on conflict within the province. Whereas the choice in Wales and Scotland has been between full union, full independence and a form of devolved government, the choice in Northern Ireland has been between full union with the UK, full union with the Irish Republic and a form of devolution that represents some kind of compromise between those two national identities.

Well-deserved praise in both the Republic of Ireland and the USA has been heaped on Tony Blair and others who managed to broker this unexpected deal. However, mediators cannot magic agreement out of thin air. It seems likely that it was the exhaustion after years of conflict, the economic prizes offered by peace and the increasing secularization of the Republic of Ireland that assuaged Protestant fears of the Catholic Church and gave rise to the dawning realization on both sides in Northern Ireland that England and its politicians were relatively neutral on the future of the province rather than being committed to the union that, together, created the context in which real peace could be established. The DUP and Sinn Fein have shown themselves capable of working together on bread-and-butter social and economic issues, including early years policy. Sinn Fein, in particular, has a strong commitment to education – something it has in common with other forms of late 19th-century republicanism, but which the party itself would relate to the illegal 'hedge schools' provided for the Catholic population during the long struggle for independence. A major feature of the new regime is increased cooperation with the Republic of Ireland, which has manifested itself in joint action to develop better child protection systems and the establishment of an all-Ireland service for children with autistic disorders.

The re-established system of devolved government achieved in 2007 has continued for almost a decade, which in itself is an historic achievement in Northern Irish politics. However, the assembly is currently under pressure, and some politicians have suggested a risk of breakdown, over welfare reform. The Stormont House agreement, reached in 2014, placed an expectation on the assembly to implement welfare and other reforms, in return for further devolved powers. What is significant in these latest developments is that previous disagreements and threats to the functioning of the assembly have generally been centred on power sharing and political issues linked to historical conflict. In 2011 a threat to the assembly, whilst unwelcome, is from domestic political issues and linked to austerity measures, as are being experienced throughout the UK.

Integration

There is still an institutional division in Northern Ireland between the care and education of young children, a division that may have been aggravated by the fact that social services in the province have institutional arrangements with many similarities to those in the Republic of Ireland, while education has more in common with England. The division manifests itself largely in a separation of childcare for the under-3s and pre-school education for 3- and 4-year-olds. This is, of course, similar to the situation in Scotland. Just as in England, some see a conflict between the demands of the National Curriculum at Key Stage 1 and the implications of the curriculum guidance for the Foundation Stage, so in Northern Ireland there is seen to be a degree of tension between the demands of the revised National Curriculum and the play-based 'Enriched Curriculum' for younger children, piloted in 120 schools across the province from 2001 to 2006 and now part of the new National Curriculum. Before the current agreement on devolution, the Department of Education had attempted to protect pre-school settings by restricting the provision of reception class places, measures that came into effect in September 2007. (Again, there are parallels with Scotland.) Northern Ireland has also promoted a new integrated approach to children's services with the creation of the posts of Children's Commissioner and, later, Children's Minister, and greater cooperation between agencies at local level.

Regulatory regimes have been less well developed in some respects than in England. For example, a new Education and Skills Authority was planned to tackle not just the issue of inter-professional coordination, but also the much more tricky issue of cooperation across the sectarian divide. However, legislation to enable this was delayed for a number of years and large-scale structural changes to the local management of education will take place with the establishment of a single Education Authority to replace the five Education and Library Boards, to better align the management of education with planned changes to local government, again showing how local, regional and national moves to devolved government are likely to impact significantly over the coming years on ECEC throughout the UK.

The Early Years (0–6) Strategy has been implemented and sets out to make links between existing early years services for 0–4-year-olds and the Foundation Stage in primary schools: it is 'a comprehensive early years strategy that focuses on the development and well-being of each child, including affordable access to high quality early years provision for families living in areas of disadvantage and poverty in urban and rural areas' (DENI, 2010: 2.5). The strategy aims to improve: transitions between early years services, pre-school and school; the quality in early years services; and the integration of services. However, the strategy will not come with new resources attached, despite chronic underfunding of the sector and existing inequalities in early years provision across Northern Ireland. Moreover, the ongoing fragmentation of early education and care is an issue that remains problematic in terms of equality in service provision and within the sector (CiNI, 2010).

Expansion

Even before the general election of 1997, Northern Ireland had taken steps towards the promotion of early years services with the establishment of inter-agency early years committees in each Health and Social Services area (as in the Republic of Ireland, Northern Ireland has a unified structure for the delivery of both health and social services through regional boards). After 1997, two reports were published from Westminster outlining plans for the development of early years learning and childcare services, plans similar to those being developed for England. By 2004, many of the targets set in those two reports had been met or surpassed. However, as discussed above, the current situation is that developments in the early years sector within the Early Years Strategy face substantial funding challenges. In Northern Ireland, the Early Years fund, which was set up in 2004, focused on providing quality early years care and education in areas of deprivation. The fund has many similarities with Sure Start in England. Funding has remained problematic, but in July 2015 the Education Minister confirmed continued funding into 2016. The fund provides support to 153 early years organizations, but has not accepted any new applications since its inception in 2004, highlighting the funding challenges for early years services in Northern Ireland (DENI, 2015b).

A significant difference between Northern Ireland and other parts of the UK is the level of funded ECEC. In Northern Ireland, under the Pre-school Education Expansion Programme (PSEEP), parents can apply for a year of funded pre-school education. Although there is provision for over 90% of pre-school children, key differences to other parts of the UK are the length of funded provision (one year) and the fact that it is not universal but allocated as part of an application process (DENI, 2015c). Through a similar array of provision as offered in England, ECEC has doubled over the past decade, but funded support for families still lags behind all other parts of the UK.

Quality, curriculum development and regulation

The quality of staff involved in early years services has been a major issue and it is only in the recent past that cooperation with the Republic of Ireland and with the rest of the UK has led to the development of something like adequate vetting procedures. Criticisms of the over-formality of teaching in Year 1 of primary education suggest the need for further work on training and qualifications. However, considerable work has been undertaken on curriculum development. There has been a government review of the Special Needs Code of Practice (largely borrowed from England). The EPPE project in England has been mirrored in a similar study in Northern Ireland (EPPNI) under the direction of Professor Edward Melhuish. Northern Ireland, often in close cooperation with agencies in the Republic of Ireland, is pioneering some interesting work in the field of special needs. One of the province's largely unnoticed achievements over the last 40 years has been the research work undertaken at the University of Ulster on cognitive development in the early years, especially where that is affected by visual and hearing impairments.

Northern Ireland and the rest of the UK

Wales and Scotland have both had significant contacts with regions in other countries that have achieved a significant measure of devolved power in recognition of their separate national identities. In particular, both the Scottish Labour Party and the SNP have had continuing contacts with the major parties in Catalonia in Spain, where interesting initiatives in early years services have occurred. There have been similar moves on the part of the Labour Party in Wales and Plaid Cymru, both of which have been interested in the 'normalization' of the Catalan language and the implications for Welsh.

Northern Ireland is unique among the countries of the UK in having a special relationship (underpinned by a growing number of institutional arrangements) with a completely independent state, the Republic of Ireland. As fears among the Unionist/Protestant community about the implications of this contact slowly diminish, these contacts could begin to prove especially fruitful and introduce new elements into the internal debate in the UK on early years services.

The introduction of the Early Years (0–6) Strategy indicates that early years policy in Northern Ireland is following similar basic principles and policy aims to the other UK countries, with a similar emphasis on improving quality provision and integration and on smoother transitions between stages of education. However, different social and structural issues may mean that implementation takes a different form to similar policies in the rest of the UK.

ACTIVITY

To develop an understanding of how policy impacts on practitioners, children and families, select two countries of the UK. If you live in a country of the UK, this would be a good selection as your first, plus one other.

Review the different policies of each country and draw out similarities and differences between them. There are different ways you could do this. A useful starting point may be to think about how different policies impact on provision or practice. For example, you could compare and contrast:

- the early years curriculum and the key areas focused on

- how young children are accessed

- access to funded ECEC

- the way that different provision is registered and regulated

- whose remit ECEC falls under (e.g. education, health, social care) and the implications of this

- the qualifications required by practitioners and the emphasis policy places on professional development.

In addition to this chapter, a useful reference point for this activity are the relevant government websites for each country, which will give information on the latest developments. The key website for each country is listed in the Useful Websites section at the start of the book. When searching, remember to ensure that you have the correct jurisdiction (i.e. English government websites end in .gov.uk; the Welsh ones end in .gov.wales; the Scottish ones in .gov.scot; and the Northern Ireland ones end in .gov.uk but generally include 'ni' as part of the name – for example, the Department of Education is deni.gov.uk).

> The overall aim of this activity is to gain an understanding of the impact of policy and of how effectively it promotes effective ECEC, supports families and promotes effective practice. It is likely that the different policies of each country will have potential benefits and disadvantages. Developing knowledge of different countries' policies will support your analysis of this.

The impact of devolution

This chapter has highlighted both similarities and differences between the countries comprising the UK and the ways in which they have influenced each other in the development of early years services.

At times, there has been a kind of competition between them, with lobbyists urging their own countries to emulate what they see as best practice in one or more of the other countries. Among the reasons have been:

- genuine concern about the well-being of young children
- the fact that there was a lack of development before devolution, so that there was a lot of catching up to do
- the lead offered by the New Labour (1997–2010) Government in London
- the new opportunities created by devolution
- the desire to respond differently to austerity than the Coalition and subsequent Conservative Government.

However, it seems likely that a perfectly natural wish to do visibly better than England, the dominant partner in the union, comes into the equation.

The fact that contrasts are often made between what happens in Westminster and the initiatives taking place under devolved governments sometimes overshadows other and equally interesting comparisons. There are, for example, many similarities between Scotland and Northern Ireland and between those two countries and France, a country whose early years policy is rarely afforded consideration in the UK. Close attention to comparisons between the countries with devolved powers, rather than between them and England, probably has some interesting lessons to reveal.

More attention might also be paid to issues of national identity and culture, particularly following the outcome of the Scottish independence referendum and the 2015 general election. The place of Welsh in the education system has been a very live issue in Wales. However, overall there is very little evidence to suggest that Wales, Scotland and Northern Ireland are developing specifically 'national' solutions to the needs of young children. This might have been expected. In Spain, the significant developments in education and social welfare policies that have taken place in Catalonia and Euskadi have been built on what has been seen as the best professional practice from abroad rather than on aspects of national identity. Indeed, some in the UK have argued strongly that the needs of children are universal and that, therefore, there should be very few differences, if any, between policies in different parts of the UK (see, for example, Kullas, 2000). This is an issue that could become increasingly contentious, not just in the context of devolution, but also in respect of allegations that 'multiculturalism' has failed.

ACTIVITY

There are some who argue that all parts of the UK should have essentially the same standards in early years services because the needs of young children remain essentially the same wherever they are.

Others argue that different developments in different parts of the UK are helpful because:

- they facilitate experimentation

- they can reflect differences in national identity

- they can reflect different demands from the public in different places.

Outline what you think are the main arguments that can be made for or against the differences in policy to which devolution has led.

SUMMARY

This chapter has shown that:

- there are a number of differences between early years policies in the four major parts of the UK

- devolution has created new opportunities to develop early childcare and education

- devolution has also, to some extent, created competition in a way that has probably helped to speed up developments in this sphere.

FURTHER READING

The sources below will help to develop a more detailed understanding of how devolution has impacted on ECEC and how different political ideologies are starting to impact on the position and direction of policy:

Clark, M. and Waller, T. (eds) (2007) *Early Childhood Education and Care*, London: Sage. This book offers an excellent description of early years policy in each of the four major parts of the UK in the earlier years of devolution (and in the Republic of Ireland). It provides much greater detail than has been possible in this chapter and has case studies that help the reader understand the impact of policy on individual children.

Palaiologou, I. (ed.) (2016) *The Early Years Foundation Stage* (4th edn), London: Sage. The chapter entitled 'The national picture' offers a very useful overview of early years curricula in the different countries within the UK.

Pilkington, C. (2002) *Devolution in Britain Today*, Manchester: Manchester University Press. This text is a good overview of the early development of devolved powers.

Rose, W. (2012) 'Incorporating safeguarding and well-being in universal services: developments in early years multi-agency practice in Scotland', in L. Miller and D. Hevey (eds), *Policy Issues in the Early Years*, London: Sage.

Welsh, F. (2010) *The Four Nations: A history of the UK* (new edn), London: HarperCollins. The book offers a useful introduction to the broad historical context.

7

THE INTERNATIONAL DIMENSION OF POLICY-MAKING

THIS CHAPTER DESCRIBES

- international agreements that impact on early years services in the UK
- international comparisons and influences on early years policies and practice
- aspects of the early years policies of eight countries.

International agreements

The UK is an independent state. It is only subject to the authority of others to the extent that it has signed up to international agreements. Even in such cases, any country ratifying an agreement may abstain from ratifying a particular aspect of it. Agreements form the basis of international law. Few of the existing ones relate directly to the early years.

The UN Convention on the Rights of the Child (OUNHCHR, 1989) is probably the one that is best known to early years practitioners here. It was agreed in 1989 and ratified by the UK in 1991, although with a number of reservations, some of which were withdrawn in 2008. The Convention has not determined law and policy in this country. However, it has often been invoked – for example, in the debate on whether England should have a Children's Commissioner.

In March 1990, an international gathering at Jomtien (Thailand) arrived at an agreement on *Education for All* (UNESCO, 1990). This laid down a framework for action, but left it to each national government to set its own goals within that framework. The first Declaration was supplemented at a conference in Dakar (Senegal) in the year 2000 (World Education Forum, 2000). Among the features of the declarations that might be noted are that:

- the emphasis is on the quality of learning rather than simply on the number of people accessing education
- the first of six 'dimensions' outlined in the declarations is an expansion of pre-school services.

Jomtien and Dakar have received comparatively little attention in the UK, presumably because of an assumption that the basic objectives have already been achieved.

As a member of the European Union, the UK is bound by EU decisions in several respects. The treaties that underpin the EU are specifically concerned with economics rather than social policy. However, the boundary line between these two cannot be absolutely clear. When early childhood services are established in the interests of children, that is a matter of social policy. If, on the other hand, it is suggested that better childcare facilities are needed to release more women for the workplace, that is a matter of economic policy and the EU does have a say in it.

In March 2002, the European Council meeting in Barcelona published an agreement that member states would seek to provide childcare for at least 90% of children between their third birthday and the official school starting age, and for at least 33% of children under 3 by the year 2010. Nothing was said about the quality of settings or the means of provision. There has been little interest in the *Barcelona Objectives* (ECESAEO, 2008) in this country, and the UK has trailed behind several other states in meeting them.

International influences on UK policy

UK early years policy and practice has long been influenced by ideas and approaches from other countries. For example, the theories of pioneers such as Froebel, Montessori, Piaget and Vygotsky have had a significant impact on thinking about early years in the UK. The launch of OMEP (*Organisation Mondiale pour l'Éducation PréScolaire*) in 1948 was only the first of a number of initiatives to foster exchange between practitioners that have generated a growing, though still far from complete, consensus among early childhood specialists across the world.

Most international exchange has been in the field of pedagogy. Approaches to the curriculum in the UK have been partially shaped by ideas from abroad, such as Headstart (developed in the USA), the approach associated with Reggio Emilia in Italy and the Te Whāriki curriculum in New Zealand. The influence of the forest schools movement in Northern Europe has been significant in securing a more positive approach to outdoor learning in England, both in policy and practice.

There is another issue – the fact that there has been less attention paid in the UK to potential lessons from abroad on what government policy might be. Reggio Emilia provides an example. At the end of the 1980s in a period of financial constraint in Italy, there were moves to limit the responsibilities of local authorities for pre-school services. With widespread approval in the community, the local government in Reggio Emilia confirmed its continuing role in the field. This example of popular support for early childhood services in a situation of budget cuts is at least as interesting as the innovations in curriculum for which Reggio Emilia is better known.

International comparisons

International comparisons between education systems in different countries have long been influential in terms of policy and practice. Comparisons tend to be either through league tables or studies that compare aspects of educational systems in more than one country. The Programme for International Student Assessment (PISA) rates countries in terms of student achievement in core subjects by testing samples of 15-year-olds every three years across 65 countries. The rating of countries in the UK has been a policy driver for some time, influencing changes to legislation and providing material for intense political debate. *The Guardian* suggests that 'Interest in the test results is always feverish' (Mansell, 2013). The PISA results from 2012, reported in 2013, were used to justify Coalition changes to education, such as curriculum amendments and school autonomy.

One of the most significant recent bases of comparison between nations in terms of the quality of early education is the Economist Intelligence Unit (EIU) research programme into pre-school environments for 3–6-year-olds, which ranks 45 countries and reports the results in their publication *Starting Well: Benchmarking early education across the world* (Watson, 2012). The research takes into account social context, availability, affordability and quality in the ranking, with quality contributing 45% of the score. The key findings are that Nordic countries such as Finland, Sweden and Norway top the league table because of their long-term commitment to prioritizing and investing in the early years to the point that this is a significant and embedded cultural factor in these countries.

As such, the study concluded that the main elements of a 'good, inclusive early years environment', drawn from the experiences of the leading countries, are:

- a comprehensive early childhood development and promotion strategy, backed up by a legal right to such education
- universal enrolment of children in at least a year of pre-school at ages 5 or 6, with nearly universal enrolment between the ages of 3 and 5
- subsidies to ensure access for underprivileged families
- where provision is privatized, the cost of such care being affordable relative to average wages
- a high bar for pre-school educators, with specific qualification requirements – this is often backed up by commensurate wages, as well as low student–teacher ratios
- a well-defined pre-school curriculum, along with clear health and safety standards
- clear parental involvement and outreach
- a broad socio-economic environment that ensures that children are healthy and well-nourished when they enter pre-school. (Watson, 2012)

The authors also found that although the wealth of the nation was a significant factor in the ability to provide good early years education, some wealthy countries did not succeed in this. The USA, Australia and Canada were found to have variable quality standards in their early years provision, which was not available or affordable for all. On the other hand, less wealthy countries with lower average per capita income, such as the Czech Republic and Chile, have made pre-school provision a right for all children. The study also revealed that budget cuts and austerity policies threaten pre-school education despite the proven reduction a good pre-school system has in future spending on social support for some young people and adults.

This has significance for current early years policy in England, where budget cuts have affected aspects of early years provision, despite a stated commitment by government to quality, affordability and accessibility for all (Watson, 2012).

Perhaps the most important finding was that teacher quality is the most significant aspect of quality and that investment in this must be protected. On the other hand, 'using standardized tests to measure student performance and holding teachers accountable based on the test scores' is not a practice that is recommended by or found among the top-scoring nations (CIEB, 2012). This has implications for UK policy in terms of the commitment to testing and scrutiny that dominates educational policy for older children.

Caution in using international comparisons

International comparisons and policy borrowing, however, need to be treated with some caution. For example, international education league tables, such as PISA, have had a strong influence on determining school policy in the UK for some time. Perceptions that UK educational policy is somehow failing because of the relatively low position UK countries hold in PISA league tables have become a major influence on English education policy (Mortimore, 2009). There are two aspects here – making comparisons between countries and using these to amend policy in the less successful country, and using the country's position in the league tables to promote particular political ideologies in policy-making. However, both approaches have been described as simplistic, both in terms of failing to recognize that transplanted policy will not easily produce the same results in different cultural, social and economic contexts, and because the league table position may simply not reflect the true status of an education system due to the limitations of the measures used (Mortimore, 2009).

As long ago as 1900, Sadler said:

> We cannot wander at pleasure among the educational systems of the world, like a child strolling through a garden, and pick off a flower from one bush and some leaves from another, and then expect that if we stick what we have gathered into the soil at home, we shall have a living plant. (Sadler, 1900: n.p.)

League tables such as PISA have been criticized because as tools of comparison they merely provide a 'snapshot' of the attainment of 15-year-olds in core subjects (maths, literacy and science) in each participating country every three years. They do not cover the whole range of subjects or provide longitudinal data and there is no teacher input. Although contextual material is part of PISA studies, political agendas mainly focus on the 'topline' – the place of the participating country in the league tables (Mortimore, 2009).

The Starting Well report on early years education, which ranks 45 nations (Watson, 2012), has generally been welcomed and seen as a useful tool for promoting quality, inclusive early education provision. However, it has been suggested that the perspective of the study may contribute to the relatively poor ranking of Asian countries, where maternal employment is lower and, as such, the infrastructure of early education services is less well developed (CIEB, 2012). The authors do however acknowledge differences between the social and cultural contexts of the nations involved and also priorities in terms of the developmental stage of early education services in different countries.

Crossley and Watson (2009) also argue that using international comparisons to develop policy promotes a competitive and economic approach to educational policy-making that results in the testing and scrutiny approach that has dominated educational policy for some time in the UK. Policies that focus on improving PISA scores have been linked with efforts to become more internationally competitive as a nation. However, the resulting emphasis on assessment and its by-products, inspection and scrutiny, have been seen in some quarters as producing education policy that is so focused on test results that it negatively impacts on equity and social justice as educational goals. There are concerns that early years policy goals, which are currently aimed at raising the attainment of disadvantaged children, can be seen as part of this push towards better scores, without the necessary focus on all aspects of young children's development and welfare.

Interestingly, countries that have done well in recent PISA studies, such as Finland and Korea, may have very different educational approaches, making it difficult to analyse what factors contribute to an excellent educational system. However, one factor they do seem to have in common is a positive view of and approach to educational professionals – a 'trust-based culture' which values teachers and their work (Lloyd, 2014). This contrasts with developments in UK policy which have lowered the status and value of teachers, such as the attempt to introduce performance-related pay and the annexing of 'failing schools' when targets are not met.

Similarly, comparative studies in education policy between countries need to be treated with caution in determining policy or supporting political agendas, as unless there are strong similarities between the contexts, the transplantation of policy is unlikely to produce similar results elsewhere. Although comparative studies are seen as useful interchanges between countries through the sharing of policy ideas and practice approaches, there has been concern among researchers in this field about the possible use of these studies to simplistically promote particular political agendas (Crossley and Watson, 2009; Adamson, 2012).

To summarize, as discussed in earlier chapters, policy in education and early years is not neutral. It is the product of particular cultural and social mores of the time, previous policy history and prevailing political ideologies. Different ideologies will influence the purposes and practices of policy at particular times. Some of the key influences on UK policy can be contradictory, such as the drive to social justice and equality versus the drive to improve market position and economic competitiveness in the international arena. The result is that national policy is shaped by many forces and is peculiar to its country of origin. Therefore, it is possibly naive to think that policy approaches can be borrowed from other nations and used to produce the same results as they did in their homeland, when there are such marked differences between nations in their cultural approaches to children and childhood, early years and education, and where there are also differences in political ideologies, economic situation and myriad other aspects of the national context (Garratt and Forrester, 2012).

CASE STUDY

Hannah is a student on an undergraduate course in early years teacher training. Her ambition is to work in a school-based nursery with children aged 3–5 years. As part of her course, she has the opportunity to spend one semester in Finland, working in an early years setting. Consider the following questions:

- What would be the value of this experience for Hannah?
- How could she prepare for it effectively?
- What might be the pitfalls?
- Why do you think Finland was chosen as one of the countries where students on this course could do an international placement?

Comparing countries

For the rest of this chapter, and bearing in mind the cautions discussed above, we offer introductions to early years policy in eight different countries. Each country has its own characteristics and the attempt to learn from what they have done must be based on an appreciation of that fact (Glass, 2001).

We chose two issues: (1) the administrative integration of different services for young children, and (2) inclusion in its widest sense, to make comparisons with policy in the UK. The limited survey undertaken here also demonstrates the significance of the issue of how much money is invested in the supply side (i.e. how much money the government invests in provision, either directly by the state or by commissioning work by other organizations) and the demand side (i.e. how much money the government invests in financially supporting parents to place their children in settings of their choice).

ACTIVITY

Consider the reasons why it is important to learn about early years care and education in other countries. What may be the benefits? What may be the pitfalls?

Search for information about another country's early years services. What information can you find? How can you judge the quality of this? What are the most useful sources?

France

For most of the 19th century and the first half of the 20th century, people in Britain who wanted to further the cause of early childhood services looked to France for inspiration. When political backing for such services went into a steep decline in the UK in the 1950s and 1960s, interest in the French model diminished. When there was renewed pressure for better services from the 1970s onwards, other European examples dominated. However, there has been a continued interest in France's commitment to childcare since that time (Frean, 1997; Martin, 2010).

France has led the field in many ways in government support for services. Crèches to allow mothers to seek paid employment were pioneered in the 1840s. In 1862, the French government began to subsidize such initiatives, recognizing them officially in 1869 as being of *utilité publique*. In the 20th century, a book by Norvez (1990) aroused fears that France might face a declining birth rate and an ageing population, although it was not until 2003 that an increase in the birth rate became an official policy objective. Such concerns encouraged the idea that the state should facilitate early years services to make it easier for families to raise children. This has resulted in considerable state funding for a range of early years provision, income-related fees and employer contributions to funding family policy.

Since the 1970s, there has been an increase in state-provided day care settings for children aged 0–3 years, as maternal employment has grown. This provision includes the *halte-garderies* that were originally set up to help mothers deal with emergencies but have come to be used by many women working part-time or outside the standard working week. These are now often found in *multi-accueil* centres, which provide a range of flexible childcare including *jardins d'enfants* (out-of-school and occasional care for ages 2–6) and *crèches* as well as the *halte-garderies*: 18% of children with two working parents now attend these centres, which open typically for 11 hours a day (Fagnani and Lloyd, 2013).

The private sector played little role in the provision of day care in France until recently, with day care centres starting to appear only from about 2003. These include workplace nurseries which comprise only about 3% of the provision (Fagnani and Lloyd, 2013). These for-profit day care centres are state-subsidized and required to meet quality standards. As with other provision in France, payment is income-related in an attempt to promote social justice for all children.

Childminding has also been supported (Algava and Ruault, 2003). In 1990, a new legal framework was introduced (with further measures in 1992). Registered childminders (*assistantes maternelles*) now enjoy most of the protections offered to other employees. Their qualification requirements are stricter than in the UK, although in other respects they are less closely regulated than they are here. In 2004 the required number of hours training was increased to 120, and there are now 500 childminder support centres in France. One-third of all children in this age group are placed with childminders, making childminding the main source of external care for working parents (DREES, 2002; Fagnani and Lloyd, 2013).

Pre-school education has an even stronger position than day care. In the early 19th century, philanthropists developed a type of infant school for the children of the poor called the *salle d'asile*. Such schools were made subject to the *ministère de l'instruction publique* as early as 1836. In 1881, the term *école maternelle* was officially adopted for these settings. Teacher training colleges began to recruit students who intended to work specifically with the youngest children from 1884. The law of 30 October 1886 made *écoles maternelles* part of the state school system, with a decree the following year laying down a basic curriculum and rules on the training and qualification of staff. In 1910, a system of inspection (drastically revised in 1972) was established. The law of 11 July 1975 gave every 5-year-old whose parents wanted it the right to attend an *école maternelle* (or a primary school if a local *école maternelle* was not yet established). The overwhelming majority of children over 3 now attend these schools. So much do primary schools rely on this fact that special 'transition initiatives' (*actions passerelles*) have been put in place to assist children who have missed out on pre-school education.

Ecoles maternelles are free and full-time for children aged 3–6 years and for some 2-year-olds (Fagnani and Lloyd, 2013). However, the proportion of 2-year-olds has fallen from 30% to 13% in the last ten years, possibly due to the growth of other provision for this age group or possibly because of pressure on places. All teachers are graduates with four years of professional training. Ratios are 1:25 plus one assistant per group (1:20 in education priority zones, usually linked to economic and social deprivation) (Fagnani and Lloyd, 2013).

There are some similarities with the UK, in that France also has a complex and fragmented system of early childcare and education provision, divided by age group. However, the majority of children over 3 years of age (97–100%) in France attend free, full-time, state-funded *ecoles maternelles* or similar provision, whereas in the UK the picture is less clear, with many children attending private settings in this age group and currently receiving only 15 free hours per week. As England moves towards 30 hours of free provision for working parents, there will be fewer differences in funding, but in France this provision is available whether parents work or not. There is a strong principle of equality and social justice in early years provision in France which compares to the more market-driven approach in the UK. In France, responsibility for early years provision is still split between the Ministry of Education (*écoles maternelles*) and the Ministry of Social Affairs (other under-3 childcare) (Scottish Government, 2013).

The French 2002 curriculum guidelines for pre-school education lay down five curriculum areas – language development, living together, self-expression, discovering the world, and creativity. The English EYFS 2014 is different in emphasis, with three prime areas of learning: personal, social and emotional development; communication and language; and physical development, along with four specific areas of learning: literacy; mathematics; expressive arts and design; and understanding the world, but there is considerable overlap, with more emphasis on formal subjects in the English curriculum.

A less obvious but also significant contrast lies in the way in which pre-school education in France enjoyed official backing from a much earlier stage than it did in Britain. One of the key figures in the development of early childhood pedagogy in France is Pauline Kergomard who was (from 1879 to 1917) the *inspectrice générale de l'école maternelle*. Both in her work as a civil servant and in her publications, she argued cogently for the relevance of the new science of child development and the importance of learning through play, and helped bring about a much closer linkage between professional opinion and political decision-making than has ever been enjoyed in this country (Plaisance, 1996).

As well as day care and pre-school education, there are a number of other early childhood services that are well established, including:

- various forms of playwork settings known under the general heading of *acceuil collectif de minuers*
- toy libraries (*ludothèques*), which are often free-standing and have their own national association
- regulated agencies that provide care workers of various kinds, including nannies, operating in the homes of clients
- *lieux d'acceuil parents–enfants* (LAEP) centres (similar to Sure Start centres), which provide supportive services to parents in group settings
- *maisons d'assistantes maternelles* – a recent development where registered childminders work together outside their own homes.

As well as investing heavily in the supply of early childhood services, the French state has developed an extensive system of financial assistance to parents. A complex collection of different mechanisms was replaced in 2004 by the *Prestation d'Acceuil de Jeune Enfant* (PAJE), which reduced the existing system to two complementary benefits – one to offset the costs of early childhood services, and the other to support either parent in taking up to three years off work to care for a young child.

State commitment to early childhood services has had the intended effect of making it easier for parents, especially mothers, to afford to have children. Even before an increase in the birth rate was set as a formal policy objective by the government, France had seen:

- a reduction in the rate of poverty among two-parent families (albeit with a lower success rate for single-parent families)
- a major increase in the birth rate – which is unusual among the wealthier European nations. (OECD, 2004)

This has won approval from some, but questions have also been raised as to whether the care system has benefited employers, who now have a more flexible workforce, more than it has children (Fagnani, 2009).

In terms of sheer provision of early childhood services, France has achieved more than the UK. Progress towards the integration of services has been less of a preoccupation there than it has here. Pre-school care and education are separated at every level between local settings to those of central government. In addition, playcare activities for children below school age are closely linked to similar services for older children and come under the aegis of the Ministry for Youth, Sport and Social Life. Moreover, the principal national playwork qualification – the *brevet d'aptitude aux fonctions d'animateurs* (BAFA) – is at a much lower level than those of the professional staff in day care and pre-school education. The promotion of LAEPs by social workers rather than staff working in other early childhood settings has been a further complication.

On the other hand, more recently there have been several initiatives to encourage closer coordination of day care and education for children under 6:

- Since the late 1980s, many local authorities have employed staff to coordinate the work of different kinds of early childhood settings (Baudelot and Rayna, 2000). Some areas, such as the city of Nantes, have developed their own overall plans for early childhood.
- Since 2000, each day care setting has had to have a set of policies and procedures that, among other things, spell out the pedagogical aspects of the work undertaken.
- In 2001, there was legislation to strengthen the educational content of playcare activities.
- In 2002, each *département* (the largest unit of local administration) has had to establish a commission to bring together different interests in early childhood provision in order to generate greater coherence in provision.
- There are now many *établissments multi-acceuil* – multi-functional settings where different kinds of service operate on the same premises.

Another contrast with the UK is in the way in which policies on inclusion have developed. In the 18th and 19th centuries, France was the world's leading country in the development of education designed to meet the needs of the visually and hearing impaired and of children with learning disabilities. In more recent times, it has made the inclusion of children with special educational needs a key element in the policy manuals of day nurseries. However, the central concept has remained – that of 'special needs' rather than 'inclusion' – and there has been no real effort to take other possible sources of disadvantage in the educational system into account. On the contrary, the focus that has been in place since the late 19th century on education as an area where French identity is emphasized and differences of faith and culture downplayed, has discouraged the development of any wider sense of inclusion.

There are, therefore, significant differences between France and the UK. It is also worth noting the fact that recent developments have placed the educational aspect of such services in greater question than before. Worries about the effectiveness of the primary school system generated criticisms that the *écoles maternelles* were doing too little to make children school-ready (Haut Conseil de l'Éducation, 2007). This led to an official report in 2008 suggesting that school-readiness should become a much more central focus for pre-school education.

The Netherlands

A major reason for examining early childhood policy in the Netherlands lies in the close similarities between that country and our own. Both are constitutional monarchies with a strong tradition of liberal democracy. Both have ageing populations that are a potential source of economic and social difficulty. Both have large black and minority ethnic groups (BME) and have experienced controversies over multiculturalism.

There are also some relatively recent political similarities. The 'Polder Model', adopted by recent governments, is a collective political approach similar to the concept of 'partnership' as the key to a 'third way' in politics that was advanced under New Labour (1997–2010). The Dutch new-style policy agreements in various areas – the *Bestuursaccorden Nieuwe Stijl* (BANS) – and the decentralization of aspects of social policy that went with it have some parallels with the Local Area Agreements introduced by Blair. However, the move towards decentralization in the Netherlands has been more whole-hearted. The development of childcare is one of the fields in which local authorities have gained greater freedom of action.

There are also parallels in early childhood services. The Netherlands is one of the few countries where the UK's playgroup movement has been widely imitated, with the *peuterspeelzaal* (playgroup) forming part of local provision. State-subsidized playgroups are still a significant part of provision, particularly for children from ethnic minorities (Scottish Government, 2013). More important similarities lie in the long-established institutional differences between care and education services for young children in both countries and in the reliance in both governments on demand-side initiatives to promote early childhood services. For example, the Department for Social Affairs and Employment has responsibility for childcare, while early education remains with the Department for Education, Culture and Science (Scottish Government, 2013).

A reluctance to see the mothers of young children in paid employment has been a feature of public opinion in many European countries for some time and this has been particularly true of the Netherlands. As late as 1997, survey evidence showed that 20% of the Dutch population disapproved of working mothers and 50% particularly disapproved of placing children in day nurseries (van Praag and Niphuis-Neil, cited in Ministry of Health, Welfare and Sport and Ministry of Education, Culture and Science, 2000: 24). What is striking about this is that these figures were taken to demonstrate a strong shift in the 1990s *towards approval* of working mothers and day nursery care.

It was economic pressure that began to alter attitudes from the mid-1980s, when new policies were first devised to encourage women into paid employment to make up what was seen as a potential shortage of workers. The early 1990s saw 'stimulative measures' designed to encourage the development of some 49,000 new childcare places.

In the 21st century, there was a decisive shift towards reliance on subsidizing demand rather than supply in Dutch childcare services. Meeting the needs of employed parents through increased childcare became the driving force of early years development rather than educational issues. The key event was the passing of the Childcare Act (*Wet Kinderopvang*) of 2005 (amended 2010 and 2012). Although there had been a considerable increase in provision, there was still unmet need and at the same time many facilities were under-occupied (Diemet, 2009):

- The Childcare Act established a system under which payment for childcare was shared by parents (at a level that depended on family income), the national government and employers, although the employer's contribution was in the end voluntary. The subsidies were only available to families if both parents were employed (or the parent in a one-parent family was in work).

- Government subsidies were available for childcare costs up to a maximum level. (It was, of course, open to parents to purchase more expensive childcare if they could afford it.)
- Subsidized childcare fell within new regulations. These included childminders (*gastouders*), who had to be linked to approved agencies. Grandparents or others caring for children to whom they were related could, however, be subsidized if they registered as childminders.
- A previously existing system of regulations on quality (mainly relating to health and safety) was replaced by a new simplified system, with area health authorities made responsible for inspection and enforcement (much like the system in England and Wales from 1948 to 1971). Essentially, childcare is largely deregulated, however amendments to the Childcare Act 2005, in 2012, led to some re-regulation.

The system introduced in 2005 entailed a number of difficulties:

- While employers were often willing to subsidize the childcare costs of skilled employees in order to secure their services, they were reluctant to subsidize the childcare of the unskilled and low-paid.
- The cost of childcare subsidies rose far more significantly than had been anticipated. It became clear that a very significant part of the increase was due to grandparents registering as childminders. In other words, the policy of funding the demand side was not leading to a major increase in services, but to a large subsidy going into a type of informal care that was already there (Lloyd, 2008).

The Dutch government tackled these issues which were both costing it a considerable amount of money. In 2007, the right of employers to back out of childcare subsidies was curtailed. Since 2007, employers have had to pay a percentage of their employees' salaries, whether they have children or not, to the government to contribute to childcare costs. In 2011, this was 0.34% of the total salary. Also in 2011, changes were introduced that severely restricted the ability of parents to secure subsidies for the use of grandparents as carers. All registered childminders had to be willing to take children other than those to whom they were related and had to secure a diploma in care at level 2.

As a result, publically funded childcare has largely disappeared, leaving childcare to market forces, with public–private partnerships being a main policy target. In terms of coherence, 'There is no consensus on how ECEC should be organised, and as a consequence, a variety of programmes and methods can be found within the system' (Scottish Government, 2013).

Pre-school education has also undergone development. As long ago as 1985, the Dutch government ended the provision of separate nursery schools and integrated those that existed with primary schools, which now cater for children aged 4–12 years. Hence, there is no official pre-school service, although there are many playgroups that fall under the aegis of the Ministry of Education, Culture and Science rather than forming part of the welfare system. Out-of-school playcare services also fall within the ambit of the Ministry of Education.

Such services have an important role to play in childcare since the Dutch school system entails a long break in the early afternoon – something that poses a particular problem for parents in employment. The extended school (*brede school*) is now an important aspect of the primary school system, and schools (whether state-provided or the equivalent of our grant-maintained schools) are obliged by law to provide out-of-school-hours care.

As in the UK, systems of day care and early education have developed quite separately, and in many respects the integration of nursery and primary schools in the 1980s has reinforced this separation. The integration of care and education is not high on anyone's agenda. However, the *Onderwijs Raad* (Education Council), an advisory body, has been pressing for more attention to pedagogy in childcare settings and has even begun to use the term *leeropvang*, equivalent to the British 'educare'. The BANS for children and young people lays particular emphasis on cooperation between different agencies providing services for families with children aged 0–6 years. However, the clear separation of day care and education inhibits such moves. The authors of an official report on early childhood services in the Netherlands noted that some believe that pre-school playgroups have an important pedagogical function, but would not commit themselves to adopting this point of view (Ministry of Health and Ministry of Education, 2000: 70).

The fact that the care and education systems are so separate has also probably had an impact on the progress of inclusion in early childhood services. The Netherlands is committed to inclusion in schools, a policy that takes the needs of BME communities as well as those of children with disabilities into account. In recent years, an increasing number of children with special needs have been included in mainstream schools (Muskens and Peters, 2009). However, this has not had much impact on childcare services. The regulations (being mainly concerned with health and safety) have little to say on the kind of pedagogical practice that might support inclusion. There has even been in the *Samenspel* ('playing together') programme a tendency to provide separately for the children of recent immigrants.

There are significant ways in which early childhood services in the Netherlands differ from those in the UK:

- the specific demands made of employers in the childcare subsidy system
- the much greater commitment to extended schools
- the greater success of childminding
- the relative lack of regulation in childcare.

On the other hand, early childhood services in both countries have been shaped significantly by:

- continuing controversy as to whether the mothers of young children should be in paid employment
- the continuing distinction between care and education
- the reliance in the recent past on demand-side rather than supply-side policies in the promotion of early childhood services.

The Czech Republic

For most of the 20th century, the Czech lands formed part of Czechoslovakia. In 1993, Slovakia gained its independence and the Czech Republic was formed.

The Communist regime that was in power from the end of the Second World War until 1989 had wanted to encourage mothers back into the workplace, partly to support economic development, partly to promote gender equality. A widespread system of local authority *jesle* (crèches) formed a critical part of this policy. When the regime fell, antagonism towards the Communists helped to reinforce traditional ideas about the family (Valentova, 2009). These ideas focus on the importance of the mother–child bond, resulting in mothers staying at home with younger children almost exclusively. This was reinforced by the withdrawal of state funding, the provision of generous maternity leave and the perception that crèches provide low-quality care based on a health model. Most of the municipal *jesle* were closed in the 1990s, with 20% of under 3s in crèches in 1989 and only 1% now. They were not replaced on any significant scale by day care services run by the voluntary or commercial sectors, although there is some private provision which is very limited and expensive. Effectively, there is barely any under-3s childcare left in the Republic, with fewer than 70 crèches still open in the whole country. However, 16.7% of women with children under 3 are in some form of paid employment (OECD, 2006). Their children are normally cared for by a relative or by a *chu° va* (the Czech word covers nannies, babysitters and au pairs). The employment of nannies is expensive and restricted to the affluent, but the number of families doing this appears to be increasing. Nannies are often secured through professional agencies, but there is no obligation to do this and neither agencies nor independent nannies are subject to any specific regulation. Although pre-schools are not intended to provide a care service for children under 3, about a quarter of the children in that age group attend their local *mateřská škola* at least part of the time. The extent to which this is a way of getting round the lack of group day care or is a practice of parents who wish to see their children get an early start in their education is unclear. Many primary schools also have their own *školni družina* (after-school club).

The principal form of pre-school education is provided by the *mateřská škola*, for children aged 3–6. Most are run by local authorities, a few by voluntary organizations, even fewer by private companies. A majority of children attend these pre-schools for at least part of the time before compulsory schooling starts at 6 (67% of 3-year-olds and 98% of 5-year-olds in the last year before school age), but the rate of participation is lower than in other European countries. Local authorities are required to provide early education for any families who want it, effectively providing children with an entitlement to early years education when aged between 3 and 6 years. Hours are determined locally and can be full- or part-time. These settings fall under the Ministry of Education, Youth and Sport (as opposed to *jesle* which come under the Ministry of Health in most cases, but under the Ministry of Social Affairs in the case of those that have an explicit 'therapeutic' function). The great majority of practitioners in pre-schools have qualifications from a four-year secondary-level course offered at 18 vocational schools across the country.

This training has in the past been significantly focused on creative activity and sport rather than on the foundations of literacy and numeracy or knowledge and under- standing of the world. Most of the teaching staff are low-paid, their salaries being equivalent to three-quarters of the average wage for all full-time employees in the Republic. Those that are graduates are rather better paid. The curriculum is deter- mined by the General Curriculum for Early Childhood Education, established by the Education Act 2004, which extended the range of skills expected of children leaving pre-schools for primary education, with an emphasis on interpersonal skills, and also defined the relationship between parents and educators as one of partnership (OECD, 2006). The guidance is cast in fairly general terms, leaving scope for differ- ent approaches, especially in the voluntary sector. This has facilitated the development of pre-schools following the Waldorf-Steiner and Montessori patterns and more individual settings, such as the *Detsky Klub Šárynka*, an innovative forest school.

The children's day care and pre-school education systems are quite clearly sepa- rated in the Czech Republic, from the level of central government downwards. The question of how far care and education can be integrated in early childhood services has, however, barely arisen because day care services are so little developed. Now that the Republic has to a large extent shrugged off its Communist past and Czechs are becoming more aware of early childhood services in other countries, the idea that the state should keep out of family affairs unless forced to intervene because parents cannot meet their responsibilities is beginning to gain acceptance.

The Czech Republic has long had a network of special schools for children with various disabilities. In response to influences from abroad, there have been recent moves towards including more children with disabilities in mainstream schools. The policy of seeking greater inclusion in the mainstream has been mainly directed at children with identified disabilities. However, it could have wider implications since the Republic is one of the Eastern European states that was accused by the European Monitoring Centre on Racism and Xenophobia of over-readiness to identify Roma children as having learning disabilities and sending them to special schools on the basis of faulty diagnoses. Similar accusations led to a successful case being taken to the European Court of Human Rights in 2007 (Devroye, 2009). However, many educationists in the Republic support the idea of special provision for Roma children because of the difficulties they are seen to encounter and present in mainstream schools.

Controversies about early childhood services have been and remain an issue in the Czech Republic. This illustrates how the ways in which services are organized tend to reflect recent history and raise questions about the values of a society.

Uruguay

After an 11-year period of military rule, the Latin American republic of Uruguay returned to civilian government in 1984. For some time after that, power was con- tested, mainly between two right-wing parties, but in 2004 the *Frente Amplio* (Broad Front), an alliance of communists, socialists and progressively minded Catholics, won the election. Tabarè Vázquez, the new head of government, initiated a wide-ranging programme of economic and social reform. When he retired in 2010, he had an 80% approval rating in the opinion polls. The *Frente Amplio* won the election that year and, although there were some changes of key personnel in the government, social policies (including those relating to early childhood) were continued.

Uruguay already had a number of early childhood services. One unusual feature of the country was that the lack of services was greatest in urban rather than rural areas (Llambi et al., 2009). The reverse is normally the case, whatever the level of development of the country in question. To a significant extent, this was because of the uncontrolled influx of families into the capital Montevideo, which now has about half the population of the entire country. As in Britain, the provision of childcare was seen largely in terms of helping women, especially single mothers, into work. It was also similarly seen as a way of tackling child poverty (Llambi et al., 2009; Perera and Llambi, 2010).

In general, universal education for all is advocated in Uruguay, and the country has led the way in education as a means to citizenship and economic success within South America. In the late 1990s, there were major reforms in the education system, which included making pre-school compulsory for two years, for children aged 4 and 5 years old. Expansion in pre-school provision was rapid during this period, with an increase of 76% between 1995 and 2004, and an even higher rate for children from disadvantaged backgrounds (Berlinski et al., 2008).

The action that has been taken in relation to early childhood services has had several defining features:

- *The policy has been the clear responsibility of the central government.* More specifically, it has been the responsibility of the *Instituto del Ninõ y Adolescente del Uruguay* (INAU), a government agency under the direction of the *Ministerio de Desarrollo Social* (MIDES), which was created by the Vásquez government in 2005 as a key part of its social and economic strategy. INAU's strapline is *Nos importan todos los niños* (which could be translated as 'Every Child Matters'). Responsibility for pedagogical aspects of children's services rests with the *Ministerio de Educación y Cultura* (MES) and a civil service agency, the *Administración Nacional de Educación Pública* (ANEP).
- *Work on early childhood services and, in particular, day care for children under 3 forms part of ENIA (Estrategia Nacional para la Infancia y Adolescencia), a general plan for advancing the interests of children*, first put forward in 2008. The plan incorporates childcare, family support, health, education and child protection, and relates initiatives in all these areas to each other. Uruguay has also taken the lead in developing SIPI (*Sistema de Información para la Infancia*), a software system designed to support safeguarding activity that has now been adopted by several Latin American countries. ENIA was originally intended to run to 2015. It has now been extended to 2030, by which year it is intended that childcare should be available to all children whose parents want it.
- *Although MIDES and ENIA control the strategy, a good deal of the work of supporting children (including day care and pre-school education) is provided by centres for the care of children and their families (Centros de Atención a la*

Infancia y la Familia – CAIFs), which are run by voluntary (usually Catholic) and commercial bodies. CAIFs have been instrumental in increasing the length of the school day and improving the quality and quantity of day care provision. The principal feature of early childhood policy is the development of such bodies. In other words, the expansion of children's day care and early education has been based on increasing supply rather than on assisting parents to meet the costs of services set up on other kinds of initiative.

- *Uruguay has adopted a policy of close coordination of early childhood services, but – unlike Britain – has not done so by giving education the lead role.*

ENIA has led to a significant increase in the number of children able to attend day care centres and pre-schools, although the number of places is still inadequate. However, between 2006 and 2012 day care centres increased from 109 to 168. By 2009, 40% of children under 3 were in day care, with an increase in 10% recorded between 2006 and 2011. Research is ongoing as to how far this has helped mothers into paid employment and whether other initiatives are needed to assist them with this. The emphasis has been on expansion. There is some evidence that the services for younger children that existed in 2004 had a positive effect later on in the school system (Berlinski et al., 2008). This suggests that there was good quality practice at that stage.

It is clear that the care and education services provided for young children are well integrated in Uruguay, at least at the level of central policy-making and planning. The intention is that they should also be closely integrated within the local CAIFs. A commitment to inclusion has gone along with this.

What has happened in Uruguay is an impressive example of services for preschool children being driven forward by a government committed to them and to seeing them as a full and integral part of its social policy. The *Frente Amplio* has also developed a supply-side strategy for expansion while still leaving room for action by voluntary and private institutions in the provision of early childhood settings and other related services.

Kenya

Kenya faces the challenge of all previously colonized countries of finding a way of combining the best of traditional and European ideas on early childhood services and has achieved a great deal in this respect (Adams and Swadener, 2010). The matter is complicated by the fact that Kenya itself is made up of many different ethnic groups that are sometimes in conflict. The lead role in early childhood services has been played by education, specifically by the Ministry of Education, Science and Technology (MOEST). This emphasis dates back to the Ominde Commission Report of 1964, published soon after independence from Britain, which spoke of the significance of education in the building of a new nation. Kenya has what may be the most highly developed education system in sub-Saharan Africa. However, recent economic and social challenges have impacted on the development of early years care and education, including rapid urbanization, the spread of HIV and AIDS, loss of the extended family through modernization and poor economic circumstances, poverty and the growth of single-parent families.

Formal primary education begins at the age of 6. It has been free since 2003, but is not compulsory. This reinforces the tendency for poorer families not to use early childhood services, since they now wait until free education begins. Another consequence is that girls are often kept away from school to provide care for their younger siblings while their parents work. Thus, free primary education has bene-fited boys much more than girls. Those who purchase pre-school education are often the better off and more ambitious, and such parents frequently demand 'proper education', that is to say formal teaching of literacy, as early as possible – a demand that conflicts with the views of more experienced practitioners. This is, of course, a familiar situation, but one that appears to be particularly acute in Kenya. There is also a high drop-out rate among staff that has undermined the efforts of the World Bank and others to invest in their training.

The coordination of early childhood services in Kenya is the responsibility of a project management support group chaired by the deputy director of primary edu-cation in MOEST and involving high-level representatives from MOEST itself, the Teacher Service Commission, the Ministry of Finance, the Ministry of Health and Kenyatta University.

MOEST recognizes seven types of early childhood setting:

- nursery schools
- pre-unit classes – these are similar to British reception classes
- kindergartens – this term is not very clearly defined but usually refers to settings that have both care and educational objectives
- day nurseries – such settings have limited pedagogic aims; they are often run by faith or other voluntary agencies for children from families facing particular difficulties
- playgroups – Kenya has a number of playgroups based on the British model
- madrassas or Islamic schools
- home-based care centres – these are parent support settings rather than agen-cies focused primarily on children.

In some ways, this range of services reflects the models derived from the former colonial power or from international bodies such as the Bernard Van Leer Foundation, the Christian Children's Fund, the Aga Khan Foundation, UNICEF and the World Bank, which have been active in the promotion of pre-school educa-tion in Kenya. There are a number of other initiatives that reflect more local traditions and concerns:

- Many communities in Kenya still follow a pastoral, nomadic style of life that does not fit well with attendance at school or early childhood settings in fixed premises. This has had a significant impact on the participation in schooling of the Maasai people, among others (Phillips and Bhavnagu, 2002). One particu-larly interesting and highly influential approach to this issue was developed by staff from a number of international agencies and the Kenya Institute of Education in the Samburu District of Northern Kenya. Believing that existing work on pre-school education in the area had been too focused on the training of staff and on fixed premises, they looked at traditional ways of caring for young children. Older women provided young children with care and education (especially in the form of traditional story telling), usually in shady outdoor enclosures (*loipis*), while their parents worked. In return, parents supplied the older women with many of their necessities. More than 80 new centres based on the Loipi model were set up in the district. Health personnel worked alongside the women to provide better physical care (including immunization). Parents were helped to create toys that had an educational function for their own Loipi settings (instead of the charities supplying Western-made equipment of this sort). By 2008, although Samburu is the second poorest district in Kenya, it had the highest proportion of children in pre-school education. The model was taken up by other nomadic peoples in Kenya and by neighbouring African states (Bosire, 2006; Van de Linde and Lenaiyasa, 2006).

- Another innovative development that seeks to blend traditional and Western approaches is the *Mwana Mwende* programme run by Anne Njenga. (The name of the programme means 'the child that is loved'.) This was launched in 1997 by a number of local voluntary organizations concerned about the welfare of children under 3 and of teenage mothers. The objective has been to raise the self-esteem, commitment and abilities of the young women for their own sake and that of their children. The programme has attempted to blend care (including health care) and education concerns and has worked through supporting the mothers of the children concerned rather than trying simply to rescue the children in some way. A key feature has been work on the inclusion of children with disabilities. The American Beth Blue Swadener and her colleagues have argued that *Mwana Mwende* represents a significant turn to more collaborative approaches to early childhood services between Africans and those from more economically developed countries (Swadener et al., 2000; Kabiru et al., 2003).

- A third example of blending local and Western approaches is provided by the work of the Aga Khan Foundation in establishing pre-schools in areas with large Moslem populations, following a more 'holistic' approach than some of the longer established madrassas or Islamic schools.

Experiments such as these have proceeded alongside a programme to develop the training of early childhood practitioners in ways that link education and care together closely and link both of those to more general community development. For some time, the National Centre for Early Childhood Education (NACECE) has encouraged local adaptation of their national guidelines by their district counterparts to ensure the relevance of the work undertaken. In general, pre-school education has been a carefully considered part of both NACECE's capacity-building programme and the political commitment to the Kenya Education Sector Support Programme (KESSP), which is one of the fast-track programmes devised in just nine countries under the Education For All (EFA) project. A key role in all this has been played by Henry Manani (2005, 2007), the coordinator of NACECE and deputy director of the Kenya Institute of Education.

However, despite the progress made so far there are major challenges to early years education and care in Kenya. The provision of free primary education in 2003 led to a rapid expansion of early years provision in the private sector but state funding is very low and quality remains a serious problem. The focus on primary schools has led to resources being sucked from the early years, and state provision has been very limited. Low participation rates among children (65% of 3–6-year-olds do not attend) reflect access issues as private providers control pre-school provision and quality variations affect provision in urban slums and rural areas. There is a lack of clear policy to support the growth of early years services, despite efforts in the past to promote these, resulting in uncoordinated growth which is often unregulated. Teachers are often not trained and pay rates vary according to the location and provider, affecting teacher motivation. Competition to enter good primaries has led a move away from a play-based curriculum towards an over-emphasis on school readiness and the three Rs. This approach is supported by teachers and parents as preparation for school is a key goal in private provision. However, despite this, the uncontrolled nature of expansion and a lack of regulation and supervision have led to poor transitions to primary for some children, with a resulting high drop-out rate from primary school (Mbugua, 2004; Githinji and Kanga, 2011).

One of the other concerns expressed has been the failure to identify or meet the needs of children with special educational needs (SEN) through some centres, due to a lack of awareness on the part of teachers and parents. Overall, long-term investment in early years care and education and a stronger approach to educational philosophy and policy are needed to improve provision and to make this inclusive for all children (Mbugua, 2004; Githinji and Kanga, 2011).

China

One reason for examining early childhood services in China is the sheer importance of the country. It also offers an opportunity to reflect on the innovation that may come from the interaction of Western and other approaches to such services.

Mutual learning is particularly relevant in the development of the early childhood curriculum. Two examples may be given:

- In the early stages of primary school, Chinese children are taught techniques of drawing in a way that contrasts vividly with the approach to creativity in the UK. The American Ellen Winner, who first reported this in the West, has developed an interesting approach that learns from and develops what has happened in China (Winner, 1989, 1993).
- Music played a significant role in Confucian (ethical teaching system) ideas on moral development and still has a major role in schools and pre-schools in China today (Yim and Ebbeck, 2009). Some settings in the UK – such as the Ellesmere Children's Centre in Sheffield – that have had contact with those in China have picked up on and implemented Chinese approaches successfully.

As China began its unusually swift economic development, a new emphasis on day care for young children began to appear. More and more parents needed such services and also valued pre-school education as a way of helping to ensure their children's success in later life. The well-established policy of pushing couples into having only one child has added to the reasons for seeking access to childcare and education services. It is seen as a way of giving the single child the experience of living with peers and as essential to prevent 'spoiling'. Initially, it was the state that provided early childhood services. The more recent past has seen the development of private enterprise in this field to fill the gaps left by low state funding and lack of prioritization of early years education and care. Private development included not only large Chinese companies (such as the Shanghai-based Xiehe chain with its 30 pre-school settings) but also foreign companies, such as the American Family Box chain, which opened its first kindergarten in China in 2009. By 2009 less than a quarter of day care centres across the country were run by the state (Luo et al., 2009: 13).

Access to day care and early education is a major problem. The primary contrast is that between rural and urban areas, as is the case in most of the world. Even where they exist, early years settings in rural areas are often poorly staffed and equipped. Only 12% of the staff in the rural settings studied by Luo et al. (2009) were considered by the authors of the report to be fully qualified. Where services are set up in rural areas, they are often close to production zones. There are frequently serious dangers to health and safety associated with them. The lack of pre-school provision in rural areas and the poor quality of some of what does exist make for longer-term problems. There is evidence that of the six dimensions on the scale of school-readiness devised by Dr Ou (a scheme that has been widely used, although it does not have official backing), most children in rural areas are only ready for school in terms of their gross motor skills (Luo et al., 2009: 14–15).

However, the key issue is not so much the contrast between rural and urban areas but between the poor and the wealthy. Early in 2010, the Western press covered the story of a single father in a large city who could only keep his young child safe while he worked by chaining him to a piece of street furniture and leaving him with food. Less anecdotally, Qinghua et al. (2005) found that low-income families in the capital of Beijing faced serious childcare problems in terms of availability and price. Many low-income parents in cities are recent migrants who have come to improve their standard of living and make use of grandparents in their original rural homes to care for their children. As in other countries, there is little support for grandparents playing that role (Nyland et al., 2009). However, despite variations within urban areas, access here is much better, with some rural areas having such little provision that families are unable to send children to pre-school even if they want to.

Wealthier families also face such problems and often find it difficult, with long working hours, to make use even of those pre-school services they can afford. Residential nurseries which were once (as they were in the UK in the first half of the 20th century) largely a resource for children whose low-income parents were incapable of providing care, are now more often used by affluent parents (Tobin et al., 2009: 33). Many couples have opted for the expensive but convenient option of having a live-in *ayi* ('nanny'). These are often very young women with little or nothing in the way of training, but who do at least provide some continuity of care as well as cover when parents are working late. Parents who cannot afford this option sometimes send younger school children to settings which offer after-school tutoring. They may be thinking, not only of their children's education, but also of the solution these after-school settings offer to childcare problems towards the end of the working day.

A major issue in pre-school settings has been the demand of ambitious parents that their children should be made to learn formally (Zhu and Zhang, 2008). Tobin et al. (2009: 91) argue that the growth of the private sector (especially in the major coastal cities) is likely to make settings more open to such demands. There have, however, been a number of developments in the pre-school curriculum in recent years.

In 1989, the first regulations for early years settings in China were issued (although Hong Kong, still then a British colony, had produced guidelines for kindergarten practice in 1981). The guidelines were considered by Carter et al. (2007) to have 'consolidated progressive influences'. However, they also felt that serious difficulties had been encountered in translating the principles of the 1989 regulations into practice. In 2001, the Ministry of Education issued further guidelines for pre-school education on a trial basis, with a plan to evaluate its effectiveness. This was followed by a plan for early childhood settings for the period 2003–7.

There has been some evidence that official guidelines have influenced practice, especially in urban settings. At the very least, there are indications of a growing acceptance by more senior staff of the kind of pedagogical ideas that are widespread among practitioners and theorists elsewhere (Hsueh and Tobin, 2003; Jiaxiong and Nianli, 2005). Yu and Pine (2006) report on an action/research project they conducted in the major cities of Nanjing and Beijing. Up until 2001, pre-school practitioners had been forbidden to do anything about literacy. This was changed by the new guidelines, but little was done to assist practitioners to develop the relevant skills. The researchers introduced practitioners to ways of encouraging 'emergent literacy'. They found that, not only were these techniques successful with the children, but also the staff gained enormously in self-confidence and interest in their work.

The issue of inclusion has also failed to get very high up the agenda of many practitioners, although both provision for special educational needs and the principle of inclusion have had official backing since the National Education Committee issued its *Educational Guidelines for People with Disabilities* in 1994. There are continuing difficulties caused by the widespread prejudice against children with disabilities (Gargiulo and Piao, 1996). The early years curriculum guidelines drafted in 2001 made 'recognition of individual differences' a key aspect by which early years pedagogy was to be assessed, but the shortage of facilities as well as prejudice continued to inhibit the development of inclusive practice, even in the major cities, where at least some settings have adopted an active policy in this respect (Hu and Szente, 2010). Apart from disability, there are issues relating to other aspects of inclusion. The Communist Party has been committed from the start to gender equality, but low-income parents, especially in rural areas, still tend to see the education of boys as being more important than that of girls (Carter et al., 2007: 17–18). At the same time, worries about separatist movements have hampered the development of teaching in minority languages.

The provision of early childhood education and care has been strongly affected by recent economic growth. The heavy reliance on the market to meet demand (to the point where many local authority settings have been privatized) has had a serious impact, not only on the availability of services, but on the nature of the services themselves. There has been some progress in the improvement of premises and general health and safety, but not as much as might have been expected, and many settings have staff groups that are small and poorly qualified. Practitioners are often unaware of developments elsewhere (in relation to behaviour management, inclusive practice and the foundations of formal learning) that might help them achieve greater competence and self-esteem.

However, since 2010 the government has made a commitment to fund early years education and since that announcement provision for young children has become a national priority. The Outline of China's National Plan for Medium and Long-term Educational Reform and Development commits the government to increased funding, support for private providers, better and more consistent teacher training, provision of buildings and more support for rural areas and disadvantaged families. Since the plan was put in place, the number of children accessing early years education has grown significantly, with 45% of children aged 3–6 attending kindergarten in 2009 and 70.5% by 2014. The focus of other targets relate to the quality of provision in terms of teacher quality, the curriculum and access. Much work remains to be done in these areas before the divide between rich and poor and urban and rural children can be breached (Zhou, 2011).

USA

The USA is an interesting comparison to the UK because of its status as a high-income country and its federal structure, which means many differences exist within the country as well as between the USA and other countries. The relationship between federal government and state government and the overall national preference for limited government involvement in social and family affairs are all part of the backdrop to the current state of early years and childcare policy. However, there are similarities to the UK in the development of a mixed market of provision and a long period of neglect of early years policy by government. The development of compensatory programmes has been a significant contribution in both countries, although the US Head Start programme preceded Sure Start by more than 30 years.

The development of early years childcare and education in the USA began in the 1830s with the establishment of day care centres (often overcrowded and poor quality) for children of the working poor and the development of nurseries, and later kindergartens, to provide early education. Day care grew rapidly in the 20th century in response to social changes, increased numbers of working women and waves of immigrants expanding the population. Kindergartens grew more slowly, providing an enhanced curriculum for better-off children. Both forms of care expanded rapidly in the 1960s to 1970s as more women started entering the workforce, and the War on Poverty led to increased interest in early education as a positive factor in promoting children's life chances. In the 1960s, the Head Start programme was developed to support low-income families and their children by enhancing early years health and education. This programme was the inspiration for the UK Sure Start programme developed in 1999 with similar goals. At present, Head Start provides free day care and pre-school places for 1 million children under 5 years old, although this is only a proportion of the eligible children. However, since the 1970s further attempts to produce a national strategy have been blocked by conservatives in the government and little development has taken place for some time. Overall, the care and education of young children has rarely been a policy objective in the USA in the past, except when women were needed for the workforce in the Second World War and the Lanham Act 1940 was passed to create state-run day care for their children. This lapsed after the war due to pressure for jobs to be vacated for returning veterans. As a result, national childcare policy in the USA has fallen far behind need, resulting in a fragmented and widely varying map of provision, with variable access, costs and provision, as well as widely variable quality across the nation.

There are a number of different forms of childcare and early education in the USA:

- family day care – similar to childminders in the UK, 22% of under 1-year-olds are in this type of care; requirements for training and qualifications are minimal and not all states require registration and inspection
- informal care – half of children under 1 year old in non-parental care are with relatives
- organized day care:

  o kindergartens – universal provision for 5-year-olds in the year before starting school, overwhelmingly publically provided
  o pre-kindergartens – for 4-year-olds, these are the most rapidly expanding provision at present with 42 states providing pre-kindergartens (although there are variations in attendance patterns between full- and part-time)
  o day care centres – for under 3-year-olds, often supporting low-income families
  o compensatory education, such as Head Start, for low-income families (see above).

This provision is marked by huge variations in quality, staff training, regulation and inspection requirements and cost. As in the UK, there is a mix of private, non-profit and public provision across the range (Kamerman and Gatenio, 2003). Currently, 42% of under 5s are cared for by relatives, 33% are in non-relative care including family day care, and 25% are in organized day care. Overall, 12 million children under 5 spend an average of 33 hours per week in day care in the USA.

Although childcare is now a key issue for families in the USA (where 60% of mothers work), costing up to 40% of income for low-income families and averaging at 7.2% of income for all families, government involvement has been low in terms of developing a comprehensive, good-quality childcare and early education system in the USA. Watson (2012) concludes in *Starting Well: Benchmarking early education across the world*, that the low position of the USA in the rankings for good quality early education identifies it as one of the high-income countries where the link between high income and good-quality early years care and education is not apparent. This is to do with the lack of consistency in access, affordability, quality and inclusion across the country, although excellent provision does exist.

It is difficult to comment on some aspects of quality as funding and participation vary greatly between states, making generalizations not meaningful. However, major issues in quality include workforce training and qualifications, with low wages and high turnover (31% a year) contributing to problems of quality provision and care. Regulation of qualifications and training of staff is minimal in some states. Costs to parents also vary between and within states but are generally increasing, meaning low-income families struggle in many areas. An NICHD study in 2007 found that only 10% of day care provision was found to be good and the rest was fair or poor.

US policy, such as it is, has been to support the demand side with child tax credits and to provide compensatory education in response to overwhelming research findings which support the view that early years care and education are a national investment. State-funded provision of kindergarten places for 5-year-olds demonstrates a commitment to early education which has more recently been extended to 4-year-olds through pre-kindergarten provision. However, the real problems lie in the lack of consistency and quality in day care for children aged 3 and under and the high costs to families where working parents need this provision.

In the last 10 years, there have been indications of a greater interest in supporting and promoting early years care and education through renewed political interest and legislation. The Strong Start for American Children Act 2013 offered, among other things, free early years education for low-income children, focusing mainly on 4-year-olds. There has been increased spending, with 40 states now funding pre-school programmes, usually from age 4. The Right Start Child Care and Education Act 2013 increased access to child tax credits. In his 2015 State of the Nation speech, President Obama declared childcare a 'must have' for working parents, proposing much increased tax credits and plans for greater investment in the infrastructure of early years provision.

In comparison to the UK, there are distinct similarities between the ad hoc development of a mixed market of provision with unequal access for some children in the USA. However, the issues of quality are different, with national quality regulations and inspection in the UK providing better conformity of standards than in the USA. Similarly, more regulatory attention to staff qualifications and suitability seems to be evident in the UK as opposed to the USA.

Finland

It is well known in the ECEC field that the Scandinavian countries, Finland, Norway and Sweden, have what are considered the best early childhood care and education systems in the world, and this is confirmed by their ranking in the Starting Well index (Watson, 2012), where these three countries take the top places. 'Finland, Sweden and Norway top the Index, thanks to sustained, long-term investments and prioritization of early childhood development, which is now deeply embedded in society' (p. 6). Therefore, Finland is included in this chapter in order to explore the key factors in this success and what we can learn from them.

In Finland, provision of comprehensive and high-quality ECEC has been a feature of social policy for decades, and current policy is focused on improving an already established and generally successful ECEC system, rather than developing ECEC services from a low base, as we have seen in other countries discussed in this chapter. There is strong commitment from government and citizens supporting the provision of good quality ECEC to all children, underpinned by a firm belief that the outcomes of ECEC are well worth the costs. The success of the Finnish ECEC provision has been well documented, with links made between this positive early start for Finnish children and the high performance in PISA rankings of 15-year-olds' test scores in core subjects (Pascal et al., 2013). Other outcome indicators are also positive:

> Regarding the indirect or direct outcomes and results of Finland's ECEC policies, Finland performs above the OECD average on most outcomes: the country's fertility rates are slightly higher than in most other OECD countries; Finnish students at the age of 15 perform well on PISA assessments for reading, mathematics and science; and there is very little child poverty. (Taguma et al., 2012: 9)

In Finland, there are two main goals for the provision of ECEC – day care for working parents and quality early education for young children. ECEC policy is linked to equality issues in terms of women's rights to work and shared responsibility for children between both partners. Provision is based on a national ECEC strategy and services are delivered by local municipalities that are also responsible for quality and supervision. ECEC has been the responsibility of the Minister of Education and Culture since 2013.

Most women return to work following the birth of a child after up to a year's maternity leave. All children have a right to ECEC from birth to 7, with parents entitled to this within two weeks of starting work or study. Children have access to day care from birth up to age 6, which can be in publically subsidized private care or publically funded day care. At age 6, children attend pre-school for a year, which involves a half day of early education and then day care for the rest of the day (Watson, 2012). Nearly all 6-year-olds were in free pre-primary education in the year before school starts up until recently (98%), but this became mandatory from August 2015. Pre-primary education takes place in schools and day care centres.

Fees are income-based and subject to the number of children in the family, although taxes are high to pay for the services. Although Finland has low levels of child poverty, unlike many other countries, such as the USA and to some extent the UK, poor children receive high quality pre-school and day care, rather than suffering a postcode lottery as to quality.

Types of care include:

- day care centres for children aged 0–6
- family day care/group family day care for ages 0–6

- pre-primary for children aged 6 in the year before starting school
- private and voluntary service provision.

Pre-school-age children in Helsinki are cared for in the following facilities:

- 59% attend municipal day care centres
- 5% attend private day care
- 25% receive care through a home care allowance payment (delivered by parents)
- 5% receive family day care
- 6% receive care through a contract or purchased service.

One of the key features of effective ECEC identified by Pascal et al. (2013) in the international comparison is staff training and qualifications, on which Finland scored highly. Teachers have good pay and status, and are well-qualified, studying for 3–4 years to gain a degree and with many going on to to complete a Master's. Their studies focus on curriculum planning and design, and leadership, as teachers also have responsibility for the curriculum. Minimum qualification standards are set and are generally high compared to other countries. Teachers are also trusted and this leads to a system of only light-touch inspection and testing. There is also a mandatory commitment to staff development, funded jointly by the employer, the individual and the state (Taguma et al., 2012).

Staff requirements are as follows:

- at least a secondary-level degree in the field of social welfare and health care
- one-third of the staff in a day care centre must have a degree, e.g. Bachelor of Education
- pre-primary teachers should have either a Bachelor's or a Master's degree in education.

According to Taguma et al. (2012): 'The main strengths of Finland's ECEC work-force are related to staff preparation, the nature of professional development, and staff working conditions' (p. 10). However, as teachers are mainly female and over 40, the authors argue for development of the workforce to include younger people from a wider variety of professional and academic backgrounds.

Regulation of ECEC in Finland across both private and public provisions is linked to high quality, scoring highly in the study by Pascal et al. (2013) in comparison to other countries. Quality is also linked to above-average public spending on the supply side, linked to high staff–child ratios in centres:

- 1:4 for 0–3-year-olds
- 1:7 for older children in ECEC
- 1:4 in family day care.

In terms of curriculum and pedagogy, integrated care and education is the norm, and early education is delivered through a play-based curriculum. There is a strong emphasis on outdoor play and activities, despite a generally cold climate.

The language of instruction in day care can be Finnish, Swedish or Sami and other languages are also supported.

The curriculum is guided by the National Curriculum Guidelines on ECEC (2003) for children 0–6 and the Core Curriculum for Pre-Primary Education for children in their last year before school. Unlike the UK, the curriculum sets aims for staff and centres, but not for individual children.

The core content areas of ECEC are:

- mathematical orientation
- natural sciences orientation
- historical/societal orientation
- ethical orientation
- religious/philosophical orientation.

The success of Finnish ECEC policy is reflected in the outcomes for children and families and the international acclaim for their services and structures, pedagogy and philosophy. In comparison to the UK, there is very little emphasis on scrutiny and testing of children; instead, teachers are trusted to deliver the curriculum successfully. While regulation is in place to maintain and promote quality, there is no sense that it is used to critique the workforce, and staff are both paid well and respected. High levels of investment in state provision have meant that all children, whatever their economic and social background, access good quality ECEC and therefore escape the link between socio-economic disadvantage and more limited and/or poorer quality provision that is found in other countries. Access to childcare for all families at affordable costs is a key element to engaging children in quality childcare and allowing mothers to return to work. Finland seems to have avoided the mish-mash of varied and variable provision and complex childcare arrangements common in the UK by investing thoroughly over a long period of time. Perhaps, most importantly, it has fostered and embedded a social and political commitment to ECEC, to the extent that it is considered a norm in Finnish society and therefore is safer from political and economic vagaries than elsewhere.

Lessons from different countries

- There are many successful ways of providing early years services and the effectiveness of these will depend on the context in which they are applied, therefore there is no one model of good early years practice, merely some indicators that are present in all successful countries, such as good-quality teachers.
- We should be careful about making over-simplified use of international comparisons.
- Concerns about aspects of early years services in one country may not be relevant to another. For example, a majority of countries have retained institutional distinctions between care and education and those that have gone for close integration have often – like Uruguay – chosen a different institutional route to achieve this.

- Supporting the demand side (by tax credits or subsidies to parents) is less successful in promoting early years services than investment in the supply side (by the provision of settings directly by the national or local state or by other agencies working under contract to the state).
- It is important that we recognize what we have to learn from countries outside Europe. There is still a lingering tendency to ignore the lessons we may have to learn from Latin America, Africa and Asia. Innovative approaches there to both provision and the curriculum are relevant to the developed world.

ACTIVITY

Looking at one or more of the countries discussed above or another country of your own choosing, compare the early years care and education services of that country to the main elements of a 'good, inclusive early years environment' summarized in the report *Starting Well* (Watson, 2012) (see p 98 of this chapter).

How does the country you are looking at compare? Where are the areas that still need development? What might be the barriers to further development?

SUMMARY

- The international dimension of early years and childcare policy development is important in terms of understanding global development and the progress of developing effective services for young children.

- Examination of the early childhood policies of several countries shows how much variation there is, suggests some of the reasons for this variation and, therefore, helps us to a critical understanding of our own circumstances.

- International comparisons, such as league tables and rankings or comparative studies, need to be treated with caution as the development of early years policy and services is locally determined by social, cultural, economic and many other factors.

FURTHER READING

The trade journal *Nursery World* and various academic journals frequently include articles covering early childhood services in other countries.

The most comprehensive surveys available are the OECD's *Starting Strong* series of reports on different countries (2001, 2006, 2012). Bear in mind when they were published and that policies in this field – as in other areas of social policy – may change significantly over time.

The latest is *Starting Strong III*, with further details at: www.oecd.org/edu/school/starting-strongiii-aqualitytoolboxforearlychildhoodeducationandcare.htm

Starting Well: Benchmarking early education across the world is an index and comparative commentary on the relative merits of early education in 45 countries: www.economist insights.com/sites/default/files/legacy/mgthink/downloads/Starting%20Well.pdf

Some shorter pieces that can be recommended are:

Penn, H. (2009) 'A mother's place is in the home?', *Nursery World*, 12 March, 1041. This article looks at differences between European states in the role of day care for young children.

Reed, M. and Walker, R. (eds) (2015) *A Critical Companion to Early Childhood*, London: Sage. Chapter 20, 'Policy into practice: implementing the early years learning framework for Australia from a Western Australia perspective', offers a fascinating insight into recent Australian early years practice.

Waller, T. (2005) 'International perspectives', in T. Waller (ed.), *An Introduction to Early Childhood: A multidisciplinary approach*, London: Paul Chapman. This chapter looks at the international dimension of early childhood services but with an emphasis on pedagogy and the curriculum rather than on policy.

White, L.A. (2009) 'Explaining differences in child care policy development in France and the USA: norms, frames, programmatic ideas', *International Political Science Review*, 30, 4, 385–405. This article provides a useful analytical framework.

8
THE IMPACT OF POLICY

THIS CHAPTER

- explores how policy development impacts on the early years sector and overall provision

- explores how policy developments impact on three key groups – practitioners, children and parents

- aims to show how policy can offer potential benefits for one or more of the groups but at the same time may also create tensions.

Chapter 5 provided an overview of how policy is devised and implemented and clearly highlighted how the raft of policies within early years has led to a significant expansion of service provision, and stated government policy suggests this will continue. On one level this can be welcomed, as it would seem likely that this would lead to improvements for children and families. Nonetheless, it is necessary to explore the likely impact of the diverse policies on different stakeholders.

Since 1997, there have been some major shifts in early years policy. In many respects, as discussed in earlier chapters, the National Childcare Strategy provided an impetus that has led to significant changes in early years services, and the Childcare Bill (2015) suggests this will continue. Over the past few years, the expectations of government, local authorities, other services and parents in regard to early years services have risen and there have been year-on-year increases in provision, including part-time funded places for 2–3-year-olds. For example, 99% of 4-year-olds, 94% of 3-year-olds and over 157,000 2-year-olds (58% of those eligible) now access funded provision (DfE, 2015b). There is a much greater focus on having practitioners with professional qualifications, although this is less evident in more recent developments as the focus appears to be on level 3 qualifications (e.g. Early Years Educator), a more rigorous inspection process to drive up quality throughout the sector and an expectation that future service provision will work in partnership not only with parents but also with a range of other services (e.g. health). Overall, these changes seem positive, but to understand the impact on the sector, practitioners, children and parents requires more in-depth consideration.

Early years sector

It is difficult to predict accurately what impact the intended increase in funded places for 3–4-years-olds will have when the Childcare Bill (2015–16) is enacted, and the effect on the early years sector. The overall economic environment is likely to impact on the number of parents working. For example, if employment prospects are positive, more women, who often take responsibility for childcare, may decide to work longer hours as ECEC is more affordable and childcare can be seen as more manageable by parents in families (Raley et al., 2012). It is also known that early years policies impact disproportionately on women, both as mothers with young children, and as practitioners, the vast majority of whom are female (Lea, 2014). However, it is likely to lead to increased demand on the sector. Alongside this, in the recent past there has been a gradual decline in the overall number of Ofsted registered providers (e.g. there was a decline of 1% in the number of providers in September 2014 compared with six months earlier), and in particular the number of childminders has declined year on year from over 60,000 in 2009 to just over 50,000 in 2014. In contrast, the number of places in the sector has increased slightly, suggesting that larger providers (e.g. nursery chains) are providing more places per provider (Ofsted, 2014). However, providers are reporting difficulties in recruiting good quality practitioners, the level of staff turnover is increasing and there is concern about the ability of the sector to support the expansion to 30 hours for 3–4-year-olds that will be piloted from 2016 (NDNA, 2015). Combined with this, funding to the PVI sector often does not cover the hour-for-hour costs of provision, meaning that expanding this provision will lead to reduced income from non-funded places, which makes this financially unachievable (House of Lords, 2015) and led to a detailed review of funding of ECEC.

There are also concerns about the impact of the myriad of policies on the overall quality of ECEC in the sector. For example, there has been an increase in the number of providers employing practitioners with a recognized professional qualification at degree level or above (e.g. qualified teaching status (QTS); Early Years Professional Status (EYPS); Early Years Teacher Status (EYTS)). However, whilst there has been an increase in the number of practitioners with these qualifications (i.e. from approximately 6,000 in 2014 to approximately 8,000 in 2015), the number of registered providers with practitioners qualified to this level fell back to 41% in 2015 compared to 45% in 2014 and 42% in 2012 (DfE, 2015b). This suggests that fewer smaller settings are employing professional graduates and/or more are securing employment in maintained settings, such as schools. This highlights the lack of clear development pathways and the need to enhance the professional standing of the sector (Nutbrown, 2012) to make it more attractive as a career route. It is also well documented by research that the higher the level of staff qualifications of the workforce, the better the quality of the setting and outcomes for children (Siraj-Blatchford et al., 2008; Nutbrown, 2012; House of Lords, 2015). To achieve the best outcomes for children, particularly those accessing targeted funding to raise attainment, there needs to be more coherence in the government's overall objectives for childcare. As an example, over 90% of 2-year-olds are in private, voluntary and independent provider provision whilst the majority of staff with higher qualifications are in the maintained sector (DfE, 2015b; House of Lords, 2015). To address this and gain the best outcomes for public investment in ECEC, the government needs to consider how the status, qualification base, career progression opportunities and quality of provision can be enhanced to enable the sector to fulfill the commitment to 30 hours of funded ECEC for young children (Osgood, 2009; NDNA, 2015).

Practitioners

The early years workforce is diverse, in terms of the qualifications and experience it holds. However, there are some areas where this diversity is not evident, for example in age, where around a third of the workforce is below the age of 25. It is also significant that approximately 98% of early years practitioners are women, few are from ethnic minorities, few have disabilities and the majority hold a qualification at or below level 3 (for example, Modern Diploma, BTEC National Diploma). Another significant difference is that over half work in the profit sector, compared with less than 10% of teachers, although there has been a fall in the number of private providers and a rise in the number of voluntary providers (DfE, 2015b). One reason for these differences, which has been discussed in previous chapters, is the division of responsibility between care and education. The terminology used for the sector varies. For example, 'early years care and education' was often used, with the aim of breaking down artificial barriers between care and education as the boundaries between each are generally unclear and young children need both, not one or the other. This is also reflected in local authorities with the merger of child social services and education departments and the creation of Director of Children's Services posts to lead the formed departments. In Scotland and Wales, ECEC is often used as it is in European contexts. Nonetheless, even when account is taken of these developments, care has often been seen as inferior to education and this is reflected in the qualification levels, perception, training opportunities and salary levels of practitioners, with those practitioners within the early years sector who are not qualified teachers being less highly regarded than those with qualified teacher status. In terms of conditions of employment as well as low pay, this often entails working longer hours and an absence of other benefits such as sick pay and time/ funding for professional development (Osgood, 2009; NDNA, 2015). The Nutbrown (2012) review of the qualifications and standing of early years as a profession confirms that many of these issues persist.

When this is seen in the context of government plans for workforce expansion and professionalization, it raises fundamental questions. The ten-year strategy, released by the previous government, set out plans for early years services, identifying the importance of the early years workforce in achieving the ambitious strategies of the plan (HM Treasury et al., 2004). These points have been reiterated in recent government plans aimed at increasing provision for funded places for 2-year-olds (albeit in targeted areas) and the new Statutory Framework for the Early Years Foundation Stage (HM Treasury, 2011; DfE, 2014a, 2015b). Although both these policies are aimed at children and families, they have a significant impact on practitioners. They stress the importance of practitioners having the appropriate qualifications and skills to work with children. This shows the inter-relatedness of policy: documents are produced by government on the basis of manifestos, political ideologies, expert reports or even public opinion. However, for successful implementation, turning the policy into practice will at least require alterations to practice and possibly a fundamental overhaul of provision and practice. The basis of this is a simple realization, but it is important to acknowledge that the quality of early years settings is clearly integrated with the quality of practitioners. The EPPE project (Sylva et al., 2004, 2012), which has tracked outcomes for over 3,000 children who have experienced various types of day care (for example, LEA-run nurseries, community playgroups and integrated centres), found that:

- the higher the qualification level of practitioners, particularly the leaders in each setting, the better the quality of the setting and the outcomes for children, particularly those with a poor early years home learning environment
- settings led by graduates were particularly effective and this has to be seen in light of the current situation where qualification levels are low
- access to training was variable in a significant number of settings, particularly those in the profit sector where there is an extremely high turnover of staff, which creates inconsistency and difficulties in sustaining a workforce that is able to continue its professional development over time.

Based on government plans for child and family services, this presents significant challenges in achieving many of the ambitious targets in two main areas: leadership of early years settings and creating a sustainable workforce.

Leadership in the early years workforce has not received the same level of attention as in other sectors of education, particularly schools. One difficulty for the early years sector is the fragmented range of services that make up provision. This ranges from multiple-site private nursery chains to integrated centres that provide a range of health, social and educational services, to community-run playgroups (which in some places, such as rural areas, may be the only provision available). In expanding services, the Labour Government, in its attempt to keep a central hold on developments, took a managerialist approach to funding and provision, which has led to a range of demands on setting leaders, including increased administration, a range of targets to achieve and complicated requirements to attract and maintain funding (Osgood, 2009). This raises issues about the balance between the complexity of centrally imposed management requirements and the demands on each type of provider. For example, a large Children's Centre or community hub may be able to respond to a broader range of requirements than a childminder working independently and offering provision for a group of children at varied times during the week. This is not meant to suggest that large-scale private provision is better or more effective. In fact, some of the most successful provision, previously designated as Early Excellence Centres (these would now mainly fall under the umbrella term of Children's Centres, many of which also evolved from Neighbourhood Nurseries and Sure Start Local Programmes), started as locally based voluntary sector provision (Osgood, 2009). Within these settings, there was an emphasis on collaborative and cooperative working, at the same time as responding to the government's agenda of reducing social exclusion. For policy development and implementation, this emphasizes the need to consider further developments carefully and ensure that account is taken of the need to develop collaborative practice, rather than simply assuming that policy alone can achieve this.

As part of its ten-year strategy for childcare, the Labour Government (1997–2010) signalled a commitment to increase the number of Children's Centres to 3,500 by 2010. These centres provide an integrated range of services to meet the social, health and educational requirements of children and families. However, under the Coalition Government, there was a reduction in the number of integrated Children's Centres and a cut in funding of approximately 20%, putting more centres at risk of closure (4Children, 2014). The diverse range of provision that children's services aim to provide will require leadership from appropriately qualified and skilled practitioners if the full potential of the policy for integrated services is to be realized. In response to this, the government, for the first time, has acknowledged the need for a range of skilled practitioners, including graduates in early years (HM Treasury et al., 2004), and the need for highly qualified practitioners has been consistently confirmed by varied sources (e.g. Sylva et al., 2004, 2012; Siraj-Blatchford et al., 2008; DfE, 2012). This move is welcome as there is a large body of evidence that shows the need for effective leadership in education, although less on leadership in early years (Muijs et al., 2004; Close and Wainwright, 2010). Kagan and Hallmark (2001) argue that leadership in early years encompasses a number of roles:

- administrative skills
- pedagogical leadership
- an ability to lead community services and initiatives
- the ability to act as an advocate for groups and show political awareness.

This highlights the need for effective education up to degree level and effective leadership training. Leadership is complex and, to be effective leaders, practitioners need to develop the characteristics associated with a leadership identity (Woodrow, 2008; Nutbrown, 2012). Other groups, such as universities providing Early Childhood Studies courses, children's organizations and sectors of the academic community, have argued the need for this for several years. A positive development was the announcement of the Graduate Leader Fund (DCSF, 2008a). The fund, which replaced the transformation fund, was allocated to local authorities, and the Children's Workforce Development Council (CWDC) (2007) aimed to raise standards and enhance quality through the provision of graduates in settings. The fund was intended to provide scope to attract new graduates into the sector and provide resources to enable practitioners already within the sector to train to graduate level. A welcome development with this fund was the commitment to provide resources through this channel until at least 2015, which was designed to enable local authorities and early years settings to plan on a more long-term basis rather than from year to year. In addition, the fund was primarily focused on the PVI sector, where only 3% of the workforce, compared with over 40% in the maintained sector, are graduates. However, the Graduate Leader Fund was closed on 31 March 2011 and funding through the early intervention grant has also subsequently been redirected to the schools budget.

The two main graduate opportunities available within the sector are Early Years Professional Status (EYPS) and the National Professional Qualification in Integrated Centre Leadership (NPQICL). These routes offer either graduate or postgraduate training for practitioners. With EYPS, which the CWDC saw as having equivalency to qualified teacher status, practitioners were trained to take a lead role in planning and delivering the curriculum. With NPQICL, which was similar in nature to the National Professional Qualification for Headship (NPQH), holders generally took a management and leadership role (National College for School Leadership, 2008). The full impact of these being withdrawn will become clear over time, but evidence has shown that the presence of graduate leaders with Early Years Professional Status leads to significant quality improvements within a setting. A review of the NPQICL also took place and this ceased in August 2014. This is contrary to a raft of evidence that emphasizes the positive impact on quality and children's outcomes of having professional graduates and leaders in early years settings (Mathers et al., 2011; Nutbrown, 2012; House of Lords, 2015). This is a clear example of how policy decisions are made on the basis of multiple factors, and of how changes in direction do not always reflect the evidence of positive impacts. In 2013 the government introduced the Early Years Teacher Status (EYTS) to focus on and lead high-quality practice. To access training as an EYT, applicants need to be graduates, and training is designed to ensure that those who complete it meet the early years teaching standards. While this is welcome, concerns remain, as the terms and conditions of those with EYTS are not automatically equivalent to those with qualified teacher status (QTS) in school-based settings. In addition, there is no recognized career development pathway to enable those with other qualifications to progress to this level. To address this, the NDNA (2015) argues that early years needs to be a greater priority for the College of Teaching.

In addition to having good leaders in the early years sector, in order to achieve the ambitious expansion plans and targets set out in policy documents, a systematic overhaul of the early years workforce will be needed. As well as the importance of the early years workforce in terms of sustainability, there is a clear link between the skill level of the workforce and quality (DCSF, 2007; Tickell, 2011; DfE, 2012; House of Lords, 2015). At present, early years practitioners cover a continuum of experience and qualifications. This ranges from little past experience and no formal qualifications to level 3 qualifications, such as the CACHE diploma or the BTEC in Early Years, to a degree, in Early Childhood Studies for example, or qualified teacher status (Nutbrown, 2012). For those with qualified teacher status, who usually work in school environments, either within maintained nurseries, reception classes or foundation units, their terms and conditions of service are set within national agreements or are guided by these. But, as stated earlier, for the majority of practitioners within early years, the level of reward, working conditions and opportunities for development and progression do not match those of practitioners with qualified teacher status, and the majority are not covered by national agreements on pay and conditions.

To address this situation, there will need to be a radical rethink on how policy can take account of and be applied to the fragmented range of early years services.

This will need to explore how best to support and develop the workforce to ensure that early years care and education services are of high quality, sustainable and take account of the expectations of children and parents. An Integrated Qualifications Framework (IQF) was under development, but the emphasis on this was lost with the disbanding of the CWDC in 2012. Within early years, practitioners cross a number of traditional professional boundaries. In addition, there has been an exponential increase over the past two decades in the range of qualifications for early education and childcare (from less than 20 in 1990 to approximately 160 in 2010), and the challenges of developing a coherent, fit-for-purpose qualification framework to ensure appropriate training and progression opportunities for the early years workforce continue (Nutbrown, 2012). In September 2014, Early Years Educator (EYE) status was introduced for those with specialist and relevant level 3 qualifications. A positive aspect of this is that it provides a way to recognize the myriad of early years qualifications under a common standard. Concerns have been expressed though at the requirement for GCSE mathematics and English to achieve the status and be counted in staff ratios. Whilst this seems a reasonable requirement, the decision not to allow equivalent qualifications in lieu of these requirements (e.g. key or functional skills) is seen as a further step in limiting the number of potential recruits to the sector.

Over a decade ago, in 2004, a National Audit Office report of early years services identified three key issues in creating sustainable provision: the lack of premises, the withdrawal of start-up funding and the lack of a trained workforce (NAO, 2004), and the latter still clearly exists. One of the greatest challenges still in terms of sustainability could arguably be ensuring an adequate supply of appropriately qualified practitioners for expanding early years services and ensuring there are processes in place that value and reward these people once they are in post.

ACTIVITY

Think about each of the following and, if possible, talk to practitioners with different experiences to gain their perspective:

- What level of qualification should early years practitioners have? Explain why you think this.

- Is there a need for some/all practitioners within early years to be educated to degree level? Explain why you think this.

- What may be the barriers to attracting people to work in early years services?

- What measures are needed to keep practitioners within early years services?

- Is there a clear career progression pathway for practitioners in early years? If not, what would need to be done to establish one?

When thinking about each of these points, an important consideration should be the diversity of early years services. Unlike schools, which generally have a similar pattern of organization (but do not necessarily offer the same experience for children), early years services span a range of providers. For example, there are childminders who may work predominantly in isolation in local communities; private organizations with multiple sites; and Children's Centres, which may be voluntary or local authority operated and which provide a diverse array of educational, social and health support services. What is clear from an accumulating body of evidence is that the higher the overall qualification of practitioners, the greater the quality of early years care and education they offer (Brind et al., 2011; DfE, 2012; Nutbrown, 2012). Arguably, the workforce issue and, up to a point, the issue of providing more consistent frameworks for developing practitioners has been tackled, but several years on, even in light of the Childcare Act 2006, which set out expectations of training for practitioners, significant challenges remain. However, to achieve the ambitious plans previously outlined, future policy will require far more than simply putting graduates into the workplace – particularly given the withdrawal of funds to specifically support this. Moss (2004) draws attention to Target 26, set by the European Commission Childcare Network in 1995, which set the ambitious aim, for the UK at least, of ensuring that a minimum of 60% of practitioners working with children have completed at least three years of post-18 training (for example, degree level) and that the remainder of staff without this should have access to it either at training institutions or through continuous professional development. Even so, increased training levels alone are not enough. To value practitioners with increased levels of training, there also needs to be a rethink of salary levels, clearer progression routes and a career framework that makes this possible (HM Treasury et al., 2004; Nutbrown, 2012), and over the past few years there has been little progress here. Various governments have outlined a commitment to addressing these aspects, but over recent years the issue has received much less attention, and the aim of creating a sustainable workforce clearly remains that – an aim. The CWDC had primary responsibility for creating an appropriately qualified and trained workforce to effectively meet the needs of children and young people (DCSF, 2008b). In 2012, the Teaching Agency was formed with two main aims in relation to early years provision: (1) the supply and retention of the workforce; and (2) the provision of a quality workforce. However, in March 2013 the Teaching Agency merged with the National College for School Leadership to form the National College for Teaching and Leadership, and the focus on the early years sector is clearly not as evident as it was.

During the term of the Coalition Government, there was a renewed emphasis on providing integrated early years services, but the historic set-up of services, with the split between the PVI and maintained sector and across traditional service boundaries (i.e. health, education and social care), in many ways made this difficult to achieve. Evidence of this can be provided by exploring two different examples. For a number of years, there has been a decline in the number of registered childminders, and this shows no signs of abating. To provide integrated services, it is necessary for practitioners to work in partnership with a range of stakeholders. For childminders, this can involve working with the local authority, the NCMA and parents.

Although this may seem unproblematic, when it is considered alongside other aspects of their role, such as meeting the expectations of the Early Years Foundation Stage (DfE, 2014a), marketing their service, attending training and managing finances, it shows the complex nature of the role and potentially highlights how the mismatch between expectations and reward has led to a significant reduction in numbers. To support childminders, some local authorities employ coordinators, and there are some childminder networks organized on a formal or informal basis. However, there has been a decrease in the number of childminders, from 71,500 in 2006 to 57,900 in 2010, and by 2014 numbers were below 52,000 (Brind et al., 2011; Ofsted, 2014), and as expectations increase, which is likely through the curriculum, inspection and other demands, this may be exacerbated and have a negative impact on provision and parental choice.

With the change in service organization and integration, it seems an ideal time to consider the roles of those who work within early years services. Questions exist about whether the current division of roles is appropriate to meet the demands which current and planned early years policies will place on providers and practitioners. Again, the Labour Government acknowledged this in its ten-year childcare strategy by stating that a new profession, combining learning and care, is needed that will exist alongside teachers (HM Treasury et al., 2004). Moss (2004) draws attention to the need for such a role, often described as a pedagogue, and similar to that seen in many European countries. The role of a pedagogue needs to be viewed as different to that of a teacher and to have its own clear identity. Pedagogues will take a holistic approach to each child and family member and encompass a number of skills that will enable them to take account of the individual social, emotional and cultural identity of each person they work with. Similarities are likely to exist in terms of the training they receive, as they will be educated to degree level. Graduates from Early Childhood Studies degrees have followed courses focusing on the holistic needs of children and families, but in employment these skills are often not fully utilized, which is partly attributable to the lack of appropriate professional roles. In a number of European countries, a pedagogue role exists, which encompasses supporting children's education and care and spans health, social care and educational contexts (Fitzgerald and Kay, 2008). The Early Years Professional role covers aspects of this position but it is heavily focused on leading the curriculum in early years settings, and in the move to multi-agency working it may not help to achieve this. Anning (2004) refers to the need to develop 'a community of practice' within early years where knowledge is used in action and developed in ways acceptable to the community. This raises issues for integration and emphasizes the need for practitioners with a high level of skill in different aspects of early years care and education, as well as a high standard of education – points supported by varied evidence (e.g. Nutbrown, 2012; House of Lords, 2015) – and could be seen as further support for the role of pedagogues who are able to use their skills and knowledge to engage in and make decisions to benefit children and families without over-dominance from the managerialist style that is often indirectly enforced through current arrangements and funding. The debate around workforce structure and roles continues. The Children and Families Act 2014 addresses the need for better working between services to best support vulnerable children. While there seems to be no intention in this legislation to introduce radical changes in roles, the fact that increased integrated working is still an aim after many years, past legislation and significant organizational change, raises questions about whether the current roles and professional boundaries within the early years sector are fit for purpose.

Children

The significant expansion of early years services now means that nearly all 3- and 4-year-olds have some type of early years care and education. This may be in the form of one to two sessions per week in a pre-school setting, five funded sessions in a nursery or a mixture of provision from different providers on a full-time basis. When considering the impact of the many policy changes, it is important that the implications for children are considered. For example:

- Is increased provision appropriate for all children?
- Is the curriculum offered appropriate to the needs of children?
- Do practitioners have the necessary qualifications, experience and access to training?
- Is there support in place to meet the diverse developmental needs of each child?

When considering these issues, it is unlikely that there will be a simple yes or no answer. It is also important to understand that policy alone cannot be blamed for failures or praised for success. To make an evaluation of the provision for children, it is necessary to evaluate whether policies have laid the basis for high-quality and appropriate provision.

For children, one of the most significant changes in ECEC has been the introduction of a unified Statutory Framework for the Early Years Foundation Stage (EYFS) (DfE, 2012), which brought together *Birth to Three Matters* (Sure Start Unit, 2002) for children from birth to 3 and the *Statutory Framework for the Early Years Foundation Stage* (DfES, 2007), which was updated again in 2014. Over the past decade, the Foundation Stage has received much greater attention and is now seen as being as relevant as other key stages, which has led to positive changes both within early years settings and schools. This has included the appointment of Foundation Stage coordinators, who are often members of school management teams, access to additional training for teachers in appropriate pedagogy for early years, a greater focus on outdoor play, and more flexible and child-directed activities. But there are still concerns with provision in the Foundation Stage, particularly in some reception classes. For example, the qualifications of many practitioners may not be specific to early years, there are often low levels of support staff and some schools have mixed Foundation and Key Stage 1 classes, which can lead to an inappropriate curriculum for young children, particularly as the number of pupils in Key Stage classes over 30 has increased. This remains an issue in a number of schools, particularly smaller ones. A number of settings also have very limited outdoor space that children are able to access freely, which is an important pedagogical tool for early years (Miller, 2015). It could be argued that many of these concerns cannot be attributed to policy failings, but new policy has not necessarily brought improvements.

ACTIVITY

Think about the issues above and any other possible concerns that you have seen or discussed relating to foundation provision and jot them down. Then answer the following questions:

- Which of the issues can be linked to potential policy shortfalls and which may have other origins?

- Are there any that have multiple causes or are difficult to place in one list or the other?

In terms of structural issues, such as the building or outdoor space, it can be argued that new policy developments which focus on appropriate pedagogy for early years cannot be linked with inopportune building design. With other issues, such as practitioner qualifications and training, it is more difficult to separate them. In many respects, introducing a curriculum appropriate to the needs of young children is a positive step, but it would not be difficult to envisage that practitioners would be likely to need significant support and training to implement this policy to its full positive effect, particularly given the myriad of early years qualifications at different levels. The decision to have a separate curriculum for children from birth to 5+ and then in Key Stage 1, could also be seen as continuing with poor policy, as it does nothing to reduce the issue of fragmentation in early years care and education provision and the start of formal schooling for younger children, nor does it introduce a coordinated approach to learning (in contrast to Wales). This also links to the current policy on school-starting age that many criticize as being too young and inappropriate for children (Dowling, 1999; Sharp, 2003; Paton, 2013). The provision of curriculum documents alone is also not the complete solution as there are still clear requirements on practitioners to promote and sustain interactions between children and ensure that activities provided are appropriately matched to children's levels of development (Siraj-Blatchford and Sylva, 2004; Siraj-Blatchford et al., 2008; Sylva et al., 2012).

Since the National Curriculum was introduced, there has been increasing criticism of the impact it has had on reducing the place of creativity within education (Robinson and Aronica, 2015). This was particularly acute for children in Key Stage 1 and reception classes, where the didactic approach of the Numeracy and Literacy Strategies was (and still may be for children in Key Stage 1) experienced on a daily basis. In comparison, the child-centred pedagogical approach advocated in the Foundation Stage curriculum guidance, which has been further developed in the reviewed EYFS (DfE, 2014a), was welcomed as a positive step forward and was seen as more likely to lead to child-initiated activities, sustained and extended by interaction between practitioners and children, and this positive step has been further developed in the new EYFS curriculum. The provision of the new document alone will not guarantee this, but the approach advocated throughout it (for example, giving children time to explore, gain understanding, problem-solve and make discoveries) is clearly in line with effective early years practice. However, this is not meant to suggest that direct teaching is wrong. As Siraj-Blatchford and Sylva (2004: 726) highlight, 'Direct instruction is not harmful; it is the balance that is important', which again points to the need for skilled practitioners. Interestingly, though, the move to embedding creativity as a key component of early years education took many years. Plowden (DES, 1967) highlighted the need for appropriate early years provision but in terms of acquiring knowledge and skills, whereas the Rumbold Report (DES, 1990) emphasized the need for a creative approach to ensure a greater coherence between education and care and to provide effectively for all aspects of children's development. It is only several years later, though, that this has been partially realized for children up to the age of 5.

Another important consideration for children is whether there is a holistic policy approach to meet the emotional, social, health and physical aspects of development as well as the educational aspects. Kurtz (2003) identifies a wide-reaching policy approach to promote the health and well-being of children, not least through the Sure Start initiative, which placed health at the centre of its agenda through the aim to tackle and reduce the impact of poverty and the links this has with low educational standards (Glass, 2001). In the early part of this century, there were reductions in poverty, infant/child mortality and accidental injury rates, which suggest a successful policy agenda, although there are claims that the first of these has risen recently. However, different interpretations can be made of the same data based on the definition of poverty used (Lister, 2004). In terms of absolute poverty (when a family lacks enough money to meet basic needs), progress has been made, but in terms of relative poverty (when a family lacks resources to have a good diet, participate in society and have access to amenities that are seen as customary in society) progress is more debatable. This is significant though as the central aim of Sure Start was to promote the inclusion and participation of disenfranchised families. The introduction of the National Service Framework for Children, Young People and Maternity Services, which sets ambitious health and treatment targets for all children, also confirms that there is a wide-ranging policy agenda to support all aspects of children's development (DoH/DfES, 2004). The National Service Framework has made advances, however the ambitious targets set for all children continue to present a clear challenge to finding ways to implement the policy across boundaries between networks of public, private and voluntary service providers (Masterson et al., 2004). It still remains to be seen whether the challenges this presents can be overcome in the Children and Families Act 2014.

Parents

The issue of partnership between providers and parents has become more significant over the past few years, and there is now a clear expectation, and rightly so, that providers need to work in a way that acknowledges the contribution parents make, and that they value and respect their opinions. But the issue of partnership is often misunderstood and the term may be bandied about without full acknowledgement of the needs of parents (Fitzgerald, 2012). As the complexity of early years services has increased, this has raised a number of issues for parents. To work effectively with parents requires policies that are joined up and responsive, which cannot be achieved through the provision of services alone. Services need to be available at times when parents require them, and must be accessible, affordable and integrated to provide consistency.

There are a variety of ways that practitioners can work in partnership with parents. Swap (1993) describes a continuum of partnership models that can still be effectively used by early years care and education settings, but which also provides a basis for other services to assess their level of partnership working with parents:

- *The protective model* – this operates along the lines of a business and requires parents to delegate responsibility for education to the setting, as the aims of home and the setting and the roles of practitioners and parents are different.
- *The school-to-home transmission model* – this recognizes the importance of the family but only places an emphasis on one-directional communication – from the setting to the home – and assumes a level of parental agreement with decisions taken by the setting. In this model, there is likely to be little sharing of ideas between the setting and the community.
- *The curriculum-enrichment model* – this recognizes the benefits of collaborative learning between practitioners, parents and children, and integrates knowledge from families and the community into the curriculum and learning. There is a focus on the curriculum as this is seen as an important vehicle for impacting on learning.
- *The partnership model* – this is built on long-term commitment, mutual respect and widespread involvement of families and practitioners at different levels, such as joint planning and shared decision-making. It reflects the fact that children are embedded in and influenced by the home, the setting and the community.

ACTIVITY

Think about each stage of the model and the settings that you have worked in or been on placement at:

- What examples have you seen of partnership working and which stage of the model would you place them at?

- Have you seen any particularly effective or poor examples of partnership working? What was it that made them effective or poor?

- Think about one aspect of partnership working with parents (you could base this on something you have seen in practice) and write a brief outline of it.

- Identify where on the model you would place the setting.

- Draw up an action plan to work out how you would develop partnership working to the next stage of the partnership model. Compare the strategies you have identified with a partner.

The introduction of policies can lay the basis for partnership working with parents (and between professionals), but policy alone cannot ensure that this will be achieved. Achieving high levels of partnership working requires practitioners and families to work together in an open and respectful way. This means practitioners need to communicate effectively with families and each other, which can be challenging, particularly when services are delivered by a number of agencies. In this respect, the challenges ahead for practitioners from different disciplines to work effectively with parents are significant.

The availability and accessibility of services is another key issue for parents. There is clearly a body of data to show that there have been significant increases in early years provision over an extended period (DfE, 2011a, 2015b), but it cannot be taken for granted that this equates to good levels of availability and accessibility for all children and families. To think about this more analytically, a number of questions must be asked:

- Are services available equally in all areas (for example, urban and rural areas)?
- Is there a range of services, by different provider types, to meet different family requirements?
- Are services affordable for all families?
- Are services available when families require them?
- If children attend more than one setting, are the different providers coordinated to ensure smooth transitions between them?
- Are there adequate transport facilities available for families to access the different providers they may need?
- Is the full range of services required by families provided in the same location?

Families living in rural areas still often face significant challenges in accessing appropriate and affordable services and this is likely to exacerbate with the introduction of funded places for 2-year-olds. This may be because there is simply a shortage of provision or that what is provided is either not able to offer early years care and education for the required amount of time or not at affordable rates, but this is not confined to rural areas alone. Another challenge faced by parents is organizing the daily family routine around early years care and education provision, and this becomes particularly challenging when there are children of different ages within the family (especially if there is a child below statutory school age and a child above). Being able to access the different range of providers and fit this in with work and other family commitments can involve the family in negotiating complex plans, making numerous journeys and still often having to rely on informal care networks throughout the week (Skinner, 2003; Truss, 2012).

In terms of accessibility, there has been success in government policy in attracting parents to services that previously may not have been affordable. In the early 2000s the Neighbourhood Nurseries Initiative (NNI), which expanded childcare provision in the 20% most disadvantaged wards in England by providing start-up funding to support new provision, was partially successful. Bell and La Valle (2005) found that:

- two-thirds of families using Neighbourhood Nursery provision had not previously used childcare facilities
- the provision was used by over half of parents in the early morning and late afternoon
- the level of satisfaction with the provision was generally high and almost a fifth of parents had been able to enter work since accessing the nursery.

More recently, the increase in childcare provision has continued but differences have been seen in the distribution between the more and less deprived areas.

Notably, 73% of full day care in Children's Centres and 58% of nursery schools were located in the 30% most deprived areas. In contrast, 19% of both sessional care and childminders were located there (DfE, 2011a). In contrast, provision which is more usually paid for by parents (e.g. sessional care) is disproportionately located away from more deprived areas. This raises concerns when seen alongside the recent reduction in the number of Children's Centres and highlights the importance of funding to ensure equality of access. With the removal of ring-fenced funding, this may also mean less use of early education among more deprived families, which is contrary to the aims of the government as set out in the spending review (HM Treasury, 2011). More recently, there has been a shift away from deprived neighbourhoods to individual families. This is evident in the policy to provide funded ECEC for 2-year-olds where parents are in receipt of certain benefits and tax/universal credits. In addition, the government is launching online childcare accounts in 2017 (initially planned for 2015) to contribute up to 20% of childcare costs for working parents for children up to age 12 up to £10,000.

Another factor that can impact on participation in service provision is the attitude of current users. The aim of many Children's Centres is to attract 'hard to reach' families, but practitioners need to be aware of how the attitude of current users may impact on potential new users so that cliques do not stop potential new users feeling excluded. This can be a particular concern if a setting is located in a catchment area that draws families from varied socio-economic backgrounds (Sheppard et al., 2008). The Family Parenting Institute argues that there is a need for an overarching family policy to include often excluded groups from services, for example children with disabilities or parents with mental health problems. The number of policies that impact on families is vast and they generally develop in a piecemeal way across many government departments, and each needs to be 'family proofed'. A particular issue that still requires much more detailed attention is the level of support that is provided to families in the first 12 months after the birth of a child (Family and Parenting Institute, 2005). There have been limited advances in this area with the introduction of the Parenting Fund, which provided three rounds of funding for promoting good practice for family and parent support services (Family and Parenting Institute, 2008), although this concluded in 2011. To address this, a much more sustained effort will need to be made to support all parents, as well as targeting those in disadvantaged areas, if the outcomes for all children are to be optimized.

The government agenda of reducing disadvantage and social exclusion is often tied to the success of policies that provide childcare places and enable parents, who previously were not employed, to return to work. This may be one method of judging the success of policy developments, but other issues need to be considered for parents. The issue of work–life balance has developed momentum over recent years and is particularly significant to families with young children (DTI, 2004). In response to this, the government announced extending the length of maternity and adoption leave to 52 weeks, with financial benefits for 39 weeks. There have also been positive moves towards allowing parents of young children to ask their employers to consider adopting a flexible approach to working hours and the introduction, albeit minimal, of paid paternity leave. The right to flexible working, shared parental leave and paid time off for attending up to two antenatal appointments was further developed by the Children and Families Act 2014. These issues highlight the need for policies to address a range of issues and to be focused on more than simply moving parents back into the employment market. The emphasis placed by government on the move from welfare to work is to some degree understandable as there is a correlation between being employed, the number of adults in a family and levels of poverty. Caution is still needed if new issues, such as reliance on a variety of providers for childcare and increased family stress levels, are not addressed in the developments. There is little point in formulating policies that move parents into work but simply replace one set of difficulties with another. To avoid this, policy-makers need to consider the holistic needs of families and ensure that policies are able to respond effectively to the diverse needs of each family. One way that this has evolved is through the development of community hubs, but this is on an informal basis and is not based on policy or a stated government intention.

ACTIVITY

You have been asked to write a short evaluative account of the impact of the Early Years Foundation Stage curriculum over the past decade as part of a review of early years provision for the National College for Teaching and Leadership. The account will be read by a range of providers, government departments and parents.

When planning your account, it would be useful to think about the impact in terms of the overall sector, practitioners, children and parents. This will help to ensure that the response takes account of the impact on the key stakeholders and is more likely to identify the benefits of and any difficulties in the curriculum.

An important aspect of any written response to this type of activity is to support all claims with relevant evidence. This could come from a range of sources, including other reports, policy documents (including policies from other parts of the UK), academic papers, research studies and other relevant texts, such as books on child development. It may be helpful to present your response in key headlines, each supported by relevant points.

Your response is likely to have included a range of positive impacts and some drawbacks. There is a broad range of information that you could have drawn on.

You may also have identified other relevant stakeholders that you feel should be considered. Further, you are likely to have made reference to the diversity of the early years workforce. For example, the practitioner group could include people with very varied experiences. It may include individual practitioners who work in a large voluntary setting, an individual childminder or an owner/manager of a private nursery. This diversity within the initial groups may seem challenging. However, considering the perspective of a range of interested stakeholders and responding to this, particularly where it is supported by evidence, will include the quality and level of analysis within your response. The points below summarize some of the issues you may have considered for each group.

Sector
- Since 2010, a government commitment to have at least one graduate in every setting, to deliver the curriculum, has been lacking, and this is likely to have impacted on continuing professional development and career progression.
- There is challenge in ensuring an adequate workforce in terms of numbers and qualifications.

Practitioners
- The current curriculum draws together and builds on information from a range of sources to show development over time (for example, *Birth to Three Matters*, *Curriculum Guidance for the Foundation Stage*, primary national curricula) and may lead to a more coherent and less bureaucratic burden for practitioners.
- The current curriculum places the role of practitioners in supporting children's development and welfare as central and this could help to professionalize the workforce.
- The demands of the curriculum will have different impacts. For example, for childminders it could add significantly to what is expected of them and they may not have access to appropriate support and training, or the resource implications of gaining this could be prohibitive.
- Linked to previous points, the increased expectations and development opportunities need to be formally recognized and a career structure is likely to aid the progression and retention of practitioners (to achieve the stated government aim of having a world-class workforce).
- The curriculum could aid inter-agency working, as all registered practitioners and settings will be working to the same unified and coherent curriculum.
- There is emphasis on the need to have well-trained practitioners and leaders (e.g. an EYP) to lead the curriculum, but how does this contrast with the lack of professionally qualified practitioners/leaders in the PVI sector?
- The curriculum could impact other government policies (e.g. the intention to extend funded ECEC to 30 hours).

Children
- The EYFS has a coordinated and joined-up curriculum.
- It has a play-based curriculum, which is appropriate to supporting children's development.

- It takes a holistic approach, which places equal value on social, emotional, physical and cognitive development.
- It takes careful account of children's welfare needs.
- It emphasizes that children develop at different rates and that this is part of expected development.
- It provides a consistent approach across all settings, which will be particularly beneficial for children attending more than one setting.
- It promotes equality for all children and recognition of diversity.
- It views all children, from birth, as competent learners and sees them as capable.
- Children are encouraged to participate in their own learning, which is in line with the principles of the UNCRC.
- The appropriate approach to learning advocated by the curriculum is in stark contrast to the Key Stage 1 curriculum and children may find the transition point difficult.

Parents

- The current EYFS curriculum sees parents at the heart of supporting their child's learning and development.
- It sets out clearly what parents can expect from early years care and education providers.
- For young children, particularly if parents are not familiar with early years care and education, the approach may seem very formal.
- The documented approach to early years care and education may be interpreted by parents as being superior to the care they, or family members, can provide.
- The curriculum lays the foundation for the inclusion of all children.

Your response to this activity may also include points which, although not directly related to the introduction of the statutory curriculum, are closely interlinked with it. This highlights both the challenges and fascination of gaining a clear insight into how policy has a widespread impact on practice and all those linked with it. What we hope is clear is that it is not possible to have a full understanding of how practice impacts on all stakeholders without at least some understanding of the policy that has led to current provision.

SUMMARY

- This chapter has explored the impact of policy on the sector and different stakeholders by examining each group in turn, but in many respects the divide is artificial.

- The purpose of this approach, however, was to show that it is important to consider how one policy can have both positive and negative impacts on different stakeholders.

(Continued)

(Continued)

- When presented with any policy, it is important to think carefully about these issues but also to consider how the policy as a whole fits with other policies and services.

- It is only through careful analysis that those to whom the policy applies will be able to take a more central role in the shaping of future policy as well as in the implementation of current policy.

FURTHER READING

To understand the impact of policy on practitioners, children and parents, it is helpful to read documents and reports that may be aimed at each of these groups. A number of government publications, particularly from the Sure Start Unit, are relevant and their websites are listed at the start of the book. In addition, the following publications may be of interest:

Department of Health (DoH)/Department for Education and Skills (DfES) (2004) *National Service Framework for Children, Young People and Maternity Services: Executive summary*, London: DoH/DfES. This framework has been published for over a decade but continues to have relevance as an overall direction for this broad array of services, many of which impact on the family.

Pascal, C. and Bertram, T. (2013) *The Impact of Early Education as a Strategy in Countering Socio-economic Disadvantage*, London: Ofsted.

Sylva, K., Melhuish, E., Sammons, P., Siraj-Blatchford, I. and Taggart, B. (2012) *Effective Pre-school, Primary and Secondary Education 3-14 Project (EPPSE 3-14) - Final Report from the Key Stage 3 Phase: Influences on Students' Development from Age 11-14*, London: DfE. The EPPSE project was a significant piece of research from 1997 and followed over 300 children from pre-school until the end of KS3. There are a number of publications from this project that will be useful to readers, but particularly the findings from the first phase, which tracked children through to the end of Key Stage 1. This paper outlines how EPPE (the early part of the study is often referred to as EPPE, as this does not include findings from the final phase – KS3) investigated practice and identified how improvements could be achieved. It includes an in-depth discussion of the qualitative findings from settings identified as providing high standards of practice.

The Study of Early Education and Development (SEED) project will build on the work of EPPSE. The longitudinal study will follow 8,000 children aged 2 until the end of Key Stage 1. The study will explore the impact of childcare and early education and aim to identify what contributes to high-quality provision. Publication of the findings will be released at regular time intervals (for details, see www.seed.natcen.ac.uk).

9

ANALYSING POLICY

THIS CHAPTER EXPLAINS

- a number of approaches that can be taken to analyse policy, including examples drawn from current policies to set this in a practice context and to promote an understanding of how drawing on research evidence and comparison with other countries can assist in this analysis

- how analysis and many of the questions posed would apply equally to the range of policies in ECEC services.

When analysing the potential impact of any policy, it is important to look broadly. It can help to think about this in terms of completing a jigsaw puzzle. At the start, you connect the edges. This gives an outline shape and some information about what the finished puzzle will look like, but it does not provide the whole picture. Over time, you try different pieces together, move them around and gradually the whole picture starts to fall into place. By the time the puzzle is complete, it is likely that you will have handled each of the pieces several times and will have thought carefully about how they fit together, and referred frequently to the box to compare the emerging puzzle and complete picture. Analysis is very similar to this. The pieces of the puzzle can be seen as representing policies. To gain a more in-depth understanding of different policies is difficult, but there are a number of approaches that you can take to help achieve this. Analysing policies is about looking at how they fit with current policies and practice, looking at how different parts of the policy impact on the sector and different stakeholders and how all this fits together in providing appropriate and responsive services for children, families and the wider community.

To analyse policy, you can contrast current approaches with historical evidence, consider how policy impacts on varied stakeholders, consider themes running through different policies or contrast the approach in the countries of the UK with that of other countries. It can also be helpful to think about the ideologies underpinning different policies. By drawing on one or more of these methods, it is likely that you will be able to identify the benefits and areas for development within policies and begin to gain a more analytical view of the impact of policy on the lives of children, parents and practitioners.

Why analyse policies?

Policy formation and implementation is a complex process that can take a considerable amount of time. A challenge for all policies is reconciling different priorities between those whom the policy will affect, such as practitioners, parents and children (Daly, 2011). A number of different elements also need to be considered, including the implementation costs, the ability of services and service providers to deliver the policy aims, the potential benefits, the impact on different stakeholders and sustainability. Many policies aimed at children and families can cover a broad remit. For example, Children's Centres (many of which were former Sure Start local projects) bring together health, social services, education and voluntary services to respond to the requirements of individual families or sections of the community. It is also likely that the broader a policy, i.e. one which covers many policies in the area of children and family services, the more likely it is to impact not only on other people but also on other policies. A potential risk with this broad approach is that the policy may not benefit all those whom it is intended to help. Sanderson (2003) contrasts the approach of evidence-based practice and the belief in government departments that 'what counts is what works'. At a simple level, this does not seem problematic. In the context of complex policies, though, it is likely that an approach to analysis that simply aims to say whether a policy is working or not working will not capture the true impact of the policy, which is likely to include positive and negative elements. Sanderson (2003) highlights other problems with this approach. What is meant by the term 'what works'? Just because a policy is working for a parent does not mean it works for a child, or a policy that works in one area may not work in another. There is also a heavy government focus on measuring outcomes, usually through targets, but not everything is easily measurable or attributable to one specific policy. Since the change of prime minister, there have been signals that a broader approach to measuring policy/service outcomes, rather than service outcomes alone, will be implemented. However, this remains to be seen across service providers. To overcome this, it is important to take a systematic and detailed approach to analysing the impact of policies that may provide the means to:

- understand the political ideology underlying the policy context
- decide if the information is accurate and how it will impact on practice
- argue why some aspects of policy are preferable to others
- identify aspects of good practice
- identify where there are shortcomings
- ensure high-quality services
- identify gaps in policy and service provision
- highlight how policy is meeting the requirements of different stakeholders
- offer a critical appraisal of a new approach to service delivery
- offer a critical appraisal of a local, regional, national or international policy.

The election of Labour in 1997 brought an unprecedented focus on ECEC. The National Childcare Strategy set out the government's intention to increase provision across the maintained, voluntary and private sectors through a number of initiatives. Children's Trusts, which were implemented in most areas by 2006, aimed to integrate locally based education, social services and some health services for children and young people (DfES/DoH, 2004). The Children's National Service Framework set out long-term plans for sustained improvement in health from birth through to adulthood (DoH/DfES, 2004). In 2007, the Children's Plan (DCSF, 2007) set out intentions to enhance the role of Children's Trusts, place schools at the centre of the community and integrate service provision; all with the aim of improving outcomes for children and families.

This continued during the Coalition term of government. However, during the Coalition term, the policy was focused more on effective use of reduced funding, such as on moving towards targeted rather than universal services, removing ring-fencing for varied early years grants and increasing the role of the PVI sector to compete for tenders (Sylva et al., 2012). The Coalition Government did not follow a dramatically different policy direction, although it commissioned a number of reviews, which led to the removal of many funding streams (i.e. the Graduate Leader Fund; and also reduced funding to Sure Start Children's Centres) and structural changes (i.e. closure of the CWDC; merging two bodies to form the National College for Teaching and Leadership; stopping the EYP training programme). The Coalition also put in place a number of reviews (e.g. the review into the role of the Children's Commissioner in England; the Nutbrown review of the early years workforce, status and qualifications; consultation on and subsequent publication of the 2012 Children and Families Bill). Consequently, when analysing the impact of these policies, it will be necessary to explore which objectives have been met, which have not and if all those intended to benefit from the policy have done or are likely to do so.

The 2015 general election led to the formation of a Conservative majority government. One of the first high-profile announcements of the Conservative Government in 2015 was the intention to double-fund provision for 3–4-year-olds with working parents during the current parliament. There were also changes announced during the Coalition term, beginning with Online Childcare accounts, suggesting that the focus on child and family policy would continue.

Levels of policy

Policies can be designed and implemented at different levels. National policies, which set out detailed arrangements, are often formulated in response to legislation. For example, the Children and Families Act (DfE, 2014e) led to policies being implemented that will impact on: the organization of children's services; the relationship between education, health and social care services; strategies to improve the well-being of all children; and support to address the diverse needs of looked-after children. In response to this, organizations, local authority service providers and ECEC settings may amend existing local policies or implement new ones to ensure that working practices take account of new expectations and potentially new legislation. Analysis can be carried out on policy at each of these levels. This approach can provide valuable information in seeing how far a policy is meeting the stated aims and objectives, and whether the statements and philosophies of the policies are evident in practice (Fitzgerald, 2004).

Approaches to analysing the impact of policy

As seen in earlier chapters, policies can impact on different aspects of service provision and take time to become embedded. Policies can also be analysed at different stages – from initial design, at implementation, through to ongoing maintenance of the policy (NAO, 2001). Glass (2001) argues that when analysing what works, it is necessary to think broadly. For example, when looking at poverty, policies that link to housing, the quality of public services and the urban environment can all contribute to reducing it. The creation of Sure Start Children's Centres, Health Action Zones and the New Deal are all examples of past policies that can contribute to tackling the impact of poverty on children and families in communities with high levels of deprivation and social exclusion. A clear challenge for any analysis of policy is to consider not only the benefits of individual policies, but also whether different policies complement each other and enhance well-being, or, potentially, the complexity leads to confusion and a lack of clarity about the overall aims and objectives.

Political ideology

Child and family policy is subject to political ideology, and the overall thrust of policy generally reflects the ideology of the political party that devises and implements policy. Ideology is about values, beliefs and ideas about the world and is informed by history. Political ideology is also often dichotomized and, simply stated, policies are seen as leaning to the left or right. Political parties that lean to the 'left' are traditionally about social equality and justice and the redistribution of wealth from the richest to the poorest to create a fair state. This is traditionally underpinned by state ownership of key industries and the provision of services by the state. An overall term to describe this type of approach is welfarist. Political parties that lean to the 'right' are traditional about the defence of individual rights, promoting ownership of private property and relying on free markets and competition to reduce state bureaucracy (this approach is based in neo-conservative and neoliberalist political ideologies). They are also seen to promote traditional family values. These different positions are often referred to as political discourses (Adams, 2014). A discourse is the language and text of politics (policies are part of these) and through these discourses power is exercised. Each policy can either provide or remove power from groups of people and in doing so conveys the political ideology of the political party enacting legislation and policy (Parker, 2013).

However, these traditional boundaries are not as evident as they were historically. For example, the Labour Government (1997–2010) encouraged private involvement in many parts of the education system (such as academies and the expansion of private nurseries). This does not match with the historical ideological grounding of the labour movement. In contrast, the Coalition Government introduced the Early Years Pupil Premium and universal school meals for children up to the age of 7, and the Conservative Government has recently announced an intention to legislate for a significant rise in the minimum wage level to support those on low incomes. This shows the fluidity of this dichotomy and how political parties are enacting policies across the ideological divide. However, an area where more traditional *right*-leaning policies have been seen is in the focus on traditional subjects, seeing a primary purpose of ECEC as preparing young children for school and advocating a reduction of the role for local authorities in education (e.g. the intention to force a number of schools to become academies). Therefore, this provides a tool to support the analysis of policies and enables questions to be asked about how each policy reflects the traditional political ideology, or otherwise, of the governing party.

Does policy represent the perspectives of all stakeholders?

Most policies will impact on a range of stakeholders, including children, parents, practitioners and, often, members of the wider community. Policy can also create differences between stakeholders within the same category. For example, when changes were introduced to childminding, the increased professionalism and impact of regulation caused some childminders to stop working and led to a significant decline in numbers. This was seen as a problem by some and as an advantage by others. When analysing the impact of policy, it is important to consider whether policies have succeeded or failed in addressing the diverse issues of the different stakeholders who are affected by the policy. Over the past decade, the UNCRC could be seen as one vehicle that has helped policy to move beyond a welfarist perspective. For children, this has potentially positive benefits: it sees them as having rights as well as being the recipients of adult protection, and places expectations on governments to ensure the rights of children are respected, addressed in policy and the outcome evaluated. The impact of this is that the interests of children should now be paramount in policy design and implementation; children should be able to exercise rights and their views should be requested and acted upon (Lansdown, 2001; Mitchell, 2014). Although this may not happen in all instances, it does provide a basis on which an analysis of policy in respecting and promoting the right of children to be consulted can be assessed.

ACTIVITY

Read the following scenario, which describes a typical daily scene for almost every young child in England, and think carefully about the policies that the education provision is based on and how well each of them takes account of the perspective of the child.

Sarah is 6 years old and is in Year 1 with 28 other children. She is with some of her friends from the reception class but her best friend from reception is in the other Year 1 class. She has had some difficulties with reading and now has one-to-one reading support from a teaching assistant three times a week.

She enjoys being at school but misses being able to play with different toys and outside on the bikes and climbing frame. Her favourite lesson is art as she likes to paint the people she has heard about in stories. Sarah likes to write some words on her paintings about the characters in stories and her teacher helps her to do this.

Initially, it may seem that there are very few explicit policies here but this may be because so many policies are taken for granted. Each of the following aspects of policy or practice could potentially impact on Sarah:

- school starting age
- the revised National Curriculum
- special educational needs and disability policy
- legal expectations placed on registered providers against which they are judged by inspectorate bodies in the UK
- school results targets
- Ofsted judgements on the setting
- governing body decisions.

From this list, the only clear reference to the need to consult children is contained in the Special Educational Needs and Disability Code of Practice (DfE, 2015a), which emphasizes 'the importance of finding out the ascertainable wishes and feelings of children and involving them when decisions are made that affect them' (section 4. 3). This would only apply if Sarah had been identified as having a special educational need, which may not be the case. The important point from this, however, is that just because there is an expectation, through the UNCRC, that children will be consulted, it does not automatically mean they will be, and this needs to be highlighted in any analysis of policy. Although the National Curriculum may have strengths, it could be argued that the pedagogical approach to learning is not the most appropriate for young children and it is likely that, if consulted, children in Key Stage 1 would choose an approach to learning that resembles more closely that of the Early Years Foundation Stage (DfE, 2014a).

Generally speaking, one of the areas in the UK where the impact of various policies is felt most by children is in education, but it is potentially the area where their views have the least impact or are not considered at all. Even where children are consulted, however, this may not equate with their views being respected and acted upon. Tisdall and Davis (2004) raise questions about the effectiveness and ethical considerations of some approaches to consultation based around school councils and whether they lead to democratic communities. This is not meant to suggest that all attempts to consult children are flawed, but it does highlight the need to look systematically at the strategies that are in place to allow organizations to claim that children are consulted. The following questions clearly show how careful analysis can help to appraise the approaches in place to listen to and act upon the views of children:

- Do all children have the right to participate or is participation focused on more articulate or older children?
- Do the approaches provide the basis for children to take on decision-making positions?

- Is consultation acted on or is it simply tokenistic?
- Is feedback provided to the representatives to show what progress has been made?

The Scottish Executive has undertaken a number of consultations with children, in areas such as school food (Shoolbread, 2006), proposed amendments to the Children and Young People's (Scotland) Act 2014 and special educational needs (SEN) policy. The SEN review aimed to involve children at different stages of the process. This was achieved by consulting an initial group of 39 children, further consultation with a group of 46 children and young people, and finally question-naires completed by a group of over 100 children and young people. The strengths of this process were that it included children with disabilities and those with English as an additional language, and the views of the respondents were used to inform policy-makers at early stages of policy design. During the process, feedback was offered to each group but no regular involvement of children or young people in the policy development group was put in place, although this was asked for. Overall, the involvement of the children and young people led to some changes but there were limitations on what was implemented, which shows that the imbalance of power between children and adults still existed (Tisdall and Davis, 2004). Even though there were limitations to this approach, it does show how children can be involved and provides a basis for analysing whether the perspective of children is in evidence at the policy-design, implementation and maintenance stages. In England, the Children's Plan made a greater attempt to include the views of chil-dren through the 'Time to Talk' consultation, which was a welcome development given that children are at the heart of planned developments and it is an area in which England has been poor in the past. More recently in England, there has been less attention given to consulting children as part of policy development.

Another example of how a major policy can impact on young children is in the introduction of the entitlement to 15 hours of early education a week for 2-year-olds and the proposed expansion for 3–4-year-olds to 30 hours per week (for 38 weeks of the year). This will undoubtedly help parents, particularly working par-ents, with the cost of childcare, which recent evidence suggests is expensive in Britain (Truss, 2012; Rutter, 2015). However, this policy may seem to only have potential benefits for some children between the ages of 2 and 4.

ACTIVITY

Think about the increase in entitlement to free early education for 2-, 3- and 4-year-olds. List some of the potential benefits and disadvantages of this policy for early years practitioners, teaching staff, children and parents.

(Continued)

(Continued)

Your benefits and disadvantages may have included some of the following:

Table 9.1   Benefits and disadvantages of free early education for 2-year-olds

Potential benefits	Potential disadvantages
Children receive more support to aid their educational development at a young age	Children spend more time in formal education and care settings from a younger age
Increased employment opportunities for practitioners	There may not be adequate levels of highly trained practitioners to provide high-quality care and education for younger children
Increased career opportunities for practitioners	Changes are driven by the need to increase the number of parents in work, rather than by what is most appropriate for the child
Access to early education and care at a younger age to support parents with childcare	There is less choice for parents with lower income levels in caring for and educating their young children at home full time
Support for working parents through increased funding	Access is initially targeted at areas of high social deprivation (for 2-year-olds) and 3–4-year-olds with working parents, further stigmatizing these communities as being in need of support
	Funding, where available, only covers 38 weeks of the year
Significant expansion in the system	Sector does not offer adequate supply in all areas (approximately half of authorities have shortages of ECEC provision)

The fact that there are potential benefits and disadvantages to increasing government funding for the provision of early education for 2–4-year-olds does not mean that this policy is bad. The simple level of provision, which has risen from 59,000 to 1.7 million places (Rutter, 2015), is impressive. It does illustrate, though, that analysis of these points is important as it can highlight the potential advantages and disadvantages from the perspective of the different stakeholders that are affected and help to identify where further developments are necessary.

Eyres et al. (2004) support many of these points as their research found that even young children were aware of the many different adults in nurseries and found this generally helpful as long as there was a level of stability in staffing. If the split between the role of the teacher and support staff is becoming harder to identify, there may be implications for workforce remodelling and the opportunities and challenges this brings in terms of pay and career structure. This seems particularly important because if there are going to be more young children in early education, this will invariably lead to more staff due to the requirement for increased ratios. The needs and support required by 2-year-olds is also different to that needed by children at 3 years and older. It could be argued that a response to many of these potential disadvantages was addressed by the introduction of Early Years Professionals (EYPs) and the replacement training scheme of Early Years Teachers (EYTS). However, as discussed in the previous chapter, there is concern about access to these positions to support career development for practitioners and concern about employment opportunities in the PVI sector and pay and conditions. Undoubtedly, these roles, which encourage practitioners to enhance their skills, offer potential benefits, but to achieve the best from these policies a careful evaluation will be needed to see how they benefit children, those pursuing the training and other practitioners who work in early years and school settings (Fitzgerald and Kay, 2008). However, the debate over this continues as it is still not clear how this role has equivalency in terms of status, pay or progression opportunities several years after being introduced.

Parents have a pivotal role to play both within the family and when working in partnership with ECEC settings. In addition, they are stakeholders in many policies impacting on early years education and care. When parents and practitioners work together, there can be significant benefits for them in terms of self-esteem and for children who see a unified approach between the home and setting. This can also help practitioners to have a greater understanding of and respect for each family (Fitzgerald, 2012). The approach of the government to families is about providing opportunities for them to lift themselves out of poverty and break down barriers that lead to social exclusion. To achieve these aims, policies have been implemented to increase childcare provision, offer financial support to parents and provide more public funds for the education and care of young children (OECD, 2011). It is also important to analyse whether there are any implicit assumptions within policies, based on idealized images of the family. In the past, governments have championed heterosexual marriage as the most stable environment for children to be raised in (Home Office, 1998), but many children flourish in non-traditional families (Patterson, 2006; Moore and Stambolis-Ruhstorfer, 2013). Family relationships, the quality of parenting and levels of support are examples of important variables and show the potentially negative impact of conveying certain types of families as second best (Roberts, 2001). Analysing the likelihood of policies to enhance these variables, rather than focusing on promoting one type of family structure above another, is clearly important.

Using past policy reports and research evidence to appraise policy

For almost two decades, there has been a continued focus by successive governments on developing early years, child and family policy. In 1989, this commenced with the Children's Act, curriculum guidance and alterations in successive years for children aged 0–5, culminating in the current EYFS (2014) and the publication in 1993 of Every Child Matters, which set the direction of travel for a number of years across traditional departmental boundaries. In 2014, a significant policy focus was on 2-year-olds, with funded places for those eligible and the intention to double the level of funded places for 3–4-year-olds from 2017. Alongside this, there have been significant developments in the devolved countries of the UK, as discussed in Chapter 6.

Based on this, you would be forgiven for concluding that policy in this area is extremely well developed for promoting children's well-being, in the interests of all families and having established a sector that is coherent and supports ongoing staff recruitment and development. However, evidence from varied sources can be used to form a systematic appraisal of the current state of the sector for children, parents and practitioners.

ACTIVITY

Make a list of current early years policies that you are aware of. To assist with this, you could use your notes from your reading of this book; skim through earlier chapters; talk to others who have knowledge of the sector; and consult the relevant government website for your area of the UK (see the Useful Websites section at the start of the book):

1. Go through each policy and make a list of the key points. It may be helpful to think about the policy in terms of its impact on children, parents and practitioners.

2. Choose 4–5 of the policies and identify other relevant evidence that will assist you to analyse your chosen policies. This could be research reports, reviews, policies from other locations, book chapters and information from non-governmental organizations (e.g. Joseph Rowntree Foundation, NDNA).

3. Try to identify how the varied evidence available assists you to make an appraisal of the potential strengths and weaknesses of the current or intended policy.

4. Use this evidence to compare and contrast with the different policies you have identified.

There are many different policies that you could have chosen and a myriad of evidence that you could compare and contrast each policy with to support your analysis. See the example list in Table 9.2.

Table 9.2   Example list of early years policies

Aspect of policy or practice	Contrasting evidence to appraise the policy area
The expansion of funded places for all 3–4-year-olds from 570 hours to 1140 hours	Will provide additional financial support to working parents who need to access ECEC
	Not available to children of non-working parents
	Inadequate funding for parts of the PVI sector to cover the current hours of funded provision
	There is no stated intention to bring more parity between the PVI and maintained (e.g. schools) sectors
	Long-term staff recruitment and retention problems
	Inadequate career progression opportunities for current practitioners

---

Aspect of policy or practice	Contrasting evidence to appraise the policy area
Evidence confirms that the higher the qualifications of practitioners, the better the outcomes for children	There are graduate opportunities with EYT training programmes
	Terms and conditions for those with EYTS are not comparable to those with QTS
	Withdrawal of funding (e.g. the Graduate Leader Fund) makes recruitment of highly qualified practitioners difficult in the PVI sector
	Many with EYPS/EYTS are attracted to work in the maintained sector
	There is no incentive for the PVI sector to employ more highly qualified staff
	Should the aim be to ensure that all or the majority of staff who work with children are qualified to at least level 3, to benefit all children?
Expanding the number of places for young children (including 2-year-olds) in schools	Do schools have the skills and pedagogical expertise for the education and care of 2-year-olds?
	Are there appropriate facilities in schools for such young children?
	The pressure on primary school places to meet statutory requirements is high, with significant predicted future shortfalls in some parts of the country
	Will some schools be tempted to follow this route to gain additional funding to support stretched school budgets?
The stated policy for funded 2-year-old places is to bridge the gap with their peers	28% of settings with funded 2-year-olds are rated below good
	Should any setting that is not rated good or above be able to provide funded places for 2-year-olds?
	Is 15 hours of funding going to support this gap?
Promoting parental take-up of provision	The funding system is complex
	Some provision is universal (e.g. 570 funded hours for 3–4-year-olds) and the rest is targeted, meaning it is based on parental work and income levels rather than children's needs
	Targeting provision at groups of children could be stigmatizing
	The introduction of online childcare accounts will add another layer of complexity to partially funded provision
	How does this policy sit alongside the reduction in other services, such as Sure Start Children's Centres?

The aspects of policy above draw on a variety of evidence. For example, the EPPE study (2008), the Nutbrown review (2012), the House of Lords report into afford-able childcare (2015), the NDNA workforce survey (2015) and varied government statistics (from the Office of National Statistics). Whilst the evidence critiques policy, the intention is not to suggest that these are 'bad' policies. On the contrary, each of the policies above has many commendable aims, however by drawing on a range of evidence this enables a more systematic and evidence-based appraisal to be made of each aspect of policy. The examples above draw on English policy aims and objectives, and reference to other countries, such as Wales and Scotland, high-lights that other countries are putting more effort into creating a coherence between early years curricula and the first phase of statutory education (KS1 in England and Wales) and between the PVI and maintained parts of the sector. Another way to appraise policy is to look at past policy. For example, in 1998 the Labour Government published the National Childcare Strategy and this was fol-lowed in 2004 by the ten-year Childcare Strategy. Review of the policy aims above, with reference to these policies, could suggest that neither was ever completely achieved. Alternatively, it could reflect different political ideologies, which empha-sizes the dynamic nature of policy as something that is continually evolving and changing to reflect the aims of the government of the day. Each of the approaches discussed provides a basis with which to appraise policy.

The impact of policy on children

Perhaps the most fundamental question that policies need to address is 'What works for children?' The Treasury response to this during the 2000s was to impose a number of public service agreements on departments to ensure there were clear accountability measures in place. For example, Sure Start, which had the aims of improving health and well-being and lifting families out of poverty, attracted large amounts of funding to help meet the targets set out in the National Childcare Strategy, many of which are reiterated in the Children's Plan. The Plan also assumes that all families will prefer to access ECEC rather than care for their child at home. Some families may decide that caring for their child at home is their preferred option but there is far less support available for this choice (higher levels of infor-mal childcare, for example being cared for by grandparents, are evident in Scotland). This may result in some families, perhaps because of lower income levels and geographical location, feeling they have no choice but to return to work, as they are not able to manage financially.

To assess the targets set out in government policy for children and families, a range of evidence could be used. Government statistics on the number of ECEC places, levels of poverty and the average cost of childcare could help to make an assessment. Reports from the Early Years Directorate of Ofsted can look at quality in specific settings and more generally across the sector. Information from evalua-tions and early years organizations could also be useful. For example, the OECD has highlighted how ECEC provision has improved but families still face a range of logistical difficulties in accessing it because it is often provided in different locations, at times that may not fit work patterns and at an unaffordable cost (OECD, 2011; Truss, 2012). Although this relates to past provision, older evidence can be useful as, when contrasted with more recent evidence, it helps to evaluate the success of a policy over time rather than making a simple judgement that there has been either a complete success or a complete failure. The content of provision can also be assessed for quality. It could be argued that a positive development for the ECEC sector was the introduction of *Birth to Three Matters* (for children from birth to 3) (Sure Start Unit, 2002) and the *Curriculum Guidance for the Foundation Stage* (for children aged 3–6) (QCA/DfEE, 2000), which both take account of the developmental needs of young children and promote an appropriate curriculum. In contrast, the introduction of these two separate curriculum documents and the formal approach of the Key Stage 1 curriculum could be seen as adding to, rather than reducing, the fragmentation of the sector. An alternative response to this could have been to introduce one curriculum that addressed the developmental needs and well-being of children in the early years, similar to the approach being developed in Wales. This also offers a potential comparison with which to analyse the English system (Welsh Assembly, 2004). This has been partially addressed through the combining of the two curricula for children aged 0–5 but there is still a divide between the early years curriculum and Key Stage 1 in England. Contrasting past developments with recent ones demonstrates how evidence over a period of time can help to make a detailed analysis of progress to date and identify, with the support of evidence, where further development could be beneficial.

Overall, there have been benefits that are the direct result of the Children's Plan, although it can be difficult to accurately assess these. For example, since 2000 there has been a reduction in child poverty (although levels increased in 2014–15), fewer deaths of children due to injury, lower levels of infant and child mortality and an increase in the number of infants being breast-fed. Alongside this, there has been a rise in childhood obesity, increased levels of asthma and diabetes and a reduction in the number of children being immunized against measles (Bradshaw, 2002; Eisenstadt, 2011). Within different communities, there may have been a number of policies operating, such as Sure Start, neighbourhood renewal initiatives, educational projects, New Deal, Health Action Zones, Primary National Strategy and the Healthy Schools Initiative, which can make it difficult to attribute change to one specific policy. This is discussed by Kurtz in relation to conflicting evidence between policies that aim to reduce social exclusion and the different explanations that can be linked to the rise in specific disorders, which 'indicates the complexities in interpreting the relationship between overall national trends in health indicators and policy initiatives' (2003: 176). Although health measures do not relate directly to the Children's Plan, they do clearly highlight the need for caution in attributing specific change to one national policy without the evidence to link outcomes with implementation initiatives. Based on this, it could also be argued that an analysis of any national policy, especially in terms of assessing whether targets have been achieved, is best undertaken through local evaluations that are more able to identify specific benefits and disadvantages in the context of the range of policy initiatives that are likely to be in place.

Approaches to analysing policy: evaluative themes

A range of questions can be asked to promote the analysis of policy. Dowling (1999) suggests that commitment to ECEC can be seen in terms of four broad themes: insufficiency, diversity, lack of resources and commitment. These themes hold good today. To analyse the impact of policy, questions can be asked that relate to the level of commitment in terms of provision and resources to implement policy plans at a regional and local level. They can relate to how likely policies are to lead to integrated, high-quality provision for each child and family. This approach to analysing policy can be applied at different levels, for example to evaluate a broad government policy (e.g. the EYFS; DfE, 2014a) or the implementation of policy within a setting (e.g. the Special Educational Needs and Disability Code of Practice in a nursery setting).

The framework suggests a number of questions in different areas that could be applied to evaluate policy. It is unlikely, and perhaps unnecessary, that all of the questions would be applied to one policy. Decisions will need to be made about what is being evaluated and the purpose of the analysis. If it is for an essay, which is aiming to contrast the approach of central governments pre- and post-1997/2010 to ECEC, it is likely that a number of commitment and resource questions will be raised. If the aim is to evaluate the level of participation of families and children in issues that affect them in their nursery, the focus may be on questions drawn from the diversity section.

The following questions are not meant to be seen as a definitive response to achieving a comprehensive analysis of policy. They could be seen as offering a starting point to promote in-depth analysis, as a stimulus to add a critical dimension to analysing policies or as a vehicle to promote critical discussion of specific issues. If the aim is to offer a broad overview, it may be useful to include a discussion of questions from each section. For a more in-depth analysis of an aspect of policy, questions may be drawn mainly from one area. It is also likely that the initial questions asked would do two things: provide answers and raise more questions.

Commitment
- Is there clear leadership at national, regional and local levels?
- Is there a commitment to integrated services and strategies in place to achieve this?
- Is there evidence of commitment across central departments and professions to developing integrated services for children and families?
- Are messages from research being integrated into policy and practice to raise the quality of ECEC services?
- Is there a commitment to increase the level and quality of ECEC services?
- Is there a commitment to promoting the involvement of children and families in service planning and evaluation?

Insufficiency
- Does the level of provision match demand in all areas of the UK?
- Are there sufficient ECEC places for all children who require them?
- Are there differences between urban and rural locations?
- Does the timing of provision match the needs of children and families?

- Are there an adequate number of practitioners with appropriate qualifications?
- Are there policies/plans in place to overcome any gaps in insufficiency?

Resources
- Does the level of resources from central government recognize and allow for the development of the ECEC sector?
- How are resources being allocated and shared at a local level?
- Are resources being increased over time to allow the development of ECEC provision?
- Are resources sustainable in the long term, particularly outside the maintained sector?
- Are resources appropriate to the requirements of service users?

Diversity
- Does the range of provision meet the diverse requirements of children and families?
- Do all children and families have equal access to provision?
- What support and training are available to practitioners to ensure they have the skills to respond to all children and families?
- Do policies value and promote the integration of each child and family?
- Are providers aware of the diversity of family structures and do they respond to this appropriately?
- Are the voices of each child and family heard equally?

International evidence

As detailed in Chapter 7, several countries now have policy initiatives similar to those of the UK, which are aimed at providing services that respond to the requirements of children and families, particularly those with lower income levels. Another similarity of many of these countries with the UK is the emphasis on preventative responses which address all aspects of support that families may need through the provision of joined-up services (OECD, 2011). This evidence can provide another approach to analysing the likely impact of UK policy as well as providing a forum to debate the potential impacts of approaches that are similar to those in other countries.

In the USA, there has been an increase in both the number of children using day care facilities and the duration of time they spend there. In response to this, the issue of quality has arisen, but in the absence of a national plan, such as Every Child Matters, individual states have responded in different ways. But evidence of the importance of high-quality environments from the USA is very similar to that of the UK: the higher the quality of the setting, the better the cognitive, linguistic and social outcomes for children. High-quality indicators include high child/staff ratios, higher levels of qualified staff, knowledge of child development and positive interactions between staff and children. In contrast, research shows that most aspects of provision are of medium to poor quality and there is no national approach to quality assurance in the USA (Grisham Brown and Hallam, 2004;

Collins, 2012). An important message from this is that just because it is known what contributes to good quality, it cannot be assumed that this will be evident in day-to-day practice. The direction can be set out in policy documents but it will then require substantial effort to embed the principles of the policy into practice. Another message to come out of the evaluation is the importance of consulting day care providers to get an accurate reflection of early care and education initiatives (Grisham Brown and Hallam, 2004). Questions can be asked about how this compares with the UK and may suggest that revisions to quality assurance processes and evaluations are needed to take more account of the views of practitioners. Another contributing factor to quality, possibly the most significant, is the skills, knowledge and experience of the workforce. This is clearly recognized by the government as the Children's Plan contains a number of initiatives aimed at raising the skill base and career development opportunities of the workforce, but, as discussed in Chapter 8, momentum in this aspect of policy has reduced. In a number of countries, particularly across Europe, there are a significant number of pedagogues who are generally trained to graduate level, have both rhetorical and practical training combined, and work throughout a range of child and family services (OECD, 2006, 2011). Initially, it may seem that this evidence would not be useful to help evaluate planned workforce developments in parts of the UK. However, it can offer a platform to compare the similarities and differences that this may have with similar roles in the UK (such as Early Years Professional/Early Years Teacher or Children's Centre Leader), which could provide evidence to form a position on how successful ongoing or planned policy developments will prove.

In Australia, the development of ECEC services has followed a similar path to that of the UK. There has been a heavy educational focus on policy and varied initiatives have caused an arbitrary division between caring and teaching. This has led to differences in levels of training, qualifications and philosophies underpinning service provision, which in many respects remain evident. Kindergarten provision, which children usually access the year before school, is seen to be good and has an educational focus. In contrast, childcare and day care are seen to be aimed at the socially disadvantaged and to be about meeting the health and safety needs of children (Jillian, 1996). Evidence of this arbitrary division and the unsystematic development of ECEC services mirrors the historical development of UK services and provides comparisons with which to analyse the potential impact of current policies moving to less fragmented and more integrated ECEC services. The levels of ECEC offered in Australia also have some similarities with the targeted approach of providing Sure Start local projects in England, which may result in less advantaged communities feeling stigmatized and raises questions about the need for a national childcare policy that leads to national levels of provision. What is clear, though, from international evidence, is that a long-term policy commitment, backed by appropriate funding, will be necessary to bring about sustainable improvements in ECEC in the UK, and this may not always sit easily alongside the quick-fix approach to societal issues (Vimpani, 2002; Rutter, 2015).

International evidence can be useful for analysing approaches to child and family policy in the UK. Glass (2001) argues that caution needs to be applied if there is an unquestioned assumption that what works in other countries can be directly applied in UK contexts. In addition, there are differences within many aspects of policy between the countries of the UK, and this was discussed in Chapter 6. There are likely to be aspects of policy, such as service design and raising the quality of ECEC provision, that will work, but others may not. Any analysis of policy should consider this and ask what aspects of policy are transferable and what may be culture dependent. For example, the approach to funding in the USA is very different to that in the UK and introducing a policy that works well there may not achieve the same outcomes here. When using international evidence to appraise UK policy, as well as asking 'what works?', Glass (2001) suggests there is another fundamental question that needs to be considered: what is worth doing for children? This question is as valid today when appraising policy as it was in 2001.

SUMMARY

- Analysing policy is a complex process, particularly in the area of early years, as policies have become increasingly complex across a complicated sector.

- Nonetheless, it is important to be able to make an appraisal of the broad issues and how they are likely to impact on the various stakeholders (including those whom policies are intended to have an impact on and those who may be affected indirectly).

- The inclusion of targets in policies may not reflect achievable results, as evidenced by subsequent policies (e.g. contrasting the targets in the Children's Plan with recent government intentions for early education provision).

- To assist readers with this process, the chapter has suggested a number of approaches that can be helpful. They are by no means the only ways to undertake an analysis of policy but it is hoped that they provide a starting point and may generate other ideas. The approaches outlined include:

  o measuring the effectiveness of policies according to outcomes (e.g. how many additional childcare places have been created and how long these have been sustained for)

  o assessing the ability of a policy to represent the perspective of different stakeholders, particularly children who may not be empowered through policy

  o a comparison with past developments and evaluation reports

  o assessing the approach of policy against research evidence (e.g. examining whether the pedagogical approach of early years curricula is developmentally appropriate for young children)

  o evaluating policy against a range of themes, including the level of commitment from government and policy-makers, the level of resources allocated to implementation and sustainability, and the ability of the policy to respond to the diversity of stakeholders

  o a comparison with international approaches and evidence, but with attention to the level of transferability within the context of the UK and the policy approach in operation

  o the ability to accurately measure gains and to what extent they can be attributed to a policy.

FURTHER READING

One of the best ways to feel more confident in evaluating policy is to read widely to gain an understanding of how authors have approached it. An approach to evaluating early years policy can be informed by reading trade journals such as *Community Care* and newspapers such as *The Guardian* and *The Independent*, all of which can be found online.

Another important consideration is how well the views of children are taken account of in policy design and implementation. There is a general consensus that children are now more involved, but this may not always be the case.

Adams, P. (2014) *Policy and Education*, Abingdon: Routledge. This is an excellent text for providing an overview of how political discourses and ideologies impact on the formation of policy. It provides an excellent overview to allow the reader to understand how politics and policy are inextricably linked.

Tisdall, E.K.M. and Davis, J. (2004) 'Making a difference? Bringing children's and young people's views into policy making', *Children and Society*, 18, 2, 131–42. This article discusses a range of issues around the involvement of children and considers at what stages their views are taken account of and, most importantly, the impact that this involvement has. The websites for the Children's Commissioners in each of the UK countries will also have relevant sources related to how children are consulted as part of the analysis of policy.

10

CONCLUSION

In this fourth edition, we have discussed what early years policy is, how it has developed over time under successive political ideologies, what influences the development of policy has had, and how it is implemented, evaluated and analysed. The development of early years policy has been particularly prolific since 1997 when early years issues became central to the then government agenda. Following the forming of the Coalition Government in 2010, the broad direction of travel had some similarities with the approach of New Labour. However, a significant development was the number of reviews that were completed or implemented and the gradual move to more targeted rather than universal provision, such as Sure Start Children's Centres. The results of these reviews led to some changes, however limited, for example the publication of the newly revised *EYFS Statutory Framework* (DfE, 2014a) following an earlier review in 2012; the establishment of new executive bodies to administer aspects of provision and direct further development; and extending the remit of the Children's Commissioner for England to align the powers more with commissioners in other parts of the UK.

Since the 2015 general election, the Conservative Government has made clear its commitment to extend ECEC. The overall emphasis on how policy in the area is viewed is relevant as traditionally ECEC policy has been seen as social policy (and to some extent this remains the case in England), whilst in Scotland the intention is for ECEC policy to be seen as economic, which emphasizes a more universal approach. This has posed challenges in the study of early years in terms of understanding the range and complexity of policies affecting young children and their families across the UK. This emphasis on early years policy will clearly continue into the future as the Conservative Government has placed children and families firmly at the centre of its agenda, as did the previous two governments. Recent developments in policy affecting young children are the most radical for over 30 years, involving wide-ranging changes to structure and practice in children's services. Whether sufficient funding will be found to effectively implement the new policy remains in question. In England, this has been signified by the closure of Children's Centres and the increase in PVI provision in at least some parts of the country. The impact of these developments on service provision is likely to be significant for years to come. In Wales, provision from cyclhoedd meithrin (Welsh medium playgroups) and in Scotland care from family members, particularly grandparents, alongside higher levels of maintained nursery provision, mediate the need for PVI provision to some degree.

A complex range of factors, which combine to create change, influences policy development. These include historical influences, the perceived effectiveness of existing policy and the impact of lobbying by statutory and voluntary sector children's organizations and the impact of a coalition administration. An example of lobbying that has gained attention recently is linked to concerns about the sustainability of PVI early years provision with current funding levels and the planned increase in funded provision to 1,140 hours in England. However, the key factor is the perceived importance of early years issues for the government of the day, as shown by public funding of over five billion pounds per year, which is set to increase substantially with current policy developments. This in turn is influenced by many interrelated factors, including meeting wider policy commitments, the role of individual ministers and senior civil servants, and the relationship between key figures in government and the early years sector.

Implementing policy at national and local government levels involves legislating for some areas of policy, disseminating information and guidance, and a comprehensive debate about how policy will work at ground level. The shape of policy is confirmed through these processes and the extent to which there is agreement between policy-makers and those delivering policy at service level. Modern policy-making is based on principles that should produce robust, effective developments that are informed by research evidence and lessons from the past. However, recent policies influencing early years have been large and complex, and what exactly the eventual outcome for children, families and practitioners will be remains unclear. Policy direction has been impacted by the government's budget deficit actions since 2010, and evidence suggests that policy decisions based primarily on financial need may be contradictory to the evidence of best practice or outcomes. A number of chapters discuss examples of this – for instance, evidence from varied reviews confirms that the higher the qualification base of practitioners, the better the outcome for children, however support for the PVI sector to employ more highly qualified staff is absent. Similarly, international comparisons have shown us that sufficient funding and political will, supported by strong policies, are needed to achieve the best ECEC.

As the complexity of policy has increased, it has become important when evaluating policy to consider the impact it has on the various stakeholders. For example, policies may have differing impacts on parents and children. A policy to support parents returning to work may improve their employability and income but result in children spending longer in day care. Similarly, policies that have led to a significant expansion in the provision of early years services have not, so far, led to increased access to training for all practitioners, a recognition of their skills and experience and the implementation of a systematic career framework to promote progression. Nonetheless, as highlighted, potentially there are plans in place to address some of these issues, emphasizing the need for ongoing evaluation.

The aim of this fourth edition is to help readers understand their own role in policy development as students, practitioners, employees and members of children's organizations within the early years sector. Policy is the product of human activity and as such can be influenced by those involved. As stated in Chapter 1, practitioners (and students as future participants in the ECEC sector) need to understand policy in terms of how it determines their roles and responsibilities, the structures and policies of their workplaces, and the quality of service provision to children and families. Throughout the book, the content and activities have provided a basis to help the reader engage with the complexity of policy-making, implementation and evaluation across the UK. Chapters 2 to 5 discuss policy development over time, including the direction of travel under the Coalition Government. Chapter 6 deals with the current similarities and differences between policies in each country of the UK. Chapter 7 presents a basis for evaluating UK policy by drawing on international examples and evidence. However, as policy develops continually, it is very important to develop strategies for keeping up to date with new initiatives. This fourth edition provides you with a range of tools to understand and evaluate policy, but keeping up to date is your responsibility. The further reading at the end of each chapter and the Useful Websites list provide guidance to assist with this.

REFERENCES

4Children (2014) *Sure Start Children's Centres Census*. Available at: www.4children.org.uk/ Files/6f907ff7–35fe-4c6f-a3a43cb00e1a11c/Children_Centre_Census_2014.pdf (accessed 7 December 2014).

Abbott, L. (2002) *Birth to Three Matters: A framework to support children in their earliest years*, London: DfES.

Adams, D. and Swadener, B.B. (2010) 'Early childhood education and teacher development in Kenya: lessons learned', *Child and Youth Care Forum*, 29, 6, 385–402.

Adams, P. (2014) *Policy and Education*, Abingdon: Routledge.

Adamson, B. (2012) 'International comparative studies in teaching and teacher education', *Teaching and Teacher Education*, 28, 5, 641–8.

Alexander, A. (2009) *Britain's New Towns: Garden cities to sustainable communities*, Oxford: Routledge.

Algava, É. and Ruault, M. (2003) *Les assistants maternelles: une profession en développement: Études et Résultats No.232*, Paris: DREES.

Allen, G. MP (2011) *Early Intervention: The next steps*. Available at: www.dwp.gov.uk/docs/ early-intervention-next-steps.pdf (accessed 29 May 2012).

Anning, A. (2004) 'The co-construction of an early childhood curriculum', in A. Anning, J. Cullen and M. Fleer (eds), *Early Childhood Education: Society and culture*, London: Sage.

Arnold, R. (2005) *Early Years Childcare and Education – the Sure Start agenda: The Beacon Council Scheme Round 5*, Windsor: NFER.

Artiles, A. and Dyson, A. (2005) 'Inclusive education in the globalisation age', in D. Mitchell (ed.), *Contextualising Inclusive Education: Evaluating old and new international perspectives*, London: Routledge.

Audit Commission (2002) *Statutory Assessment and Statements of SEN: In need of review?* London: TSO.

Baldock, P. (2011) *Developing Early Childhood Services: Past, present and future*, Maidenhead: Open University Press.

Barnardo's (2003) Every Child Matters, *Green Paper*, 8 September. Available at: www.barnardos. org.uk/newsandevents/media/press/release.jsp?id=1153 (accessed 1 March 2005).

Barnardo's (2015) 'Barnardo's wants children's centre funding protected', 22 May. Available at: https://www.barnardos.org.uk/news/Barnardo8217s_wants_children8217s_centre_funding_ protected/latest-news.htm?ref=104819

Baudelot, O. and Rayna, S. (2000) *Coordinateurs et coordination de la petite enfance dans les communes: Actes du colloque du Créas*, Paris: Institut national de recherche pédagogique.

Bell, A and La Valle, I. (2005) *Early Stages of the Neighbourhood Nurseries Initiative: Parents' experiences*, London: DfES/Sure Start Unit.

Berlinski, S., Galiani, S. and Manacorda, M. (2008) 'Giving children a better start: pre-school attendance and school-age profiles', *Journal of Public Economics*, 92, 5–6, 1416–40.

Bertram, T. and Pascal, C. (2014) *Early Years Literature Review*, The British Association of Early Childhood Education. Available at: www.early-education.org.uk/sites/default/files/CREC%20Early%20Years%20Lit%20Review%202014%20for%20EE.pdf (accessed 2 August 2015).

Bilton, H. (1998) *Outdoor Play in the Early Years: Management and innovation*, London: David Fulton.

Bingham, J. (2012) '"Baby P panic" helped save thousands of children figures show – but care lottery continues', *The Telegraph*, 29 May.

Blades, R., Greene, V., Wallace, E., Loveless, L. and Mason, P. (2014) *Implementation Study: Integrated review at 2-2 ¹/₂ years – integrating the EYFS progress check and the HCP health and development review*. Research report, November. London: DfE.

Blair, T. (1996) *New Britain: My vision of a young country*, London: Fourth Estate.

Blakemore, K. and Griggs, E. (2013) *Social Policy*, Maidenhead: Open University Press.

Blunkett, D. (2006) *The Blunkett Tapes: My life in the bear pit*, London: Bloomsbury.

Bosire, B. (2006) 'Playing under the fig trees in Kenya', *UNESCO Courier: Learning is Child's Play*, October.

Bradshaw, J. (ed.) (2002) *The Well-being of Children in the UK*, London: University of York and Save the Children.

Brandon, M., Howe, A., Dagley, V., Salter, C., Warren, C. and Black, J. (2006) *Evaluating the Common Assessment Framework and Lead Professional Guidance and Implementation in 2005-6*. DfES Research Report RR740, University of East Anglia.

Brannen, J. and Moss, P. (eds) (2003) *Rethinking Children's Care*, Buckingham: Open University Press.

Brehony, K.J. (2000) 'The kindergarten in England 1851–1918', in R. Wollons (ed.), *Kindergarten and Cultures: The global diffusion of an idea*, London: Yale University Press, pp. 59–86.

Brewer, M., Cattam, S., Crawford, C. and Rabe, B. (2014) *The Impact of Free, Universal Pre-school Education on Maternal Labour Supply*, London: IFS/ESRC.

Brind, R., Norden, O., McGinigal, S., Garnett, E., Oseman, D., La Valle, I. and Jelicic, H. (2011) *Childcare and Early Years Providers*, London: DfE.

Bromley, C., Curtice, J., McCrone, D. and Park, A. (eds) (2006) *Has Devolution Delivered?* Edinburgh: Edinburgh University Press.

Bruce, T. (2001) 'The north and south divided', *Nursery World*, 12 July.

Butler, P. (2013) 'Hundreds of Sure Start centres have closed since election, says Labour', *The Guardian*, 28 January.

Cafcass (2012) *Three Weeks in November ... Three Years On ... Cafcass Care Application Study 2012*. Available at: www.cafcass.gov.uk/pdf/Cafcass%20Care%20Application%20Study%202012%20FINAL.pdf (accessed 29 May 2012).

Carter, C., Janmohammed, Z., Zhang, J. and Bertrand, J. (2007) *Selected Issues Concerning Early Childhood Care and Education in China: Background paper for the Education for All Global Monitoring Report – 'Strong Foundation: Early Childhood Care and Education'*, Paris: UNESCO.

Center on International Education Benchmarking (CIEB) (2012) *Global Perspectives: Starting well – benchmarking early education across the world*. Available at: www.ncee.org/2012/08/global-perspectives-starting-well-benchmarking-early-education-across-the-world/ (accessed ?).

Child Poverty Action Group (CPAG) (2012) *Poverty in the UK: A summary of facts and figures*. Available at: www.cpag.org.uk/povertyfacts/index.htm (accessed 29 May 2012).

Child Poverty Action Group (CPAG) (2015) *Child Poverty Facts and Figures*. Available at: www.cpag.org.uk/povertyfacts/ (accessed 13 June 2015).

Children and Families Directorate (2014) *Early Years Collaborative (EYC): Stock take review of years 1 and 2*. Edinburgh: Scottish Government. Available at: www.gov.scot/Resource/0047/00473734.pdf (accessed 10 May 2015).

Children in Northern Ireland (CiNI) (2010) *Briefing Paper on DE (0–6), Early Years Strategy, 6*. Available at: http://cini.killercontent.net/media/cb3d218ce0174d05ac5d e922dce9aae4CiNI%20Briefing%20Paper%2015.09.10.pdf (accessed 21 May 2012).

Children's Commissioners (2011) *The UK Children's Commissioners' Midterm Report to the UK State Party on the UN Convention on the Rights of the Child*. Available at: www.childcomwales.org.uk/uploads/publications/277.pdf (accessed 1 May 2012).

Children's Commissioners (2015) *Report of the UK Children's Commissioners*. Available at: www.childrenscommissioner.gov.uk/sites/default/files/publications/Report%20to%20the%20UNCRC.pdf (accessed 20 July 2015).

Children's Workforce Development Council (CWDC) (2007) *Children's Workforce Strategy* (updated Spring 2007), Leeds: CWDC. Available at: https://www.education.gov.uk/consultations/downloadableDocs/CWS%20update%20PDF%20version.pdf (accessed 18 December 2015).

Clark, M.M. and Waller, T. (eds) (2007) *Early Childhood Education and Care: Policy and practice*, London: Sage.

Close, P. and Wainwright, J. (2010) 'Who's in charge? Leadership and culture in extended service contexts', *School Leadership and Management*, 30, 5, 435–50.

Collins, V.K. (2012) 'Child care in the American South: poverty, costs and quality', *Early Childhood Research and Practice*, 14, 1. Available at: http://ecrp.uiuc.edu/v14n1/collins.html (accessed 4 December 2014).

Comenius, J.A. (1956) *The School of Infancy* (ed. E.M. Miller), Chapel Hill, NC: University of North Carolina Press.

Corbett, J. (2015) 'Government advised to reconsider the term "Integrated Review" for new two year olds' progress check'. Available at: http://www.daynurseries.co.uk/news/article.cfm/id/1567033/government-advised-to-reconsider-the-term-integrated-review (accessed 18 December 2015).

Craston, M., Thom, G. and Spivack, R. (2013) *Evaluation of the SEND Pathfinder Programme*. Available at: www.gov.uk/government/publications/evaluation-of-the-send-pathfinder-programme-process-and-implementation (accessed 24 August 2015).

Croll, P. and Moses, D. (2000) *Special Needs in the Primary School: One in five?* London: Continuum.

Crossley, M.W. and Watson, K. (2009) 'Comparative and international education: policy transfer, context sensitivity and professional development', *Oxford Review of Education*, 35, 5, 633–49.

Daly, M. (2011) 'Family policy: striving for sustainability', in J. Clasen (ed.), *Converging World of Welfare*, Oxford: Oxford University Press.

Daycare Trust (2005) 'Childcare and early years services in 2004', paper 1 of *A New Era for Universal Childcare?* Available at: daycaretrust.org.uk (accessed 15 March 2012).

Department for Children, Schools and Families (DCSF) (2007) *The Children's Plan: Building Brighter Futures*, London: DCSF.

Department for Children, Schools and Families (DCSF) (2008a) *Graduate Leader Fund: Further information on purpose and implementation*. Available at: www.everychildmatters.gov.uk/earlyyearsworkforce/ (accessed 2 July 2008).

Department for Children, Schools and Families (DCSF) (2008b) *Building Brighter Futures: Next steps for the children's workforce*, Nottingham: DCSF.

Department of Communities and Local Government (2015) *Cities and Local Government Devolution Bill*. Available at: www.publications.parliament.uk/pa/ld201516/ldhansrd/text/150715-0001.htm#15071539000515 (accessed 16 July 2015).

Department for Education (DfE) (2010) *The Impact of Sure Start Local Programmes on Seven Year Olds and their Families*, London: The Stationery Office. Available at: https://

www.gov.uk/government/uploads/system/uploads/attachment_data/file/184073/ DFE-RR220.pdf (accessed 18 December 2015).

Department for Education (DfE) (2011a) *Special Educational Needs in England: January 2011.* Available at: www.education.gov.uk/rsgateway/DB/SFR/ s001007/index.shtml (accessed 29 May 2012).

Department for Education (DfE) (2011b) *Support and Aspiration: A new approach to special educational needs and disability – progress and next steps,* London: DfE.

Department for Education (DfE) (2012) *Families in the Foundation Years.* Available at: www.education.gov.uk/home/childrenandyoungpeople/earlylearningandchildcare/ (accessed 1 August 2012).

Department for Education (DfE) (2013) *Teachers' Standards (Early Years),* London: The Stationery Office.

Department for Education (DfE) (2014a) *Statutory Framework for the Early Years Foundation Stage* (EYFS), London: The Stationery Office.

Department for Education (DfE) (2014b) *Early Years Pupil Premium and Funding for Two-year-olds.* Available at: www.education.gov.uk/consultations (accessed 6 June 2015).

Department for Education (DfE) (2014c) *Early Years Pupil Premium: Guide for local authorities.* Available at: www.education.gov.uk/consultations (accessed 6 June 2015).

Department for Education (DfE) (2014d) *Consultation on Early Years Pupil Premium and Funding for Two-year-olds: Government consultation response 2014.* Available at: www. gov.uk/government/consultations/early-years-pupil-premium-and-funding-for-2–year-olds (accessed 24 August 2015).

Department for Education (DfE) (2014e) *Children and Families Act 2014,* London: The Stationery Office.

Department for Education (DfE) (2015a) *Special Educational Needs and Disability Code of Practice: 0 to 25 years.* Available at: www.gov.uk/government/uploads/system/uploads/ attachment_data/file/398815/SEND_Code_of_Practice_January_2015.pdf (accessed 24 August 2015).

Department for Education (DfE) (2015b) *Provision for Children under Five Years of Age in England: January 2015.* Available at: www.gov.uk/government/uploads/system/uploads/ attachment_data/file/437598/SFR20–2015_Text.pdf (accessed 1 July 2015).

Department for Education (DfE) and Department of Health (DoH) (2011) *Supporting Families in the Foundation Years,* London: HMSO.

Department for Education and Employment (DfEE) (1997) *Excellence for All Children: Meeting special educational needs.* Available at: www.achieveability.org.uk/files/127074 0065/dfes-excellence-for-all-chil-dren-2001.pdf (accessed 20 August 2012).

Department for Education and Employment (DfEE) (1998) *Meeting the Childcare Challenge: A framework and consultation document,* London: HMSO.

Department for Education Northern Ireland (DENI) (2010) *Early Years (0-6) Strategy.* Available at: https://www.deni.gov.uk/sites/default/files/publications/de/early-years-strategy.pdf (accessed 18 December 2015).

Department of Education Northern Ireland (DENI) (2013) *Learning to Learn Framework: A framework for early years education and learning.* Available at: www.deni.gov.uk/english_a_ framework_for_ey_education_and_learning_oct_13_tagged.pdf (accessed 1 July 2015).

Department of Education Northern Ireland (DENI) (2015a) *Delivering Social Change for Children and Young People.* Available at: www.ofmdfmni.gov.uk/index/delivering-social-change/dsc-children-young-people.htm (accessed 1 August 2015).

Department of Education Northern Ireland (DENI) (2015b) *Education Minister Confirms £1.1 Million Funding for the Early Years Fund.* Available at: www.deni.gov.uk/news/ news-de-090715–education-minister-confirms.htm (accessed 31 July 2015).

Department of Education Northern Ireland (DENI) (2015c) *Pre-school Places.* Available at: www.deni.gov.uk/index/support-and-development-2/early-years-education/16–pre-school-education-preschoolplaces-pg.htm (accessed 31 July 2015).

Department for Education and Skills (DfES) (2003) *Every Child Matters* (Green Paper), London: HMSO.

Department for Education and Skills (DfES) (2004a) *Removing Barriers to Achievement: The government's strategy for SEN*. Available at: www.education. gov.uk/publications/standard/publicationDetail/Page1/DfES%200117%202004 (accessed 1 August 2012).

Department for Education and Skills (DfES) (2004b) *Every Child Matters: Next steps*, London: DfES.

Department for Education and Skills (DfES) (2004c) *Every Child Matters: Change for children*, London: HMSO.

Department for Education and Skills (DfES) (2006) *Sure Start Children's Centres: Planning and performance management guidance*. Available at: http://publications. everychildmatters.gov.uk/eOrderingDownload/SSCC- PERFORM2006.pdf (accessed 30 June 2008).

Department for Education and Skills (DfES) (2007) *Statutory Framework for the Early Years Foundation Stage*, Nottingham: DfES.

Department for Education and Skills (DfES) (2014) *Statutory Framework for the Early Years Foundation Stage* (from 1st September 2014), Nottingham: DfES. Available at: https://www.gov.uk/government/publications/early-years-foundation-stage-frame work--2 (accessed 18 December 2015).

Department for Education and Skills (DfES) Wales/Department for Communities and Tackling Poverty (DfCTP) Wales (2014) *Draft 10 Year Plan for the Early Years, Childcare and Play Workforce in Wales*, Welsh Government. Available at http://gov.wales/docs/dcells/ consultation/140922-10-year-plan-for-the-early-years-childcare-and-play-workforce-in-wales-plan-en.pdf (accessed 18 June 2015).

Department for Education and Skills (DfES)/Department of Health (DoH) (2003) *Together from the Start: Practical guidance for professionals working with disabled children (birth to third birthday) and their families* [LEA/0067/2003], Nottingham: DfES.

Department for Education and Skills (DfES)/Department of Health (DoH) (2004) *Children's Trusts*. Available at: www.dfes.gov.uk/childrenstrusts/ (accessed 1 December 2004).

Department of Education and Science (DES) (1967) *Children and their Primary Schools* (Plowden Report), London: HMSO.

Department of Education and Science (DES) (1990) *Starting with Quality: Report of the Committee of Inquiry into the educational experiences offered to three and four year olds* (Rumbold Report), London: HMSO.

Department of Health (DoH) (1991) *The Children Act 1989: Guidance and regulations. Volume 2: Family support, day care and educational provision for young children*, London: HMSO.

Department of Health (DoH) (1998) *Quality Protects: Framework for action*, London: DoH.

Department of Health (DoH)/Department for Education and Skills (DfES) (2004) *National Service Framework for Children, Young People and Maternity Services: Executive summary*, London: DoH/DfES.

Department of Health (DoH)/Welsh Office (1997) *People Like Us: The report of the review of safeguards for children living away from home* (Utting Report), London: HMSO.

Department of Trade and Industry (DTI) (2004) *Work–Life Balance and Flexible Working: The business case*. Available at: www.dti.gov.uk/bestpractice/assets/wlb.pdf (accessed 1 March 2005).

Devroye, J. (2009) 'The case of D.H. and others v. the Czech Republic', *Northwestern Journal of International Human Rights*, 7, 1, 81–101.

Diemet, L. (2009) 'Childcare legislation in the Netherlands', paper delivered at the Second ICMEC International Seminar Series at the International Centre for the Study of the Mixed Economy of Childcare, London, 23 March.

Direction de la recherche, des études, de l'évaluation et des statistiques (DREES) (2002) *Enquête: Modes de garde et d'acceuil des enfants de moins de 7 ans*, Paris: DREES.

Dowling, M. (1999) 'Early years: then, now and next', *Education 3-13*, 27, 3, 5–10.

Dunford, J. (2010) *Review of the Office of the Children's Commissioner (England)*, London: The Stationery Office.

Dwork, D. (1987) *War is Good for Babies and Other Young Children: A history of the infant and child welfare movement in England 1989-1918*, London: Tavistock.

Dyson, A. (2005) 'Philosophy, politics and economics? The story of inclusive education in England', in D. Mitchell (ed.), *Contextualising Inclusive Education: Evaluating old and new international perspectives*, London: Routledge.

Education Scotland (2012) *The Purpose of the Curriculum*. Available at: www.education scotland.gov.uk/thecurriculum/whatiscurriculumforex-cellence/thepurposeofthecurriculum/ index.asp (accessed 21 May 2012).

Eisenstadt, N. (2011) *Providing a Sure Start: How government discovered early childhood*, Bristol: The Policy Press.

End Child Poverty (2011) 'Empty strategy leaves families in growing hardship', 5 April. Available at: www.endchildpoverty.org.uk/news/news/empty-strategy-leaves-families-in-growing-hardship/23/189 (accessed 29 May 2012).

End Child Poverty (2015) *Short Changed: The true cost of cuts to children's benefits*. Available at: www.endchildpoverty.org.uk/files/short-changed/Short-Changed-the-true-cost-of-cuts-to-childrens-benefits-FULL-REPORT.pdf (accessed 17 July 2015).

European Commission on Employment, Social Affairs and Equal Opportunities (ECESAEO) (2008) *Implementation of the Barcelona Objectives Concerning Childcare Facilities for Pre-school-age Children*, Brussels: ECESAEO.

Eyres, I., Cable, C., Hancock, R. and Turner, J. (2004) '"Whoops, I forgot David": children's perceptions of the adults who work in their classrooms', *Early Years*, 24, 2, 149–62.

Fagnani, J. (2009) 'Childcare policies in France: the influence of organisational change in the workplace', in S. Kamerman, S. Phipps and A. Ben-Arieh (eds), *From Child Welfare to Child Well-Being: An international perspective on knowledge in the service of policy*, New York: Springer, pp. 385–402.

Fagnani, J. and Lloyd, E. (2013) 'France's childcare system: French lessons', *Nursery World*, 8 February.

Family and Parenting Institute (2005) *Making Families Matter: Nine steps to make Britain family friendly*. Available at: www.familyandparenting.org/Manifesto#3 (accessed 1 June 2008).

Family and Parenting Institute (2008) *About the Fund*. Available at: www.familyandparenting. org/ParentingFundAbout (accessed 1 June 2008).

Faux, K. (2010) 'Excessive weight is placed on early years says Tory MP', *Nursery World*, 4 March.

Field, F. MP (2010) *The Foundation Years: Preventing poor children becoming poor adults – the report of the Independent Review on Poverty and Life Chances: Final report*, 3 December. London: HM Government.

Fitzgerald, D. (2004) *Parent Partnerships in the Early Years*, London: Continuum.

Fitzgerald, D. (2012) 'Working with parents and families', in J. Kay (ed.), *Good Practice in the Early Years*, London: Continuum.

Fitzgerald, D. and Kay, J. (2008) *Working Together in Children's Services*, Abingdon: Routledge.

Frean, A. (1997) 'France shows way with childcare', *The Times*, 13 June.

Gargiulo, R.M. and Piao, Y. (1996) 'Early childhood special education in the People's Republic of China', *Early Childhood Development and Care*, 41, 1, 51–7.

Garratt, D. and Forrester, C. (2012) *Education Policy Unravelled*, London: Continuum.

Githinji, F.W. and Kanga, A. (2011) 'Early childhood development education in Kenya: a literature review on current issues', *International Journal of Current Research*, 3, 11, 129–36.

Glass, N. (1999) *Origins of the Sure Start Local Programmes*. Available at: www.surestart. gov.uk/_doc/P0001720.doc (accessed 28 June 2008).

Glass, N. (2001) 'What works for children: the political issues', *Children and Society*, 15, 1, 14–20.

Glass, N. (2005) 'Surely some mistake?', *The Guardian*. Available at: www.guardian.co.uk/society/2005/jan/05/guardiansocietysupplement.childrensservices (accessed 24 May 2010).

Goddard, C. (2015a) 'Early Years Pupil Premium: can nurseries make the Early Years Pupil Premium work?', *Nursery World*, 9 February.

Goddard, C. (2015b) 'EYFS best practice: an essential guide to spending the Early Years Pupil Premium', *Nursery World*, 23 March.

Grauberg, J. (2014) 'Strengthening the impact of the Early Years Pupil Premium', *Nursery World*, 21 August.

Grisham Brown, J. and Hallam, R. (2004) 'A comprehensive report of child care providers' perceptions of a statewide early care and education initiative', *Child and Youth Care Forum*, 33, 1, 19–31.

Haut Conseil de l'Éducation (HCE) (2007) *École primaire: bilans des resultants de l'école*, Paris: HCE.

HM Government (2006) *Select Committee for Education and Skills*, 3rd report, June. Available at: www.publications.parliament.uk/pa/cm200506/cms-elect/cmeduski/478/47802.htm (accessed 4 July 2008).

HM Government (2014) *Child Poverty Strategy 2014-17*, London: HMSO.

HM Treasury (2011) *Autumn Statement: Presented to Parliament by the Chancellor of the Exchequer*, London: HMSO.

HM Treasury, Department for Education and Skills (DfES) and Department for Work and Pensions (DWP) (2004) *Choice for Parents, The Best Start for Children: A ten year strategy for childcare*, London: HMSO.

Hillman, J. and Williams, T. (2015) *Early Years Education and Childcare: Lessons from evidence and future priorities*. London: Nuffield Foundation.

Home Office (1998) *Supporting Families: A consultation document*, London: HMSO.

Hope, C. (2010) 'Middle classes told to stop using Sure Start', *The Telegraph*, 11 August.

House of Lords (2015) *Select Committee on Affordable Childcare – First Report: Affordable childcare.* Available at: www.publications.parliament.uk/pa/ld201415/ldselect/ldaffchild/117/11702.htm (accessed 17 March 2015).

Hsueh, Y. and Tobin, J. (2003) 'Chinese early childhood educators' perspectives on dealing with a crying child', *Journal of Early Childhood Research*, 1, 1, 73–94.

Hu, B. and Szente, J. (2010) 'Introduction to Chinese early childhood inclusion', *International Journal of Early Childhood*, 42, 1, 59–66.

ican (2014) *A new DfE research report has been published on the 2-2 1/2 year check*. Available at: www.ican.org.uk/What_is_the_issue/ (accessed 15 August 2015).

Jeffreys, B. (2015) 'Extra free childcare: who will benefit?', BBC News, 1 June. Available at: www.bbc.co.uk/news/education-32956512 (accessed 15 August 2015).

Jiaxiong, Z. and Nianli, Z. (2005) 'A survey of current Shanghai early childhood education through director's self-assessment', *International Journal of Early Years Education*, 13, 2, 113–27.

Jillian, R. (1996) 'Early years provision in Australia in the 1990s: present status, current issues and future trends', *International Journal of Early Childhood*, 28, 1, 48–58.

Joseph Rowntree Foundation (2005) *Policies towards Poverty, Inequality and Exclusion since 1997.* Available at: www.jrf.org.uk/knowledge/findings/socialpolicy/0015.asp (accessed 25 March 2005).

Kabiru, M., Njenga, A. and Swadener, B.B. (2003) 'Early childhood development in Kenya: empowering young mothers, mobilising a community', *Childhood Education*, 79, 6, 358–63.

Kagan, S.L. and Hallmark, L.G. (2001) 'Cultivating leadership in early care and education', *Child Care Information*, 140, 7–10.

Kamerman, S.B. and Gatenio, S. (2003) 'Overview of the current policy context', in D. Cryer and R.M. Clifford (eds.), *Early Childhood Education and Care in the USA*, Baltimore, MD: Paul H. Brookes.

Kingdon, Z. (2014) 'The Early Years Foundation Stage: Tickell and beyond – a critical perspective', in Z. Kingdon and J. Gourd (eds), *Early Years Policy: The impact on practice*, London: David Fulton/Routledge.

Kullas, J. (2000) 'All God's children need to have some space', *Nursery World*, 14 December: 34.

Kurtz, Z. (2003) 'Outcomes for children's health and well-being', *Children and Society*, 17, 173–83.

Labour Party (1985) *A Charter for the Under-Fives*, London: Labour Party.

Laming, Lord H. (2003) *The Victoria Climbié Inquiry: Report of an inquiry by Lord Laming*, London: HMSO.

Laming, Lord H. (2009) *The Protection of Children in England: A progress report*, London: The Stationery Office.

Lansdown, G. (2001) 'Children's welfare and children's rights', in P. Foley, J. Roche and S. Tucker (eds), *Children in Society: Contemporary theory, policy and practice*, Basingstoke: Palgrave.

Lea, S. (2014) 'Early years work, professionalism and the translation of policy into practice', in Z. Kingdon and J. Gourd (eds), *Early Years Policy: The impact on practice*, London: Routledge.

Levin, P. (1997) *Making Social Policy: The mechanisms of government and politics, and how to investigate them*, Buckingham: Open University Press.

Levine, R.L. and Fitzgerald, H. (eds) (1992) *Analysis of Dynamic Psychological Systems, Vol. 1: Basic approaches to general systems theory and dynamics systems, and cybernetics*, New York: Plenum Press.

Lindon, J. (2005) 'Early stages', *Nursery World*, 3 February.

Lister, R. (2004) *Poverty*, Cambridge: Polity.

Llambi, C., Perera, M., Piñeyro, L. and Rovira, F. (2009) 'Effects of an expansion of public child care services on female labour supply and income distribution in Uruguay'. Research proposal presented to the 8th PEP General Meeting, Dakar, Senegal, June. Available at: www.pep-net.org/sites/pep-net.org/files/typo3doc/pdf/files_events/8th-PEPmeeting 2010-Dakar/papers/Cecilia_Llambi.pdf (accessed 19 October 2015).

Lloyd, D. (2014) 'International comparisons in education: what we can learn from PISA', *Teaching Business and Economics*, 8, 1, 18–19.

Lloyd, E. (2008) 'Dutch childcare reforms: informal care too costly', *Nursery World*, 6 November.

Luo, R., Zhang, L., Liu, C., Zhao, Q., Shi, Y., Rozelle, S. and Sharboro, B. (2009) *Behind before they Start: The challenge of early childhood education in rural China – Rural Education Action Project, Working Paper 209*, Stanford, CA: Stanford University Press.

Mackinnon, D. (2015) 'Devolution, state restructuring and policy divergence in the UK', *The Geographical Journal*, 18, 1, 47–56.

Manani, H.K. (2005) *NACECE Capacity Building Programmes*, Nairobi: Kenya Institute of Education.

Manani, H.K. (2007) 'Accelerated learning: new opportunities for children at risk', seminar paper, Addis Ababa, Ethiopia, November.

Mansell, W. (2013) 'Pisa mystery', *The Guardian*, 3 September.

Marcus, L. (2007) 'Scotland: first children's minister', *Nursery World*, 24 May: 4–5.

Martin, M.-H. (2010) 'Equality begins in the crèche: the debate over motherhood is missing the point – British mums should be fighting for the French model of childcare', *The Guardian*, 19 February.

Masterson, A., Antrobus, S. and Smith, S. (2004) 'The children's national service framework: from policy to practice', *Nursing Management*, 11, 6, 12–15.

Mathers, S., Ranns, H., Karemaker, A., Moody, A., Sylva, K., Graham, J. and Siraj-Blatchford, I. (2011) *Evaluation of the Graduate Leader Fund: Final report*, London: DfE.

Mbugua, T.J. (2004) 'Early childhood care and education in Kenya', *Childhood Education*, 80, 4, 191–7.

McVeigh, T. (2014) 'Sure Start Children's Centres face worse year of budget cuts, say charity', *The Observer*, 12 October.

Miller, M. (2015) 'Early years in school and early school life', in S. Hay (ed.), *Early Years Education and Care*, London: Routledge.

Ministry of Health, Welfare and Sport and Ministry of Education, Culture and Science (2000) *Early Childhood Education and Care Policy in the Netherlands: Background report to the OECD project* (official English language version), The Hague: Government of the Netherlands.

Mitchell, R.C. (2014) 'Reflections on the UNCRC's future from a transdisciplinary bricoleur', in M. Freeman (ed.), *The Future of Children's Rights*, The Hague: Martinus Nijhoff.

Mittler, P. (2005) 'The global context of inclusive education: the role of the United Nations', in D. Mitchell (ed.), *Contextualising Inclusive Education: Evaluating old and new international perspectives*, London: Routledge.

Moore, M.R. and Stambolis-Ruhstorfer, S. (2013) 'LGBT sexuality and families at the start of the 21st century', *Annual Review of Sociology*, 39, 491–507.

Mortimore, P. (2009) 'Alternative models for analysing and representing countries' performance in PISA', paper commissioned by the Education International Research Institute, Brussels. Available at: http://download.ei-ie.org/Docs/WebDepot/Alternative%20Models%20in%20PISA.pdf (accessed 19 October 2015).

Morton, K. (2009) '"Cool it" on early years, say Tories', *Nursery World*, 9 July.

Moss, P. (2001) 'Britain in Europe: fringe or heart?', in G. Pugh (ed.), *Contemporary Issues in the Early Years* (3rd edn), London: Paul Chapman Publishing.

Moss, P. (2003) 'Getting beyond childcare: reflections on recent policy and future possibilities', in J. Brannen and P. Moss (eds), *Rethinking Children's Care*, Buckingham: Open University Press.

Moss, P. (2004) 'Why we need a well-qualified early childhood workforce', paper presented at Regents College, London, 16 March.

Muijs, D., Aubrey, C., Harris, A. and Briggs, M. (2004) 'How do they manage? A review of the research on leadership in early childhood', *Journal of Early Childhood Research*, 2, 3, 157–69.

Muncey, J. (1988) 'The special school as part of a whole authority approach', in D. Baker and K. Bovair (eds), *Making the Special Schools Ordinary? Vol. 1: Models for the developing special school*, London: Falmer Press.

Munro, E. (2011) *The Munro Review of Child Protection Final Report: The child's journey*, London: Department of Education.

Muskens, G. and Peters, D. (2009) *Inclusion and Education in European Countries: INTMEAS project – Final Report on the Netherlands (No. 8)*, Brussels: European Union Directorate General for Education & Culture.

National Audit Office (NAO) (2001) *Modern Policy Making: Ensuring policies deliver value for money*, London: NAO.

National Audit Office (NAO) (2004) *Early Years: Progress in developing high quality childcare and early education accessible to all*, HC 268, Session 2003–04, London: NAO.

National Audit Office (NAO) (2006) *Sure Start Children's Centres*, London: TSO.

National College for School Leadership (NCSL) (2008) *National Professional Qualification for Integrated Children's Centre Leadership*. Available at: www.ncsl.org.uk/npqicl-index (accessed 15 June 2008).

National Day Nurseries Association (NDNA) (2015) *Workforce Survey 2015*. Available at: www.ndna.org.uk/NDNA/News/Reports_and_surveys/Surveys_and_reports.aspx (accessed 24 June 2015).

National Evaluation of Children's Trusts (NECT) (2004) *Children's Trusts: Developing integrated services for children in England*, Norwich: University of East Anglia/National Children's Bureau/DfES/DoH.

National Evaluation of Sure Start (NESS) Research Team (2008) *The Impact of Sure Start Local Programmes on Three Year Olds and their Families*, Nottingham: DfES Publications. Available at: www.ness.bbk.ac.uk/documents/activities/impact/42.pdf (accessed 26 June 2008).

NICHD (2007) *The NICHD Study of Early Child Care and Youth Development: Findings for children up to age $4\frac{1}{2}$ years*, US Department of Health and Human Services.

Norvez, A. (1990) *De la naissance à l'école: Santé, modes de garde et préscolarité dans la France*, Paris: INED – Presses Universitaires de France.

Nursery World (2001) 'NI children's strategy "could lead the world"', *Nursery World*, 12 July: 6.

Nutbrown, C. (2012) *Review of Early Education and Childcare Qualifications: Final report*, London: DfE.

Nutbrown, C. (2013) 'Shaking the foundations of quality? Why "childcare" policy must not lead to poor quality early education and care', University of Sheffield, March.

Nyland, B., Zheng, X., Nyland, C. and Tran, L. (2009) 'Grandparents as educators and carers in China', *Journal of Early Childhood Research*, 7, 1, 46–57.

O'Brien, N. (2011) '"Special educational needs" – or just badly behaved children?', *The Telegraph*, 9 March. Available at: http://blogs.telegraph.co.uk/news/neilobrien1/100079216/special-educational-needs-or-just-badly-behaved-children/ (accessed 29 May 2012).

Office of the United Nations High Commissioner for Human Rights (OUNHCHR) (1989) *United Nations Convention on the Rights of the Child*, Geneva: OUNHCHR.

Office for National Statistics (ONS) (2013) *Women in the Labour Market, 2013*, 25 September. Available at: www.ons.gov.uk/ons/rel/lmac/women-in-the-labour-market/2013/index.html?format=hi-vis (accessed 16 August 2015).

Office for Standards in Education (Ofsted) (2006a) *Extended Services in Schools and Children's Centres*. Available at: www.ofsted.gov.uk/assets/Internet_Content/Publications_Team/File_attachments/extended2609.doc (accessed 30 June 2008).

Office for Standards in Education (Ofsted) (2006b) *Inclusion: Does it matter where pupils are taught? An Ofsted report on the provision and outcomes in different settings for pupils with learning difficulties and disabilities*. Available at: www.ofsted.gov.uk/publications/index.cfm?fuseaction=pubs.displayfile&id=4235&type=pdf (accessed 4 July 2008).

Office for Standards in Education (Ofsted) (2008) *How Well are they Doing? The impact of children's centres and extended schools*. Available at: www.ofsted.gov.uk/assets/Internet_Content/Shared_Content/Files/2008/jan/ childcentres_exschs.doc (accessed 30 June 2008).

Office for Standards in Education (Ofsted) (2014) *Registered Childcare Providers and Places in England, August 2014: Key findings*. Available at: www.gov.uk/government/statistics/registered-childcare-providers-and-places-in-england-december-2008–onwards (accessed 20 February 2015).

Ominde, S. H. (1964) *Kenya Education Commission Report*. Nairobi: National government publication

Organisation for Economic Co-operation and Development (OECD) (2001) *Starting Strong: Early childhood education and care*, Paris: OECD.

Organisation for Economic Co-operation and Development (OECD) (2004) *Early Childhood Education and Care Policy in France*, Paris: OECD.

Organisation for Economic Co-operation and Development (OECD) (2006) *Starting Strong II: Early childhood education and care*, Paris: OECD.

Organisation for Economic Co-operation and Development (OECD) (2011) *Doing Better for Families*, Paris: OECD.

Organisation for Economic Co-operation and Development (OECD) (2012) *Starting Strong III: A quality toolbox for early childhood education and care*, Paris: OECD.

Osgood, J. (2009) 'Childcare workforce reform in England and "the early years professional": a critical discourse analysis', *Journal of Education Policy*, 24, 6, 733–51.

Parker, I. (2013) 'Discourse analysis: dimensions of critique in psychology', *Qualitative Research in Psychology*, 10, 223–39.

Pascal, C., Bertram, T., Delaney, S. and Nelson, C. (2013) *Comparison of International Childcare Systems*, London: DfE.

Paton, G. (2013) 'Start schooling later than age five, say experts', *The Telegraph*. Available at: www.telegraph.co.uk/education/educationnews/10302249/Start-schooling-later-than-age-five-say-experts.html (accessed 15 March 2015).

Patterson, C.J. (2006) 'Children of lesbian and gay parents', *Current Directions in Psychological Science*, 15, 5, 241–4.

Penn, H. (2005) *Understanding Early Childhood: Issues and controversies*, Maidenhead: Open University Press.

Penn, H. (2009) 'A mother's place is in the home?', *Nursery World*, 12 March, 10–11.

Perera, M. and Llambi, C. (2010) *Plan de Acción 2010–2015: Dimensinamiento economico de la universilazación de los servicios de atención y educación a la primera infancia: considerando los modelos existents asi como possibles modelos alternatives. Informe final*, Montevideo: ENIA.

Phillips, J.S. and Bhavnagu, N.P. (2002) 'The Masai's education and experiences: challenges of a nomadic lifestyle', *Childhood Education*, 78, 140–6.

Pilkington, C. (2002) *Devolution in Britain Today*, Manchester: Manchester University Press.

Plaisance, É. (1996) *Pauline Kergomard et l'école maternelle*, Paris: Presses Universitaires de France.

Power, E. (2011) 'Cuts threaten plans for special needs children', *The Guardian*, 9 March. Available at www.guardian.co.uk/education/mortar-board/2011/mar/09/cuts-threaten-sen-plans (accessed 29 May 2012).

Pre-school Learning Alliance (2014) 'EYPP to go ahead as government consultation reveals backing', 23 October. Available at: www.pre-school.org.uk/sectornews/269/eypp-to-go-ahead-as-government-consultation-reveals-backing (accessed 12 August 2015).

Qualifications and Curriculum Authority (QCA)/Department for Education and Employment (DfEE) (2000) *Investing in Our Future: Curriculum guidance for the foundation stage*, London: QCA/DfEE.

Qinghua, J., Yan, L., Yan, Z. and Qiong, L. (2005) 'A survey of current pre-school education of/for children from urban low-income families in Beijing', *International Journal of Early Years Education*, 13, 2, 157–69.

Quinn, G. and Degener, T. (eds) (2002) *The Current Use and Future Potential of United Nations Human Rights Instruments in the Context of Disability*, Geneva: OUNHCHR.

Raley, S., Bianchi, S.M. and Wang, W. (2012) 'When do fathers care? Mothers' economic contribution and fathers' involvement in child care', *American Journal of Sociology*, 117, 5, 1422–59.

Rawstrone, A. (2001) 'Scotland provides a good care model', *Nursery World*, 7 June: 4–5.

Ridge, T. (2011) 'The everyday costs of poverty in childhood: a review of qualitative research exploring the lives and experiences of low-income children in the UK', *Children and Society*, 25, 1, 73–84.

Robb, S. (2015) 'The Early Years Pupil Premium and you', *Nursery Management Today*, March/April.

Roberts, M. (2001) 'Childcare policy', in P. Foley, J. Roche and S. Tucker (eds), *Children in Society: Contemporary theory, policy and practice*, Basingstoke: Palgrave.

Robinson, K. and Aronica, L. (2015) *Creative Schools*, New York: Viking.

Rose, W. (2012) 'Incorporating safeguarding and well-being in universal services: developments in early years multi-agency practice in Scotland', in L. Miller and D. Hevey (eds), *Policy Issues in the Early Years*, London: Sage.

Rutter, J. (2015) *Childcare Costs Survey 2015*, Family and Childcare Trust. Available at: http://fct.bigmallet.co.uk/sites/default/files/files/Childcare%20cost%20survey%20 2015%20Final.pdf#overlay-context=childcare-cost-survey-2015 (accessed 17 May 2015).

Ruxton, S. (2001) 'Towards a "children's policy" for the European Union?', in P. Foley, J. Roche and S. Tucker (eds), *Children in Society: Contemporary theory, policy and practice*, Basingstoke: Palgrave.

Sadler, M. (1900) 'How far can we learn anything of practical value from the study of foreign systems of education?', address to the Guildford Educational Conference, 20 October.

Sanderson, I. (2003) 'Is it "what works" that matters? Evaluation and evidence-based policy making', *Research Papers in Education*, 18, 4, 331–45.

Scotland Office (2015) *Scotland Bill 2015 (Legislation and explanatory notes)*. Available at: www.gov.uk/government/publications/scotland-bill-2015-legislation-and-explanatory-notes (accessed 22 June 2015).

Scottish Executive (2001) *For Scotland's Children*, Edinburgh: Scottish Executive.

Scottish Government (2008) *Getting it Right for Every Child (GIRFEC)*. Available at: www.gov.scot/resource/doc/1141/0065063.pdf (accessed 22 October 2015).

Scottish Government (2013) *ECEC Review: International review of policy, provision and funding*. Available at: www.gov.scot/Publications/2013/03/4564/11 (accessed 8 August 2015).

Scottish Government (2014) *Children and Young People (Scotland) Act 2014*. Available at: www.legislation.gov.uk/asp/2014/8/contents/enacted (accessed 4 April 2015).

Scottish Government/Convention of Scottish Local Authorities (COSLA) (2008) *Early Years Framework*. Available at: www.scotland.gov.uk/Resource/Doc/257007/0076309. pdf (accessed 21 May 2012).

Senge, P. and Lannon-Kim, C. (1991) *The Systems Thinker Newsletter*, 2, 5.

Sharp, C. (2003) 'School starting age: European policy and recent research', *Early Education*, Spring: 4–5.

Sheppard, M., MacDonald, P. and Welbourne, P. (2008) 'Service users as gate keepers in children's centres', *Child and Family Social Work*, 13, 61–71.

Shoolbread, A. (2006) *Consulting Children on the Proposed Schools (Nutrition and Health Promotion) (Scotland) Bill*, Edinburgh: Scottish Executive.

Simpson, D. and Envy, R. (2015) 'Subsidizing early childhood education and care for parents on low income: moving beyond the individualized economic rationale of neoliberalism', *Contemporary Issues in Early Childhood*, 16, 2, 166–78.

Siraj-Blatchford, I. and Sylva, K. (2004) 'Researching pedagogy in English preschools', *British Educational Research Journal*, 30, 5, 713–30.

Siraj-Blatchford, I., Taggart, B., Sylva, K., Sammons, P. and Melhuish, E. (2008) 'Towards the transformation of practice in early childhood education: the effective provision of preschool education (EPPE) project', *Cambridge Journal of Education*, 38, 1, 23–36.

Skinner, C. (2003) *Running Around in Circles: Coordinating childcare, education and work*, York: Joseph Rowntree Foundation.

Smith, M., Oliver, C. and Barker, S. (1998) *Effectiveness of Early Years Interventions: What does the research tell us?* Comprehensive Spending Review: Cross-Departmental Review of Provision for Young Children, Vol. 2, London: HM Treasury.

Spivack, R., Craston, M., Thom, G. And Carr, C. (2014) *Special Educational Needs and Disability Pathfinder Programme Evaluation. Thematic Report: the Education, Health and Care (EHC) Planning Pathway for families that are new to the SEN system.* DfE. Online at: https://www.gov.uk/government/uploads/system/uploads/attachment_data/file/275104/RR326B_EHC_planning_pathway_-_FINAL.pdf

Stewart, K. and Obolenskaya, P. (2015) *The Coalition Record on the Under Fives: Policy, Spending and Outcomes 2010–2015*, Social Policy in a Cold Climate Working Paper 12, Centre for Analysis of Social Exclusion/London School of Economics. Available at: http://sticerd.lse.ac.uk

Sure Start (2008) *Districts that Participated in the Mainstreaming Pilot.* Available at: www.surestart.gov.uk/_doc/P0001719.doc (accessed 30 June 2008).

Sure Start Unit (2002) *Birth to Three Matters: A framework to support children in their earliest years*, London: DfES.

Swadener, B.B., Kabiru, M. and Njenja, A. (2000) *Does the Village Still Raise the Child? A collaborative study of changing child-rearing and early education in Kenya*, New York: State University of New York Press.

Swap, S.M. (1993) *Developing Home–School Partnerships: From concepts to practice*, New York: Teachers College Press.

Sylva, K., Melhuish, E., Sammons, P., Siraj-Blatchford, I. and Taggart, B. (2004) *The Effective Provision of Pre-School Education (EPPE) Project: Findings from pre-school to end of Key Stage 1*, London: Sure Start.

Sylva, K., Melhuish, E., Sammons, P., Siraj-Blatchford, I. and Taggart, B. (2012) *Effective Pre-school, Primary and Secondary Education 3–14 Project (EPPSE 3–14): Final report from the Key Stage 3 phase – influences on students' development from age 11–14*, London: DfE.

Taguma, M., Litjens, I. and Makowiecki, K. (2012) *Quality Matters in Early Childhood Education and Care: Finland 2012*, Paris: OECD.

Taylor, D. and Balloch, S. (2005) 'The politics of evaluation: an overview', in D. Taylor and S. Balloch, *The Politics of Evaluation*, Bristol: The Policy Press.

Taylor, C., Rhys, M., Waldron, S., Davies, R., Power, S., Maynard, T., Moore, L., Blackaby, D. and Plewis, I. (2015) *Evaluating the Foundation Phase: Final report.* Cardiff: Welsh Government.

Teather, S. (2011) 'To each child a fair start', *Nursery World*, 28 October: 12.

Tickell, Dame C. (2011) *The Early Years: Foundations for life, health and learning.* Available at: http://media.education.gov.uk/MediaFiles/B/1/5%7BB15EFFOD-A4DF-4294-93A1-1E1B88C13F68%7DTickell%20review.pdf (accessed 29 October 2015).

Tisdall, E.K.M. and Davis, J. (2004) 'Making a difference? Bringing children's and young people's views into policy making', *Children and Society*, 18, 2, 131–42.

Tobin, J., Hsueh, Y. and Karasawa, M. (2009) *Pre-school in Three Cultures Re-visited: China, Japan and the United States*, Chicago, IL: University of Chicago Press.

Truss, E. (2012) *Affordable Quality: New approaches to childcare*, Centre Forum. Available at: www.centreforum.org/assets/pubs/affordable-quality.pdf (accessed 20 May 2012).

Tweed, J. (2002) 'Labour's early years job "is not finished"', *Nursery World*, 14 February: 4.

United Nations Educational, Scientific and Cultural Organisation (UNESCO) (1990) *World Declaration on Education for All and Framework for Action for Meeting Basic Needs*, Paris: UNESCO.

Valentova, M. (2009) *Employment Breaks due to Childcare in the Czech Republic: Before and after 1989*, Hartford, CT: IDEAS, University of Connecticut.

Van de Linde, T. and Lenaiyasa, S. (2006) 'Influencing and developing good policy in early childhood development amongst pastoralist communities in East Africa: the case of Samburu in Kenya', paper delivered at the conference on Pastoralism and Poverty Reduction in East Africa, the International Livestock Research Institute, Nairobi, June.

Vimpani, G.V. (2002) 'Sure Start: reflections from down under', *Childcare, Health and Development*, 28, 4, 281–7.

Walker, R. (ed.) (1999) *Popular Welfare for the 21st Century?* Bristol: The Policy Press.

Warnock Committee (1978) *Special Educational Needs: The Warnock Report*, London: DES.

Warnock, M. (2005) *Special Educational Needs: A new look*, London: Philosophy of Education Society of Great Britain.

Waterhouse, Sir R. (2000) *Lost in Care: Report of the Tribunal of Inquiry into the abuse of children in care in the former county council areas of Gwynedd and Clwyd since 1974*, London: HMSO (DoH).

Watson, J. (2012) *Starting Well: Benchmarking early education across the world*, EIU. Available at: www.economistinsights.com/sites/default/files/legacy/mgthink/downloads/Starting%20Well.pdf (accessed 30 December 2015).

Welsh Assembly (2004) *Celebrating Progress in Early Years and Primary Education*. Available at: www.learning.wales.gov.uk/scripts/fe/news_details.asp?NewsID=1399 (accessed 15 November 2004).

White, G., Swift, J. and Bennett, A. (2005) *Sure Start Mainstreaming Pilots: What can we learn?* Annersley: DfES Publications.

White, L.A. (2009) 'Explaining differences in child care policy development in France and the USA: norms, frames, programmatic ideas', *International Political Science Review*, 30, 4, 385–405.

Winner, E. (1989) 'How can Chinese children draw so well?', *Journal of Aesthetic Education*, 23, 1, 41–63.

Winner, E. (1993) 'Exceptional artistic development: the role of visual thinking', *Journal of Aesthetic Education*, 27, 4, 31–44.

Wintour, P. (2006) 'Blair admits failing most needy children', *The Guardian*, 16 May.

Woodrow, C. (2008) 'Discourses of professional identity in early childhood: movements in Australia', *European Early Childhood Education Research Journal*, 16, 2.

World Education Forum (2000) *The Dakar Framework for Action – Education for All: Meeting our collective commitments*, Paris: UNESCO.

Yim, H.Y.B. and Ebbeck, M. (2009) 'Children's preferences for group musical activities in child care centres: a cross-cultural study', *Early Education Journal*, 37, 2, 103–11.

Yu, Z-y. & Pine, N. (2006) *Strategies for enhancing emergent literacy in Chinese preschools*. National Reading Conference, Los Angeles, December 2006.

Zhou, X. (2011) 'Early childhood education policy in China', *International Journal of Child Care and Education Policy*, 5, 1, 29–39.

Zhu, J. and Zhang, J. (2008) 'Contemporary trends and developments in early childhood education in China', *Early Years*, 28, 2, 173–83.

INDEX